SUPPLEMENTS

SUNY series in Contemporary Continental Philosophy

———————————————————————

Dennis J. Schmidt

editor

MARTIN HEIDEGGER

SUPPLEMENTS

From the Earliest Essays to

Being and Time and Beyond

edited by

JOHN VAN BUREN

STATE UNIVERSITY OF NEW YORK PRESS

Published by
STATE UNIVERSITY OF NEW YORK PRESS, ALBANY

© 2002 State University of New York

For information, address State University of New York Press,
90 State Street, Suite 700, Albany, NY 12207

Production, Laurie Searl
Marketing, Anne M. Valentine

Library of Congress Cataloging-in-Publication Data

Heidegger, Martin, 1889–1976.
  [Essays. English. Selections]
  Supplements : from the earliest essays to Being and time and beyond / Martin
Heidegger ; edited by John van Buren
    p. cm. — (SUNY series in contemporary continental philosophy)
  Includes bibliographical references.
  ISBN 0-7914-5505-X (alk. paper) — ISBN 0-7914-5506-8 (pbk. : alk. paper)
  1. Philosophy. I. Van Buren, John, 1956– II. Title. III. Series.

B3279.H47 E5 2002d
193—dc21
                                                                    2002075878

10 9 8 7 6 5 4 3 2 1

Contents

ACKNOWLEDGMENTS

I am grateful to my co-translators who generously and patiently worked on this project through the last ten years, especially Charles Bambach on whom I relied for important editorial advice. I also wish to thank Thomas Sheehan, who first effectively opened up research on Heidegger's earliest thought in the English-speaking world, for his generous and valuable suggestions.

We owe a debt of gratitude to Hermann Heidegger, executor of Martin Heidegger's literary estate, for his encouragement and assistance throughout the nineties to make this collection of his father's earliest writings available in the English-speaking world, echoing his decision announced in the April 1984 prospectus for his father's *Gesamtausgabe* that writings from the Early Freiburg Period would be published as "a supplement."

We are also grateful to Dennis Schmidt, editor of the Contemporary Continental Philosophy Series, and acquisitions editor Jane Bunker for their support, labors, and patience in waiting for this follow-up volume that was announced in my first edited volume in this series, *Reading Heidegger From the Start* (1994).

We wish to thank the following publishers and journals for granting the permissions that are spelled out in Chapter 1: Vittorio Klostermann Verlag; N. G. Elwert Verlag; Cambridge University Press; Dr. Frithjof Rodi, editor of the *Dilthey-Jahrbuch;* Wolfe Mays, editor of the *Journal of the British Society for Phenomenology; Graduate Faculty Philosophy Journal;* and *Man and World.*

Thanks are also due to David Farrell Krell and William McNeill for arranging to have my translation "Comments on Karl Jaspers' *Psychology of Worldviews*" appear roughly simultaneously in Heidegger's *Pathmarks* published by Cambridge University Press and in the present volume.

I also wish to express my gratitude to the Dean of Fordham College, Jeffrey von Arx, and the Vice-President of Academic Affairs, John Hollwitz, for supporting the completion of this project with a faculty fellowship, leave of absence, and teaching reductions, as well as to my research assistants and other graduate students who assisted the project, especially Kevin Hoffmann, Curt Purcell, and Robert Vigliotti.

John van Buren
Fordham University, 2002

ABBREVIATIONS

TEXTS

BTMR   *Being and Time,* tr. John Macquarrie and Edward Robinson (New York: Harper & Row, 1962).

BTS   *Being and Time,* tr. Joan Stambaugh (Albany: State University of New York Press, 1996).

GA   Martin Heidegger, *Gesamtausgabe* (Collected Edition) (Frankfurt: Klostermann, 1975ff.). Volume number immediately follows this abbreviation and then pagination. Unless otherwise indicated, references are to first editions. A list of volume titles with other bibliographic information can be found in chapter 1 of this volume.

OHF   Martin Heidegger, *Ontology—The Hermeneutics of Facticity,* translated and commented on by John van Buren (Bloomington: Indiana University Press, 1999).

RHFS   John van Buren and Theodore Kisiel, eds., *Reading Heidegger From the Start: Essays in His Earliest Thought* (Albany: State University of New York Press, 1994).

YH   John van Buren, *The Young Heidegger: Rumor of the Hidden King* (Bloomington: Indiana University Press, 1994).

References to less frequently cited secondary works, listed in the secondary bibliography at the end of this volume, are made in short form.

OTHER

KNS   Special post-war semester, from February–mid-April 1919, at the end of the First World War.

SS   Summer semester, typically from May–July in German universities.

WS   Winter semester, typically from November–February, with a month off for Christmas.

Editor's Introduction

The English-speaking world has long had anthologies of Heidegger's later essays after *Being and Time*. *Supplements* adds for the first time in any language a comprehensive anthology of the most important of his recently discovered essays before *Being and Time,* offering selections drawn from the long series of Heidegger's experimental, constantly supplemental attempts at rethinking philosophy that stretch from the earliest essays in the teens to those in the early twenties preceding *Being and Time* and pointing beyond to the later writings, when Heidegger's famous "turn" took in part the form of a "return" to his earliest writings. It presents them under a title taken from the first 1974 publisher's prospectus for Heidegger's *Collected Edition* (GA), which announced that certain texts from the Early Freiburg Period, though not included in the edition's original plan due to their anomalous character, might nonetheless later be "published as a supplement *[Supplement]*."[1] The nine milestone selections—five of which were generally not even known of in Heidegger scholarship until the mid-1990s (chapters 2, 6, 8, 9, 10)—are representative of the Student Period (WS1909–10 to SS1915), the Early Freiburg Period (WS1915–16 to SS1923), and the first years of the Marburg Period from WS1923–24 to 1926, when *Being and Time* was composed.

As explained in detail below, this new primary source will serve scholars, teachers, and students well when used as a supplemental companion volume to early lecture courses such as the editor's translation of *Ontology—The Hermeneutics of Facticity* (OHF), *Being and Time* (available from State University of New York Press in a new translation by Joan Stambaugh), and even later works such as *Contributions to Philosophy*. References to these writings have accordingly been provided. Finally, because Heidegger's early experimental essays often make for difficult reading and can at times seem quite inscrutable, this collection also has been designed so that readers can, if they wish, use it in conjunction with the editor's secondary works on the early Heidegger (YH, RHFS, and OHF). References

1

to these and other secondary works listed in the secondary bibliography at the
end of the volume also have been provided.

Four of the selections were composed or published by Heidegger as free-
standing journal articles. The remaining six were composed in different genres: a
book notice, a supplemental conclusion to a dissertation, an introduction to a
planned book, transcripts of two talks, and a letter. However, except for the letter, these too are presented in the genre of "essays," able to stand on their own
with the proper editorial introduction and in the literal sense of "essays" as
"attempts" or "experiments" *(essais)* in thinking.

Previously unpublished chapters, which make up almost two-thirds of the
body of the volume, include chapter 1 (the editor's "Chronological Overview"),
the translation in the first section of chapter 5 ("Author's Book Notice"), and the
translations in chapters 6 ("Letter to Father Engelbert Krebs"), 8 (the talk "The
Problem of Sin in Luther"), 9 (the book introduction "Phenomenological Interpretations in Connection with Aristotle"), and 10 (the talk "Wilhelm Dilthey's
Research and the Struggle for a Historical Worldview"). While chapters 3 and 4
(the journal articles, "The Problem of Reality in Modern Philosophy" and "The
Concept of Time in the Science of History"), as well as the second section of
chapter 5 (the supplemental book conclusion, "The Problem of Categories")
appeared in journals twenty to thirty years ago, they have been thoroughly
revised and reedited in collaboration with the original translators. Even chapters
2 (the journal article *"Per mortem ad vitam"*) and 7 (the journal article "Comments on Karl Jaspers' *Psychology of Worldviews*"), which originally were published in English in the nineties, have been revised to bring them up-to-date with
current research and to standardize translations of key terms and stylistic con-
ventions in this collection.

In all cases, the attempt was made to provide a translation as interpretively
faithful as possible to the original German text, while respecting equally the con-
ventions of the English language. Translations are always interpretations "in a
nutshell," Heidegger wrote in 1922 in one of his very first forays into the philosophy of translation occasioned by the challenge of writing a planned book on
the ancient Greek philosopher, Aristotle (see chapter 9 of this book, p. 127).[2]

NARRATIVE OF CHAPTERS

CHAPTER I: CHRONOLOGICAL OVERVIEW

The opening chapter provides a detailed chronology of Heidegger's education,
professional appointments, teaching, research, and publications and is divided
into four sections: Student Period: Education; Student Period: Research and Publication; Early Freiburg Period; and Marburg Period. Referring back to this
chronology, which also functions as a primary bibliography, subsequent chapters
offer representative selections of "essays" from these three periods. The selections

are flagged by daggers in the left margin of the chronology, so that when moving to subsequent chapters the reader can conveniently return to the chronology for philological and bibliographic information on the selection in question. The narrative of chapters presented below, to which the reader can return, also provides references to relevant secondary background material in the editor's previous publications (YH, RHFS, and OHF) and in other works listed in the secondary bibliography at the end of this book.

The selections are presented not only as a set of "supplements" to Heidegger's other early writings, but also as a series of "supplements" in the spirit of his own lifelong theme that his texts constituted a "path" of thinking about the relation of being, time, and human existence which was ever incomplete and undergoing supplementation with new attempts.[3] Already in 1916 he wrote that "as temporally conditioned cultural facts, the particular concrete sciences are never complete but rather always on the way in their discovery of truth" and again in 1920 that "the path leading to the 'things themselves' treated in philosophy is a long one" (see this volume, pp. 50, 74). Later in the first 1972 edition of *Early Writings*, he suggested that this predicament was pronounced in the series of "my early attempts" *(Versuche)* from the Student Period to *Being and Time*: "Stirring at that time in but a dark and uncertain and helpless manner, the question of what unifies the manifold meanings of being *remained*—throughout the many overturnings, labyrinths, and perplexities—*the* unceasing impetus for the treatise *Being and Time* which appeared two decades later."[4] Specifically regarding his "attempts" after 1919, we read elsewhere: ". . . the path of questioning became longer than I suspected. It demanded many stops, circuitous experiments, and wayward excursions."[5] What we find in the opening chapter's long chronology of Heidegger's research and publication and more specifically in the "essays" selected from it for this volume, such as the conclusion "written as a supplement" (GA1 191) for the publication of Heidegger's postdoctoral dissertation (chapter 5), is precisely a path or series of supplemental "attempts" or "essays" from the early teens to 1925, one that also "stops" for a time with *Being and Time* in the late twenties and then, occasioned by the failed experiment of this never finished work, pushes forward into the later texts with their new supplemental attempts to rework his early thought.

CHAPTERS 2–5: STUDENT PERIOD

Chapters 2–5 present essays from Heidegger's Student Period at the University of Freiburg.[6] Chapter 2, the book review article "*Per mortem ad vitam* (Thoughts on Johannes Jörgensen's *Lies of Life and Truth of Life*)" (1910), is drawn from the first anti-modernist theological phase of Heidegger's student years when, as the chronological overview in the previous chapter outlines, he was studying for the priesthood in the Department of Theology between WS1909–10 and SS1911 and produced a series of book reviews, poems, and other texts that exhibit predominantly theological, moral, aesthetic, and cultural interests. Representing the intellectual starting point of Heidegger's development, these texts basically put forth an anti-modernist Aristotelian–Scholastic position in which, following the official stand of the Catholic Church at the time, Heidegger condemns what he perceives to be the subjectivist, historicist orientation of modern philosophy and liberal culture as exemplified in figures such as Nietzsche, calling for a historical return to the realism of medieval Aristotelian–Scholastic philosophy with its commitment to an objective, timeless order of being based on God.

Using chapter 2 as a foil, chapters 3–5 offer essays from the second neo-Scholastic philosophical phase of the student years from WS1911–12 to SS1915 which is sketched out in the chronological overview. During this second phase, Heidegger, making an anxiety-ridden "turn" in his intellectual outlook and career plans from the priesthood to the academic profession, first transfers to the Department of Natural Sciences and Mathematics (WS1911–12 to WS1912–13) as he considers a career as a high school teacher in mathematics and then to the Department of Philosophy (SS1913 to SS1915) for a university teaching career, generating a series of journal articles, book reviews, and dissertations that crystallizes at the end of the Student Period in the project of an innovative neo-Kantian, phenomenological neo-Scholasticism attempting to supplement and critically renew medieval Scholasticism in the modern world by synthesizing its logic of the categories of being with the systematic concerns of contemporary neo-Kantianism, Husserlian phenomenology, the philosophy of history, philosophy of life, and German Idealism.

In chapter 3, "The Problem of Reality in Modern Philosophy" (1912), Heidegger's first publication in a properly academic journal, the critical realism of the contemporary thinker Oswald Külpe, as well as Husserl's phenomenology, is used by Heidegger to explore the aggravated modern problem of the intentional relation of consciousness to being. The article criticizes the "identification of being and being-perceived" in the traditional English empiricism of Berkeley and Hume and in contemporary epistemology, arguing both historically for the enduring validity of "Aristotelian–Scholastic philosophy, which has always thought in a realist manner," and systematically for the need to synthesize this philosophical tradition with the "new epistemological movement" represented by Külpe and Husserl. "Positive, progressive work must be its main concern," Heidegger writes of Aristotelian Scholasticism (pp. 40, 48). Speaking like a Thomist, an English empiricist, and a German phenomenologist all at once, Heidegger maintains that the structure of the intentional "relation" *(Bezug)* of consciousness to its "content" *(Inhalt, Gehalt),* i.e., being, lies in the fact that after objects have stimulated the sense organs and nervous system, creating "sense impressions," consciousness is able to abstract from the subjective factors of these impressions and to "posit" and "define" the "real being" of the "external world" by means of the "ideal being" of concepts or categories: ". . . a being that is thought is in no way identical with being in thought. What is in being here (in the phenomenal sense) is a concept whose content is intention-ally referred to transcendent being. . . . Real being is thought by means of a con-cept, but this in no way means that such being is taken inside the subject and transformed into psychical being" (p. 43).

Chapter 4, "The Concept of Time in the Science of History," which the chronological overviews shows Heidegger delivering to the Department of Phi-losophy in SS1915 as a trial lecture required for the postdoctoral degree *(Habil-itation)* and license to teach in German universities *(venia legendi)* as a lecturer *(Privatdozent)* and publishing it the following year as a journal article, now adds an exploration of the very modern theme of the historical "actualizing" *(Vollzug)* of the mind's intentional "relation" to being and value, and it is Heidegger's very first publication to do so, such that he cited it later in *Being and Time.*[7] It also is his first work to pursue this theme through an in-depth contrast between the qualitative, "significance"-charged, and "difference"-laden concept of time in the historical sciences and the quantitative, neutral, and homogeneous concept of time in the modern mathematical natural sciences (for this contrast, see also chapter 10, pp. 170ff. and §§80–81 of *Being and Time*). In this regard, and as can be seen in the chronological overview, Heidegger draws on his intensive stud-ies in the Department of Natural Sciences and Mathematics from WS1911–12 to WS1912–13, his studies in the Department of Philosophy from SS1912 to SS1915 with the philosopher of history Heinrich Finke and with the distin-guished neo-Kantian philosopher Henrich Rickert on the transcendental logic of the natural sciences and the historical human sciences, his continued studies after SS1911 with the speculative theologian Carl Braig who introduced him to Hegel's historically oriented Idealism, and his independent studies of Dilthey's and Nietzsche's philosophies of life and history from 1910 onward.[8]

Chapter 5, "The Theory of Categories and Meaning in Duns Scotus," comprises two texts also relating to Heidegger's postdoctoral degree awarded in SS1915. The first section, "Author's Book Notice," presents a notice on the 1916 publication of the postdoctoral dissertation "The Theory of Categories and Meaning in Duns Scotus," which he had submitted to the Department of Phi-losophy the year before. It conveniently summarizes the dissertation, showing that the expanding series of historical influences and systematic interests docu-mented in the chronological overview from Heidegger's first anti-modernist the-ological phase to his second neo-Scholastic philosophical phase now momentar-ily crystallized in the sweeping synthetic historical-systematic experiment of, first, a regressive treatment of "the history of problems" focusing on Duns Scotus' metaphysical theory of the "categories of being" in relation to his grammatical-logical theory of meaning and, second, a critical systematic reconstruction of this historical position within the conceptuality and concerns of contemporary phe-nomenology and neo-Kantianism. As Heidegger stated much later, the result of this neo-Kantian, phenomenological neo-Scholasticism was a metaphysical "onto-logic" (GA1 55) of categories of being that approached these categories as

a conceptual nexus of timeless ideal being by means of which intentional "judgments" gain access to real being and which is itself grounded in the absolute
being of God.

The second section of Chapter 5, "Conclusion: The Problem of Categories," presents the forward-looking conclusion "written as a supplement"
(GA1 191) to the dissertation for its publication. This supplemental conclusion
now adds an admission of deep "intellectual *unrest*" in the face of "the impression of a certain deathly emptiness" given by the treatment of categories in the
dissertation (p. 62). While restating the dissertation's ontological separation of
the realms of "time and eternity, change and [the] absolute validity [of the categories of being], world and God," Heidegger poses the perplexing problem of
understanding how the realm of the truth of ideal being and that of historical
actuality work together within an intimate living unity, arguing that this unity,
as glimpsed by medieval mysticism, constitutes the "authentic depth dimension"
of philosophy, and that future philosophy must aim at a "*breakthrough* to [its]
true actuality and actual truth" (pp. 66, 68). Drawing on his research into contemporary philosophy of value, life, and history, as well as into Hegel's Idealism
and medieval mysticism, he poses the problem more specifically in terms of
three "requirements" that a theory of the categories of being must fulfill if it is
to avoid the impression of abstract emptiness: (1) demarcating the irreducible
categorial regions of being in their relation to the actuality of different kinds of
experienceable objects; (2) seeing the categories of being in their inseparable
intentional "relation" to "the subject" and not merely the "logical judging subject," "the epistemological subject" with its "theoretical attitude" focused on in
his 1912 journal article on epistemology (chapter 3), but more deeply in line
with his 1915 talk on historical time (chapter 4), the subject as "living spirit,"
which is *"historical spirit in the widest sense of the word"* (p. 66); and accordingly
(3) "history," as the process of the "actualizing" of the subject's intentional relation to the content of the categories, *"must become a determining element for the
meaning of the problem of categories"* (p. 67). Here, as well as in the application
at the time for a research grant documented in the chronological overview, the
young self-professed phenomenological neo-Scholastic announces that he will
be dedicating his life's work to these problems, suggesting that the answers are
to be found in a neo-Hegelian approach that sees the historical "actualizing" of
spirit's "relation" to categorial meaning to be grounded in the "teleological"
unfolding of "the absolute spirit of God" and of the soul's "transcendent relation" to God (pp. 66–67).

CHAPTERS 6–10: EARLY FREIBURG AND MARBURG PERIODS

The remaining five chapters, which comprise subsequent "essays" from the Early
Freiburg Period (WS1915–16 to SS1923) and the first years of the Marburg
Period (WS1923–24 to WS1925–26),[9] tell the story that as the student-turned-

lecturer now attempted to fulfill the above three "requirements," he eventually, around 1919, abandoned his unstable neo-Scholastic onto-logic of timeless being for a new fundamentally historical phenomenological ontology, left the Catholic Church for free Protestantism, and now launched into a series of bold new experiments investigating: (1) how the demarcation of the different categorial regions of being, which make up the intentional "sense of the content" *(Gehaltssinn)* of experience, hinges upon seeing these regions to be based on the "significance" of the immediately experienced, practical world; (2) how the "subject" constituting the deepest "sense of the relation" *(Bezugssinn)* to the categories of being has the form of "factical life" in its practical situatedness and with its own categorial structures; and (3) how historical time is the deepest "sense of the actualizing" *(Vollzugssinn)* or "temporalizing" *(Zeitigungssinn)*[10] of the intentional relation to the categorial content of the world and is the condition of the possibility of this relation. The texts between 1919 and 1925 experimented with often poetic descriptions of the dynamism of historical time as a "properizing event" *(Ereignis)*, "there is/it gives" *(es gibt)*, "it worlds" *(es weltet)* (GA56/57 63–76); as a nonobjectifiable "be-ing" or "existing" (chapter 7 of this volume); as an open-ended "kinesis" or "motion" (chapter 9 of this volume); as a "whiling" *(Verweilen)* or "sojourning" *(Aufhalten)* in the "awhileness of temporal particularity" *(Jeweiligkeit)* (OHF 7ff./5ff.); and as a "happening" *(Geschehen)* (chapter 10 of this volume). This series of self-supplementing experiments would lead to the most ambitious "essay" of Heidegger's early thought, namely, the composition in 1926 of the book *Being and Time,* which exhibited a recent marked turn to the paradigm of Kant's transcendental philosophy[11] and now transformed this still little-known figure into a leading European philosopher and the more familiar Heidegger we know today.

In this second but more dramatic confessional and philosophical "turn" in his early development, which Hans-Georg Gadamer has called "the turn before the turn,"[12] Heidegger on January 9, 1919 wrote to his friend from the early teens, Father Engelbert Krebs of the Department of Theology, that "epistemological insights extending to a theory of historical knowledge have made the *system* of Catholicism problematic and unacceptable to me, but not Christianity and metaphysics—these, though, in a new sense" (p. 69). Then in February he opened his lecture course in the special post-war semester with a revolutionary call for "a completely new concept of philosophy" that would entail "the catastrophe of all (previous) philosophy," echoing this call in WS1921–22 with talk of "the end of philosophy" and "the genuine new beginning."[13] Accordingly, the remaining chapters of this volume show that Heidegger now pursued (1) a regressive "destruction"or "dismantling"[14] of the history of Western ontology back to the foundational dimensions of the practically significant world, factical life, and historical time; (2) a reconstructive "appropriation" or "repeating" of this history in a new beginning; and for the sake of this "systematic" reconstruction (3) a series of critical appropriations of the ontologically rich traditions of primal

Christianity (Augustine, medieval mysticism, Luther, Kierkegaard), Aristotle's physics and practical philosophy, and Dilthey's philosophy of life and history.

Chapter 6, the 1919 "Letter to Father Engelbert Krebs,"[15] in which he announces his profound confessional and philosophical turn, and chapter 7, the 1920 book review essay "Comments on Karl Jaspers' *Psychology of Worldviews,*"[16] belong to the first phase of Heidegger's Early Freiburg Period, when he was a lecturer at the University of Freiburg between WS1915–16 and SS1923, also serving as Husserl's assistant from 1919 onward. These texts are drawn from the body of articles, lecture courses, and correspondence in the chronological overview from 1916–1921 in which Heidegger, drawing on his Christian heritage in a new way, was especially interested in developing a "phenomenology of religion"[17] and using it to exploit the significance of the primal Christianity of figures such as Luther and Kierkegaard for rethinking ontology historically along the lines of the three requirements voiced in the 1916 supplemental conclusion to his postdoctoral dissertation. Employing the technical terms "sense of relation," "content," and "actualizing" to explore factical life's intentional relation to being, Heidegger's article deals with Jaspers' Kierkegaardian philosophy of existence, its relation to Husserl's phenomenology[18] and contemporary philosophy of life,[19] the nature of concepts as formal indications,[20] and the current fundamental tasks of philosophy.

Chapter 8, the WS1923–24 talk "The Problem of Sin in Luther,"[21] dates from the very start of Heidegger's Marburg Period, when he taught at the University of Marburg as an associate professor between WS1923–24 and SS1927 and then as professor from WS1927–28 to SS1928. Insofar as this two-part talk given in Rudolf Bultmann's seminar on St. Paul's ethics explored Luther's biblically based understanding of the dynamic being of man's relation to God, it derives from the first phase of the Early Freiburg Period mentioned above and should be read with Heidegger's 1919–20 article on Jaspers.

Chapter 9, the 1922 book introduction "Phenomenological Interpretations in Connection with Aristotle: An Indication of the Hermeneutical Situation,"[22] is drawn from the body of texts in the chronological overview from 1921 to 1924 in which Heidegger now takes a marked turn to a direct engagement with the source of Western ontology in Aristotle, combining this with his explorations of primal Christianity. The text is a draft overview introduction to a large, projected but never published book on Aristotle (planned to be published in Husserl's phenomenological journal), which was to have systematically worked out Heidegger's new historically oriented hermeneutical-phenomenological ontology by means of a critical, historical appropriation of Aristotle especially[23] but also of primal Christianity, medieval Scholasticism, and Husserl's phenomenology.

Chapter 10, the 1925 ten-part talk "Wilhelm Dilthey's Research and the Struggle for a Historical Worldview," is drawn from a group of texts in the chronological overview from 1924 to 1925 and immediately before the 1926

composition of *Being and Time,* in which Heidegger turns to a systematic engagement with Dilthey's philosophy and Dilthey's recently published correspondence
with his friend Count Yorck. A premonition of Dilthey's and Yorck's presence in
Being and Time, though without the heavily Kantian transcendental framework
that appears in *Being and Time,* this series of lectures investigates the significance
of Dilthey's philosophy of history and its relation to Husserl's phenomenology for
rethinking the question of being.

USING *SUPPLEMENTS*

SUPPLEMENTING *BEING AND TIME*

In addition to reading this new source of Heidegger's early thought on its own as
a presentation of his very first self-supplementing attempts to reformulate the traditional question of being on the basis of time, scholars, teachers, and students
can use it, along with early lecture courses before *Being and Time* such as the
SS1923 *Ontology—The Hermeneutics of Facticity* (OHF),[24] as a companion volume to supplement *Being and Time.* Since its initial appearance in English translation in the early sixties, it was very difficult to study *Being and Time* in connection with its rich history in the preceding decade and a half, simply because
few texts from this period were available either in German or English. The series
of "essays" in this book from the Early Freiburg and Marburg Periods provides
important first drafts, as it were, of *Being and Time* (see especially chapters 7, 9,
and 10), and the book as a whole is an overview of the longer history of its making from the early years of the Student Period onward. These first drafts add to
Being and Time the following supplemental material lacking in it: (1) first versions of the historical destruction of Western ontology that was to have constituted the unpublished part 2 of *Being and Time* (see §8); (2) details of the critical appropriations of primal Christianity (New Testament, Augustine, medieval
mysticism, Luther, Kierkegaard), Husserl, Aristotle, and Dilthey, which are mentioned but not fully explained in notes, the exception being Dilthey, who is
treated in §77, though in nothing like the detail of the 1925 talk on Dilthey in
chapter 10 of this volume; and (3) the first and in many respects different versions of the systematic reconstruction of ontology presented in Divisions I and II
of part 1 and to be presented in the unpublished Division III of part 1, first versions that are referred to in notes in §§15 and 54 but not summarized. "The
author may remark," the text reads, "that this analysis of the environing world
and in general the 'hermeneutics of the facticity of Dasein' have been presented
repeatedly in his lecture courses ever since the winter semester of 1919–20."[25]

Moreover, specific themes and historical references in *Being and Time* can
be supplemented and followed up with the texts in this volume. For example, §1
on the theory of categories of being in the history of Western philosophy can be
supplemented especially with the texts from 1916 and 1922 on the same topic in

chapters 5 and 9 of this volume; the references to Jaspers' discussions in his *Psychology of Worldviews* of a philosophical anthropology of human Dasein,[26] the "limit-situation" of death,[27] and Kierkegaard's concepts of "existence," "temporality," and the "moment"[28] supplemented with the long 1920 article on Jaspers' book in chapter 7; §43(a) on the problem of the external world with the 1912 article on the same topic in chapter 3 and the discussion of Dilthey's approach to this problem in chapter 10; the references to Luther's critique of the concepts of man and God in medieval Scholasticism (§3), to his powerful analysis of the anxiety-ridden human condition after the Fall in his *Commentary on Genesis*,[29] and to other Christian influences on Heidegger's notions of "care,"[30] "mood,"[31] "anxiety,"[32] "death,"[33] and "conscience"[34] exerted by the theological anthropology of St. Paul, Augustine, Pascal, and Kierkegaard's "edifying writings" supplemented with the 1924 exposition of Luther's theological anthropology in chapter 8 and with the first part of the 1922 text on the history of Christian and Aristotelian anthropology in chapter 9; the truncated references to "Aristotle's ontology"[35] in his metaphysical, psychological, logical, and practical writings and more specifically to his understanding of the "ontic priority" of human Dasein (§4), "desire" or "care,"[36] "mood" (§§29–30), "discourse" (§§7[a]–[b], 33–34), the environing world of ready-to-hand equipment for practical dealings (§15), and "truth" as the "unconcealment" brought about by intellectual virtues such as "practical wisdom" and "science" (§§44, 7[a]–[b]) supplemented with the long text on Aristotle in chapter 9; §§76–77 on the science of history and the concept of historical time in Dilthey and Yorck supplemented with the 1925 series of lectures on Dilthey and Yorck in chapter 10, as well as with the 1916 article on the science of history in chapter 4 that *Being and Time* cites in connection with the problem of "time-reckoning";[37] and the references to Husserl's phenomenology[38] and the briefly stated claim that phenomenology must become a historical, "destructive" hermeneutical phenomenology of being (§7[c]) supplemented with the fuller discussions of these topics in chapters 7, 9, and 10.

SUPPLEMENTING HEIDEGGER'S LATER WRITINGS

This book also can be used, along with the earliest lecture courses, as a companion volume to supplement Heidegger's later writings after *Being and Time,* in which he made his famous "turn" from *Being and Time*'s Kantian-transcendental emphasis on human being to being itself and from its equally Kantian-transcendental conception of being as constituted by static historical structures to a more dynamic, differentiated conception of being as a difference-generating historical "event" *(Ereignis).* Ever since Heidegger's well-known letter of 1962 to William Richardson brought attention to the turn from the "Heidegger I" of *Being and Time* to the "Heidegger II" of the later writings,[39] the lack of relevant texts again made it difficult to study the historical genesis of this turn and to make sense of Heidegger's elliptical suggestions that "Heidegger II" was not only a turn to new topics and sources but also in part a critical "re-turn" to his earliest attempts before the "Heidegger I" of the Kantian-transcendental experiment of *Being and Time,* as he now attempted to supplement and rewrite this unfinished, failed experiment in later "essays" such as the 1936–38 *Contributions to Philosophy— On Event* (cf. G65 §42 "From *Being and Time* to 'Event'").[40] As we now know from the recent publication in the *Collected Edition* of the full range of Heidegger's early texts before *Being and Time* and texts after *Being and Time* in the late twenties and early thirties providing the details of the turn from "Heidegger I" to "Heidegger II," the later experimental texts critically reappropriated the nonanthropocentric, speculative, and mystical lines of thought in his 1915 postdoctoral dissertation, which had focused on the relation of language (grammar) and the categories of being and ultimately on an "inner Dasein . . . anchored in a primordial, transcendent relation of the soul to God" (p. 67). These later attempts also experimented anew with the highly innovative texts after the Student Period on the historical dynamism of factical life's relation to being, returning for fresh takes on early terms and themes such as "properizing event" *(Ereignis);* "it worlds"; "there is/it gives"; the predominantly verbal sense of "be-ing"; "whiling" and "sojourning"; historical "happening"; "mystery"; the terminological triad of "content," "relation," and "actualization"; the nature of philosophical terms as "formal indications"; the "end of philosophy" and a "new beginning"; philosophy as a perpetual "turning," "beginning," or "path"; technology; and university reform.[41] Though Heidegger certainly also criticized the very philosophy of life (Dilthey) and philosophy of existence (Kierkegaard, Jaspers) in which his thought of the late teens and early twenties was framed,[42] we nonetheless find him as early as his SS1928 lecture course reintroducing the term "to world" from KNS1919 and experimenting with it anew in relation to the pre-Socratics, telling his students that it was used "already in my early Freiburg lecture courses."[43]

Thus, along with early lectures courses such as the SS1923 *Ontology—The Hermeneutics of Facticity* (OHF), *Supplements* adds to the later experimental texts after "the turn" certain background material lacking in them: important early themes and terminology to which these texts returned and thereby a filling out of Heidegger's claim that they constituted in part a return to his "essays" before *Being and Time.* Translated later texts which, in making this claim, most clearly present themselves as a return to the Heidegger before "Heidegger I" and can thus especially be supplemented with the present volume include *On the Way to Language,*[44] which returns to the theme of the relation of language and being in the 1915 postdoctoral dissertation (chapter 5 of this volume) and that of hermeneutics in the early twenties (see chapters 4, 7, 9, and 10 of this volume, as well as OHF, "Translator's Epilogue"[45]), and *On Time and Being,* which also returns to the reading of Aristotle's notion of truth in the early twenties (see chapter 9 of this volume).[46] Another candidate connecting later texts to those before *Being and Time* is the anthology *Pathmarks*[47] which, though primarily intended to present later texts, opens with the 1920 article on Jaspers' Kierkegaardian philosophy of existence included in chapter 7 of this volume. The supplements *(Nachträge)* in this volume also can be used with later texts such as *Contributions* [Beiträge] *to Philosophy— On Event* which, though not explicitly relating themselves to the earliest texts, nonetheless involve critical reappropriations of earlier themes and terminology, including Heidegger's early theological interests in his phenomenology of religion (cf. GA65 405ff.). For example, *Contributions* returns to the technical term *Ereignis* ("properizing event") first introduced in KNS1919 (GA56/57) for characterizing the happening of factical life's intentional relation to being; "indication" *(Anzeige)* first introduced around 1920 (see chapters 7 and 9 in this volume); and the triad of terms "relation" *(Bezug)*, "content" *(Gehalt)*, and "actualization" *(Vollzug)*, which first became technical terms also around 1920 (see chapters 7ff.).[48] Similarly, essays in the English-language anthology *The Question Concerning Technology*[49] picked up much earlier discussions of technology in the late teens and early twenties (see YH 320–22, 370), and those in *Poetry Language Thought*[50] returned to poetic terms such as "it worlds" and "it events" from KNS1919 and "whiling" from SS1923 (OHF), as well as to the general theme of the relation between philosophy and art that had concerned Heidegger since his student years.

Very little has been written about Heidegger's early interest in art, but he pursued in high school and during his university studies an avid interest in the literature of Stifter, Hölderlin, Lessing, Goethe, Schiller, Dostoevsky, Rilke, Trakl, and Greek tragedy.[51] In fact, the report of Heidegger's religion teacher on his senior high school years complained that "at times he pursued German literature—in which he is very well read—a bit too much, to the detriment of other disciplines."[52] During his student years he also took at least two university courses in art history and published reviews of literary works and his own poems.[53] His interest in the relation of philosophy and art stretches from his first essay published in *The Academician* in 1910 (chapter 2 of this volume) to his 1915 postdoctoral dissertation, whose introduction underscored the importance of relating the theory of the categories of being in medieval Scholastic philosophy to the "total culture" of the Middle Ages and so promised a future "phenomenological investigation of mystical, moral-theological, and ascetic literature in medieval Scholasticism" (GA1 205). Accordingly, the supplementary "Conclusion" to the dissertation for its book publication opened with a quote from the mystical German poet Novalis and again touched upon medieval mystical literature (chapter 5 in this volume, pp. 62, 64 n. 4), just as the publication of the trial lecture on the category of time Heidegger presented along with his dissertation opened with a motto from the medieval mystic Eckhart (chapter 4, p. 49).

This interest extended into the Early Freiburg Period and then, after being eclipsed in the Marburg Period culminating in *Being and Time,* beyond into the later writings on the philosophy of art. At times taking up the neo-Kantian doctrine of the different spheres of categorial value, including aesthetic value, which Heidegger explores at one point with the "poetic" neologism "'it values' for me" *("es wertet" für mich),* the lecture courses of KNS1919, SS1919 (GA56/57), and

WS1919–20 (GA58) and the notes for the lecture course on "The Philosophical Foundations of Medieval Mysticism," originally planned for WS1919–20 but undelivered (GA60), continue in the same vein as the postdoctoral dissertation, approaching the "life-worlds" in "art history" (e.g., Hölderlin's translation of Sophocles' *Antigone*, the German Romantic poets, Shakespeare, Dostoevsky, Stefan George, Rembrandt, Bach, and mystical literature) as primordial expressions of the manner in which categorial sense manifests itself pretheoretically as an "it worlds for me" and an "it events."[54] The 1920 essay on Karl Jaspers focuses on Jaspers' inappropriate "aesthetic attitude" (chapter 7 of this volume, pp. 88ff.). The SS1921–22 lecture course discusses "the relationship between philosophy and art" in terms of an "anology" between the primordial active sense of "philosophy" as "philosophizing" and that of music as "making music" *(musizieren)* (GA61 46–50). The 1922 essay on the effective history of Aristotle in Western philosophy again takes up from the postdoctoral dissertation the question of the relationship between "the hymnology and music of the Middle Ages, as well as its architecture and plastic arts," and "the philosophical and theological anthropology of this era" (see chapter 9 of this volume, p. 125, n. 11). The SS1923 lecture course again discusses the relation between "art history" and philosophy (GA63 36–57/OHF 29–45). When Heidegger comes to work up his lecture course manuscripts into the book *Being and Time* in 1926, the earlier discussions of art are collapsed into a few elliptical comments on how art and especially poetry have to be understood in terms of the basic existential structures of human existence studied in ontology.[55] But the earlier discussions were subsequently renewed in Heidegger's later philosophy of art, so that the famous "turn" in his thought after *Being and Time* is for this reason not just a novelty but also in part a "return."

Note too that in fashioning in 1919 neologisms such as "it values," "it worlds," and "it events," which are takeoffs from a double reading of *es gibt* as both "there is" and more literally "it gives" (GA56/57 65–68), the young Heidegger also was putting to work in philosophy his abilities as a published poet since 1910. This literary crafting of new terminology for philosophy continues through the early 1920s with neologisms such as his often enigmatic translations of Aristotle's key terms in 1921–22 (chapter 9 of this volume) and the highly poetic term *Jeweiligkeit* ("the temporal particularity of awhileness") in 1923–24 (GA63/OHF) to the recycling of earlier neologisms such as *das Man* (the "they" or "everyone") in *Being and Time*. This "poetic thinking" manifests itself again in an emphatic style in the later writings, such as the *Beiträge zur Philosophie, Vorträge und Aufsätze,* and *Zur Sache des Denkens,* and so here too, then, Heidegger's "turn" after *Being and Time,* with its use of poetic vocabulary such as *Ereignis* ("event," "enownment"), *Es gibt* ("there is/it gives"), *Welten* ("worlding"), *Dingen* (thinging), and *Weilen* ("whiling"), shows itself to be in part a "return" to and radicalization of an earlier style of poetic thinking.[56] Heidegger may have been saying as much in a 1957 curriculum vitae that later served as the introduction to the reprinting of his student writings in a single volume. Referring to

the courses he took from his teachers in theology and art history, he stated that
"the decisive and therefore ineffable influence on my own later academic career
came from two men . . . the one was Carl Braig, professor of systematic theology. . . . The other one was the art historian Wilhelm Vöge."[57]

SUPPLEMENTING THE REDISCOVERY OF HEIDEGGER'S EARLIEST THOUGHT

This book carries forward into the English-speaking world the work of supplementing the originally incomplete plan of Heidegger's *Collected Edition*, which
was announced in the first publisher's prospectus in the fall of 1974 but did not
include many of the early texts before *Being and Time*, including those presented
in chapters 2, 6, 8, 9, and 10 of this volume. The prospectus, issued on the occasion of Heidegger's eighty-fifth birthday, stated that the edition was intended "to
allow the path of the question of being to be seen in the sequence of its steps
more penetratingly than before. . . . Because the *Collected Edition* is meant to
show the movement of Heidegger's path of thinking, the chronological principle
of the genesis of the texts forms the basis of each division." Nonetheless, the
admission was made that "it remains postponed for a later decision whether the
lecture courses from the early Freiburg period (1916–1923) will also be published as a supplement *[Supplement]* to the second division" containing the lecture courses from the Marburg and Later Freiburg Periods. Moreover, the
prospectus' plan for "Division III: Unpublished Essays" made no mention of
unpublished essays preceding the Marburg Period. Eventually, the fifth prospectus of April 1984 announced that the literary executor, Dr. Hermann Heidegger,
had made the decision to include the lecture courses from the Early Freiburg
Period as a "supplement." To date, ten of these courses have appeared in German
and one in English translation (OHF), with a number of others currently being
prepared for publication in English.[58] Prospectuses also have announced plans to
supplement the *Collected Edition* with previously unpublished shorter texts preceding the Marburg Period, as well as with a fuller selection of those from the
Marburg Period itself, and a good number of these shorter texts, as well as early
correspondence, have been published either in the *Collected Edition* or outside of
it.[59] With more than half of it consisting of selections from these shorter texts
added to the originally incomplete plan of the *Collected Edition*, this book is,
along with translations of early lecture courses, an important counterpart in the
English-speaking world to the ongoing work in the German language of supplementing the *Collected Edition* and thereby allowing the constantly supplemental
"sequence" of Heidegger's texts "to be seen . . . more penetratingly than before."
    For this reason, as well as because Heidegger's texts before *Being and Time*
are generally still little known in the English-speaking world, this book makes an
important contribution to the recent discovery of Heidegger's earliest thought
and the ongoing labor of supplementing our still incomplete historical picture
and critical evaluation of it. After the publication of *Being and Time*, the large

corpus of earlier published and unpublished texts comprising course manuscripts, articles, talks, books, book reviews, poems, and correspondence soon fell
into oblivion, with the exception of Heidegger's cursory, sometimes historically
inaccurate discussions of them in later autobiographical comments, anecdotal
accounts by his students such as Oskar Becker, Karl Löwith, Hans-Georg
Gadamer, and Hannah Arendt who privately circulated them and held them in
very high esteem, and eventually Otto Pöggeler's ground-breaking work *Martin
Heidegger's Path of Thinking* in the early sixties which, by using Heidegger's
unpublished manuscripts, for the first time systematically linked *Being and Time*
and later writings to Heidegger's earliest thought (Pöggeler 1987).[60] Then, with
the publication of the *Collected Edition* from the late seventies onward, the rediscovery of these lost texts gained momentum in the nineties with a series of books
presenting historical studies, philosophical evaluations, and independent experimental uses of Heidegger's early thought that were for the first time based on the
whole of his early corpus and not just *Being and Time*.[61] Five of the nine early
Heidegger texts in this volume (chapters 2, 6, 8, 9, and 10) were first discovered
in the eighties and then became known to Heidegger scholarship in the English-
speaking world only in the mid-nineties. Though it may itself need to be supplemented when additional, important shorter texts planned for publication in
the *Collected Edition* appear in the future, as may be suggested by the chronology
of the large body of Heidegger's early research and publications in chapter 1 of
this volume, *Supplements* nonetheless has, along with translated early lecture
courses, at the very least established a reliable textual basis in the English language for scholars, teachers, and students to continue studying, evaluating, and
experimenting with Heidegger's earliest "essays" before *Being and Time*. These
"dangerous supplements"[62] promise not only to add to our previous understanding of the development and significance of Heidegger's thought but also to correct and supplant it in important ways.

Chapter One

CHRONOLOGICAL OVERVIEW

Education, Teaching, Research, and Publication

JOHN VAN BUREN

The section that follows presents a chronology of Heidegger's education, and the remaining sections offer a chronology of his professional appointments, teaching, research, and publications from the Student Period to the composition of *Being and Time* in 1926 at the midpoint of the Marburg Period.[1] The ordering of data in entries on Heidegger's texts is as follows: date of composition (or if not available, date of original publication), genre, original German title if different from the title in the *Gesamtausgabe*, original publication, reprinting in the *Gesamtausgabe* if applicable, and the published English translation if available. First references to volumes in the *Gesamtausgabe* provide the volume's title with the date of publication in parentheses. Thereafter, only the volume number is given. Unless otherwise indicated, the cited edition of these volumes is the first. When no published English translation exists for a German text, an English translation of the title has been inserted in parentheses. Daggers in the left margin flag texts that can be found in subsequent chapters of this volume.

STUDENT PERIOD: EDUCATION

1889. Martin Heidegger, born September 26 in Messkirch, Germany

EARLIEST EDUCATION

1895–1903. State grammar and middle schools in Messkirch

1903–1906. State Gymnasium in Constance with residence at the Catholic archdiocesan Gymnasium Seminary in preparation for the archdiocesan priesthood

1906–1909. State Berthold Gymnasium in Freiburg with residence at the archdiocesan Gymnasium Seminary

1909. Organizes private high school circle for the study of German literature

7/13/1909. High school baccalaureate awarded with the highest possible overall grade. Academic subjects: Religion, German, German Essay, Latin, Greek, French, Hebrew, English, Mathematics (Algebra, Geometry), History, Physics, Philosophy, Singing, Gymnastics. Statement of intent regarding university studies: "theology."

9/30/1909. Jesuit Novitiate at Tisis near Feldkirch, Austria, with dismissal two weeks later for health reasons

UNIVERSITY OF FREIBURG, DEPARTMENT OF THEOLOGY

WS1909–10. Department of Theology at the University of Freiburg in preparation for the archdiocesan priesthood, with residence at the archdiocesan Theological Seminary. Courses enrolled in: Encyclopedia of Theological Disciplines, two hours (Rev. Julius Meyer);[2] Introduction to the Sacred Scripture of the Old Testament, four hours (Rev. Gottfried Hoberg); Exegesis of Paul's Letter to the Romans, four hours (Rev. Simon Weber); General History of the Church, Part I, with Special Consideration of the Post–Nicene Period, four hours (Rev. Georg Pfeilschifter); Theory of Religion, three hours (Rev. Heinrich Straubinger); Logic, four hours (Prof. Johann Uebinger, Department of Philosophy).

SS1910. Courses enrolled in: Messianic Prophesies, three hours (Hoberg); Hermeneutics with the History of Exegesis, two hours (Hoberg); Introduction to the Sacred Scripture of the New Testament, four hours (Weber); General History of the Church, Part II, with Special Consideration of the 16th Century, six hours (Pfeilschifter); Theory of Revelation and the Church, three hours (Straubinger); Metaphysics, 4 hrs. (Uebinger)

WS1910–11. Courses enrolled in: Introduction to Catholic Dogmatics: Doctrine of God, four hours (Rev. Carl Braig); Exegesis of the Holy Gospel According to John, four hours (Weber); General Moral Theology, Parts I–III, three hours (Mayer); Doctrine of Property, one hour (Mayer); Catholic Canon Law, Part I: Introduction, Sources and Constitution, four hours (Rev. Emil Göller); General History of the Church, Part III: Age of Enlightenment, one hour (Pfeilschifter); History of the German Constitution from the 16th Century to the Present, four hours (Prof. Georg von Below, Department of Philosophy); History of Medieval Mysticism, two hours (Rev. Joseph Sauer).

SS1911. Courses enrolled in: Theological Cosmology: Creation, Preservation, and Governance of the World, four hours (Braig); Special Moral Theology, Parts I–II, four hours (Mayer); The Christian Art of the 19th Century and the Present, one hour (Sauer); The Age of the Renaissance (History of the Late Middle Ages), four hours (Prof. Heinrich Finke, Department of Philosophy).

Department of Natural Sciences and Mathematics

WS1911–12. Withdraws from the Department of Theology and the Theological Seminary for health reasons, abandoning career plans for the priesthood[3]; transfers to the Department of Natural Sciences and Mathematics with the initial intention of majoring in mathematics and taking the State Examination granting the degree required for a teaching career in high schools; shortly thereafter, considers moving to the University of Göttingen to study with the phenomenologist Edmund Husserl, but for financial reasons he remains in his new department at the University of Freiburg with the intention of majoring in philosophy, while attending courses also in the Departments of Philosophy, Theology, and Classical Philology. Courses enrolled in for WS1911–12: Analytic Geometry of Space, one hour (Prof. Lothar Heffter); Exercises in Analytic Geometry, one hour (Heffter); Differential Calculus, four hours (Prof. Alfred Loewy); Exercises in Differential Calculus, one hour (Loewy); Experimental Physics, two hours (Prof. Wilhelm Himstedt); Experimental Inorganic Chemistry, five hours (Prof. Ludwig Gattermann); Logic and Epistemology, four hours (Prof. Arthur Schneider, Department of Philosophy). Seminar: Spinoza's *Ethics,* no hours listed (Schneider). Courses audited sometime after SS1911:[4] Dogmatic Theology (Braig);[5] Gospel of John (Prof. Eduard Schwartz, Classical Philology);[6] Hellenic Mystery Religions (Prof. Richard Reitzenstein, Classical Philology); Art History (Prof. Wilhelm Vöge, Art History);[7] Botany (teacher unknown).[8]

SS1912. Courses enrolled in: Algebraic Analysis, three hours (Heffter); Exercises in [Algebraic] Analysis, one hour (Heffter); Integral Calculus, four hours (Loewy); Exercises in Integral Calculus, one hour (Loewy); Experimental Physics, five hours (Himstedt); Introduction to Epistemology and Metaphysics, two hours (Prof. Heinrich Rickert, Department of Philosophy); Epistemological Exercises in Theory of Judgment (Seminar), no hours listed (Rickert).

WS1912–13. Courses enrolled in: Advanced Algebra, four hours (Heffter); Theory of Differential Equations, four hours (Loewy); General History of Philosophy, four hours (Schneider); Exercises in Epistemological Problems, no hours listed (Schneider).

SS1913. Course enrolled in: The Age of the Renaissance, four hours (Finke).

DEPARTMENT OF PHILOSOPHY

7/26/1913. Department of Philosophy recommends Heidegger for the doctoral degree in philosophy summa cum laude. Dissertation submitted with a curriculum vitae[9] on 6/30: "Theory of Judgment in Psychologism: Critical and Positive Contributions to Logic" (Die Lehre vom Urteil im Psychologismus. Ein kritisch-positiver Beitrag zur Logik) (GA1 59–188), directed by Schneider.[10] Oral examination on 7/26 on philosophy (Schneider) and the minor subjects of mathematics (Heffter) and medieval history (Finke).

8/20/1913. Application to the Freiburg Archdiocesan Chancellery Office for a Von Schaezler Grant in order "to dedicate himself to the study of Christian philosophy and to pursue an academic career" through work on the postdoctoral degree (Habilitation) and license to teach in German universities (venia legendi) as a lecturer (Privatdozent). Awarded on 9/29/1913 for the 1913–14 academic year with the stated expectation that the applicant "would remain true to the spirit of Thomistic philosophy."[11]

WS1913–14. Auditing of Finke's seminar on method in the science of history in preparation for the postdoctoral dissertation;[12] auditing of Rickert's seminar in preparation for the postdoctoral dissertation. Seminar paper therein on the limits of concept-formation in the natural sciences.[13]

SS1914. Auditing of Rickert's seminar.[14]

9/20/1914. Application for a renewal of the Von Schaezler Grant in order "to make possible the last step toward a career in the service of researching and teaching Christian Scholastic philosophy" and "the Catholic worldview." Awarded for the 1914–15 academic year.

7/15/1915. Lecture titled "Question and Judgment" (Frage und Urteil) in Rickert's seminar.[15]

† 7/27/1915. Department of Philosophy recommends Heidegger for the postdoctoral degree and license to teach in German universities as a lecturer.

Dissertation submitted with a curriculum vitae[16] on 7/2/1915: "The Theory of Categories and Meaning in Duns Scotus" (Die Kategorien- und Bedeutungslehre des Duns Scotus) (GA1 189–398), directed by Rickert.[17] Required trial lecture presented on 7/27/1915 to the Department of Philosophy: "The Concept of Time in the Science of History" (Der Zeitbegriff in der Geschichtswissenschaft) (GA1 413–33; translated in chapter 4 of this volume).

8/5/1915. The University of Freiburg officially confers the rank of lecturer with the right to begin giving courses in WS1915–16.

† 12/13/1915. Successful application for a third Von Schaezler Grant to work on the publication of his expanded postdoctoral dissertation (supplemental conclusion to be found in GA1 399–411; translated in chapter 5 of this volume), as well as of "a nearly finished investigation on the logic and psychology of late Scholasticism," and thereby to facilitate "his academic life's work [being] oriented to making the wealth of ideas inherited from Scholasticism applicable to the future intellectual struggle for the Christian ideal of life in Catholicism."

STUDENT PERIOD: RESEARCH AND PUBLICATION

Previously unpublished poems. "Fernes Land" (Distant Land), "Hast die Sonne du verloren" (Have You Lost the Sun?), etc. In "I. Frühe unveröffentlichte Gedichte" of GA81: *Gedachtes* (forthcoming). The publisher's prospectus does not state the precise years in which these early poems were composed.

† March 1910. Book review essay. "Per mortem ad vitam (Gedanken über Jörgensens *Lebenslüge und Lebenswahrheit*)," *Der Akademiker* 2, no. 5 (March, 1910): 72–73. Reprinted in GA16: *Reden und andere Zeugnisse eines Lebenswege 1910–1976*, ed. Hermann Heidegger (2000), pp. 3–6. Translated by John Protevi as "Per mortem ad vitam (Thoughts on Johannes Jörgensen's *Lies of Life and Truth of Life*) in *Graduate Faculty Philosophy Journal* 14–15 (1991): 487–91, with an introduction by Hugo Ott, who first rediscovered these *Der Akademiker* articles in the late 1980s (481–85); reprinted in revised form in chapter 2 of this volume with the generous permission of the journal.

May 1910. Book review. "Förster, Fr. W. *Autorität und Freiheit. Betrachtungen zum Kulturproblem der Kirche*," *Der Akademiker* 2, no. 7 (May, 1910): 109–10. Reprinted in GA16 7–8. Translated by John Protevi as "Förster, Fr. W. *Authority and Freedom: Observations on the Cultural Problem of the Church*," *Graduate Faculty Philosophy Journal* 14–15 (1991): 491–93.

August 27, 1910. Newspaper article. "Abraham a Sankta Clara. Zur Enthüllung seines Denkmals in Kreenheinstetten am 15. August 1910" (Abraham of Saint Claire: On the Unveiling of His Monument in Kreenheinstetten, August 15, 1910), *Allgemeine Rundschau. Wochenschrift für Politik und Kultur* 7, no. 35 (August 27, 1910): 605. Reprinted in GA13: *Aus der Erfahrung des Denkens,* ed. Hermann Heidegger (1983), pp. 1–3.

October 29, 1910. Poem. "Sterbende Pracht" (Dying Splendor), *Allgemeine Rundschau* 7, no. 44 (October 29, 1910): 775. Reprinted in GA13 5.

December 1910. Book review. "Cüppers, Ad. Jos. *Versiegelte Lippen. Erzählung aus dem irischen Volksleben des 19. Jahrhunderts,*" *Der Akademiker* 3, no. 2 (December 1910): 29. Reprinted in GA16 9. Translated by John Protevi as "Cüppers, Ad. Jos. *Sealed Lips: The Story of the Irish Folk Life in the 19th Century,*" *Graduate Faculty Philosophy Journal* 14–15 (1991): 495.

January 1911. Book review. "Jörgensen, Joh. *Das Reisebuch. Licht und dunke Natur und Geist,*" *Der Akademiker* 3, no. 3 (January 1911): 45. Reprinted in GA16 10. Translated by John Protevi as "Jörgensen, Joh. *Travelogue: Light and Dark Nature and Spirit,*" *Graduate Faculty Philosophy Journal* 14–15 (1991): 495.

March 1911. Essay. "Zur philosophischen Orientierung für Akademiker," *Der Akademiker* 3, no. 5 (March 1911): 66–67. Reprinted in GA16 11–14. Translated by John Protevi as "On a Philosophical Orientation for Academics," *Graduate Faculty Philosophy Journal* 14–15 (1991): 497–501.

March 25, 1911. Poem. "Ölbergstunden" (Hours on the Mount of Olives), *Allgemeine Rundschau* 8, no. 12 (March 25, 1911): 197. Reprinted in GA13 6.

April 8, 1911. Poem. "Wir wollen warten" (We Shall Wait), *Allgemeine Rundschau* 8, no. 14 (April 8, 1911): 246. Reprinted in GA13 6.

May 15, 1911. Book review. "Zimmermann, O., S. J. *Das Gottesbedürfnis*" in *Akademische Bonafatius-Korrespondenz* (May 15, 1911), p. 214. Reprinted in GA16 15.

July 1911. Poem. "Auf stillen Pfaden" (On Quiet Paths), *Der Akademiker* 3, no. 6 (July 1911): 140. Reprinted in GA16 16.

1911. Unpublished Poem. "Julinacht" (July Night). In GA16 17.

† 1912. Essay. "Das Realitätsproblem in der modernen Philosophie," *Philosophisches Jahrbuch der Görresgesellschaft* 25 (1912): 353–63. Reprinted in GA1: *Frühe Schriften,* ed. Friedrich-Wilhelm von Herrmann (1978), pp. 1–15. Translated by Philip J. Bossert as "The Problem of Reality in Modern Philosophy" in *Journal of the British Society for Phenomenology* 4 (1973):

64–71, reprinted with extensive revisions by the original translator and John van Buren in chapter 3 of this volume. The permission of the journal is gratefully acknowledged.

March 1912. Essay. "Religionspsychologie und Unterbewusstsein," *Der Akademiker* 4, no. 5 (March, 1912): 66–68. Reprinted in GA16 18–28. Translated by John Protevi as "Psychology of Religion and the Subconscious," *Graduate Faculty Philosophy Journal* 14–15 (1991): 503–17.

March 1912. Book review. "Gredt, Jos. O.S.B. *Elementa Philosophiae Aristotelico-Thomisticae. Vol. I. Logica, Philos. nat. Edit. II.*," *Der Akademiker* 4, no. 5 (March, 1912): 76–77. Reprinted in GA16 29–30. Translated by John Protevi as "Gredt, Jos. O.S.B. *Elements of Aristotelian-Thomistic Philosophy*, vol. 1: *Logic*, Philos. nat. Edit. II," *Graduate Faculty Philosophy Journal* 14–15 (1991): 517–19.

March 17, 1912. Letter to Josef Sauer. In Ott 1988/1993, p. 73/70–71.

October–December 1912. Essay. "Neuere Forschungen über Logik" (Recent Research in Logic), *Literarische Rundschau für das katholische Deutschland* 38, no. 10 (1912), cols. 465–72; no. 11, cols. 517–24; no. 12, cols. 565–70. Reprinted in GA1 17–43.

1912ff. Correspondence with Henrich Rickert. *Martin Heidegger/Heinrich Rickert: Briefe 1912 bis 1933 und andere Dokumente Aus den Nachlässen,* ed. Alfred Denker (Frankfurt: Klostermann, 2002).

January 1913. Book review. "*Bibliothek wertvoller Novellen und Erzählungen.* Herausgegeben von Prof. Dr. O. Hellinghaus. Bd. IX," *Der Akademiker* 4, no. 3 (January 1913): 45. Reprinted in GA16 31. Translated by John Protevi as "*Library of Valuable Novellas and Stories,* vol. 9, O. Hellinghaus, ed.," *Graduate Faculty Philosophy Journal* 14–15 (1991): 519.

1913. Book review. "*Kant Briefe in Auswahl.* Herausgegeben und erläutert von F. Ohmann," *Literarische Rundschau für das katholische Deutschland* 39, no. 2 (1913), col. 74. Reprinted in GA1 45.

1913. Book review. "Nikolai von Bubnoff, *Zeitlichkeit und Zeitlosigkeit,*" *Literarische Rundschau für das katholische Deutschland* 39, no. 4 (1913), cols. 178–79. Reprinted in GA1 46.

June 30, 1913. Doctoral dissertation "Die Lehre vom Urteil im Psychologismus. Ein kritisch-positiver Beitrag zur Logik" (Theory of Judgment in Psychologism: A Critical and Positive Contribution to Logic), submitted on this date to the Department of Philosophy at the University of Freiburg.

June 30, 1913. Curriculum vitae submitted with the doctoral dissertation. Published as "Lebenslauf (1913)" with an accompanying English translation ("Curriculum Vitae 1913") in Sheehan 1988, pp. 115, 106. Also in *Martin Heidegger/Heinrich Rickert: Briefwechsel 1912 bis 1933,* p. 92.

August 20, 1913. Letter of application to the Freiburg Archdiocesan Chancellery Office for a Von Schaezler Grant to work on his postdoctoral degree in the area of "Christian Philosophy." Excerpts in Hugo Ott, "Der Habilitand Martin Heidegger und das von Schaezler'sche Stipendium," *Freiburger Diözesanarchiv* 108 (1986): 154. Grant for the 1913–14 academic year awarded on September 29.

1913–14. Seminar paper on the limits of concept-formation in the natural sciences in Heinrich Rickert's seminar of WS1913–14. In *Martin Heidegger/Heinrich Rickert: Briefwechsel 1912 bis 1933*, pp. 77–79.

1914. Excerpts from the doctoral dissertation. "Die Lehre vom Urteil im Psychologismus" (Theory of Judgment in Psychologism), *Zeitschrift für Philosophie und philosophischer Kritik* 155 (1914): 148–72; 156 (1915): 41–78.

1914. Publication of doctoral dissertation under the same title, *Die Lehre vom Urteil im Psychologismus. Ein kritisch-positiver Beitrag zur Logik* (Leipzig: Johann Ambrosius Barth, 1914). Reprinted in GA1 59–188.

1914. A slightly revised version of the above-cited "Lebenslauf (1913)." "Lebenslauf" in *Die Lehre vom Urteil im Psychologismus*, p. 111. Reprinted in GA16 32. Translated by Therese Schrynemakers as "Curriculum Vitae," *Listening* 12 (1977): 110.

1914. Book review. "Franz Brentano, *Von der Klassifikation der psychischen Phänomene. Neue, durch Nachträge stark vermehrte Ausgabe der betreffenden Kapitel der* Psychologie vom empirischen Standpunkt" (Franz Brentano, *On the Classification of Psychical Phenomena: New Expanded Edition of a Chapter From Psychology From an Empirical Point of View*), *Literarische Rundschau für das katholische Deutschland* 40, no. 5 (1914), cols. 233–34. Reprinted in GA1 47–48.

1914. Book review. "Charles Sentroul, *Kant und Aristoteles*" (Charles Sentroul, *Kant and Aristotle*), *Literarische Rundschau für das katholische Deutschland* 40, no. 7 (1914), cols. 330–32. Reprinted in GA1 49–53.

1914. Book review. "*Kant-Laienbrevier. Eine Darstellung der Kantischen Welt- und Lebensanschauung für den ungelehrten Gebildeten aus Kants Schriften, Briefen und mündlichen Äußerungen. Zusammengestellt von F. Groß*" (*A Kant Reader: Portrait of His View of the World and Life Designed for the Non-Expert and Drawn from His Writings, Correspondence, and Oral Remarks*, ed. F. Gross), *Literarische Rundschau für das katholische Deutschland* 40, no. 8 (1914), cols. 376–77. Reprinted in GA1 54.

July 19, 1914. Letter to Father Engelbert Krebs. In Ott 1988/1993, p. 83/81. Translated also in Sheehan 1988, p. 113.

September 20 and November 23, 1914. Letters to the Freiburg Archdiocesan Chancellery Office for a second Von Schaezler Grant to continue working on his postdoctoral degree "in the service of Christian Scholastic philosophy and the Catholic worldview." Excerpts in Ott, "Der Habilitand Martin Heidegger und das von Schaezler'sche Stipendium," pp. 155–56. Grant for the 1914–15 academic year awarded on November 18.

1915. Book review. "W. Wundt. Probleme der Völkerpsychologie," *Philosophisches Jahrbuch* 28 (1915): 88–90. Reprinted in GA16 33–35.

January 13, 1915. Article. "Das Kriegstriduum in Meßkirch" (Messkirch's Wartime Triduum), *Heuberger Volksblatt* 17 (January 13, 1915).

March 1915. Poem. "Trost" (Consolation), *Heliand* 6 (March 1915): 161. Reprinted in GA16 36.

July 2, 1915. Postdoctoral dissertation "Die Kategorien- und Bedeutungslehre des Duns Scotus" (The Theory of Categories and Meaning in Duns Scotus), submitted on this date to the Department of Philosophy at the University of Freiburg. In GA1 189–398.

July 2, 1915. Curriculum vitae submitted with the dissertation. Published as "Lebenslauf (1915)" with an accompanying English translation ("Curriculum Vitae 1915") in Sheehan 1988, pp. 116–17. Also in GA16 37–39.

July 15, 1915. Lecture in Heinrich Rickert's seminar at the University of Freiburg. "Frage und Urteil" (Question and Judgment) in *Martin Heidegger/Heinrich Rickert: Briefwechsel 1912 bis 1933*, pp. 81–90. Also in GA80 (forthcoming).

† July 27, 1915. Trial lecture presented to the Department of Philosophy as a requirement for the postdoctoral degree and license to teach. "Der Zeitbegriff in der Geschichtswissenschaft." Published under the same title and in a slightly revised version in *Zeitschrift für Philosophie und philosophische Kritik* 161 (1916): 173–88. Reprinted with Heidegger's marginalia in GA1 413–33. Translated by Harry S. Taylor and Hans W. Uffelmann as "The Concept of Time in the Science of History" in *Journal of the British Society for Phenomenology* 9 (1978): 3–10; reprinted with extensive revisions by John van Buren in chapter 4 of this volume. The permissions of the original translators and the journal are gratefully acknowledged.

EARLY FREIBURG PERIOD

LECTURER, UNIVERSITY OF FREIBURG

WS1915–16. Lecture course. "Die Grundlinien der antiken und scholastischen Philosophie" (Basic Outlines of Ancient and Medieval Philosophy), two hours. No publication announced.

WS1915–16. Seminar. "Über Kant, *Prolegomena*" (On Kant's *Prolegomena*). No publication announced.

December 13, 1915. Letter to the Freiburg Archdiocesan Chancellery Office for a third Von Schaezler Grant to work on the publication of the post-doctoral dissertation, as well as of a related investigation dealing with "the logic and psychology of Late Scholasticism" and thereby to make a contribution to "the future struggle for the Christian ideal of life in Catholicism." In Ott, "Der Habilitand Martin Heidegger und das von Schaezler'sche Stipendium," pp. 156–59.

1916. Poem. "Einsamkeit" (Loneliness), *Heliand* 7 (1916): 161. Reprinted in GA16 40.

SS1916. Lecture course. "Der deutsche Idealismus" (German Idealism), two hours. No publication announced.

SS1916. Seminar. "Übungen über Texte aus den logischen Schriften des Aristoteles (mit E. Krebs)" (Exercises with Texts from Aristotle's Logical Writings [co-taught with E. Krebs]). No publication announced.

Summer 1916. Poem. "Abendgang auf der Reichnau." In *Das Bodenseebuch 1917. Ein Buch für Land und Leute,* vol. 4 (Constance: Reuss and Itta, 1916), p. 152. Reprinted in GA13 7. Translated by William J. Richardson as "Eventide on Reichnau" in William J. Richardson, *Through Phenomenology to Thought* (The Hague: Martinus Nijhoff, 1963), p. 1.

† 1916. Publication of the postdoctoral dissertation under the same title *Die Kategorien- und Bedeutungslehre des Duns Scotus* (Tübingen: J.C.B Mohr, 1916) and with the inclusion of the supplemental conclusion, "Schluß. Das Kategorienproblem." Reprinted in GA1 399–411. Translated by Harold J. Robbins as "Duns Scotus's Theory of the Categories and of Meaning," Ph.D. dissertation, DePaul University, 1978. Supplemental conclusion translated by Roderick M. Stewart as "The Problem of Categories" in *Man and World* 12 (1979): 378–86; reprinted with extensive revisions by the original translator and John van Buren in chapter 5 of this volume. The permission of the journal is gratefully acknowledged.

WS1916–17. "Grundfragen der Logik" (Basic Problems in Logic), two hours. No publication announced.

January 7, 1917. Letter to the medievalist Martin Grabmann. In Hermann Köstler, "Heidegger schreibt an Grabmann," *Philosophisches Jahrbuch* 87 (1980): 98–104.

SS1917–WS1918–19. No teaching due to conscription into war service.

† 1917. Author's book notice. "Selbstanzeige. *Die Kategorien- und Bedeutungslehre des Duns Scotus,*" *Kant-Studien* XXI (1917): 467–68. Reprinted in GA1: *Frühe Schriften,* p. 412. Translated by John van Buren as "Author's Book Notice" in chapter 5 of this volume.

1917. Informal talk. "Über das Wesen der Religion" (On the Essence of Religion). In GA60: *Phänomenologie des religiösen Lebens,* ed. Matthias Jung, Thomas Regehly, and Claudius Strube (1995), pp. 319–22. GA60 translated by Jennifer Gossetti as *Phenomenology of Religious Life* (Bloomington: Indiana University Press, forthcoming).

1917–19. Notes on phenomenology of religion and medieval mysticism that were to be used in the canceled lecture course of WS1919–20, "Die philosophischen Grundlagen der mittelalterlichen Mystik" (The Philosophical Foundations of Medieval Mysticism). In GA60 301–37.

June 15, 1918ff. Correspondence with Elisabeth Blochmann. Martin Heidegger and Elisabeth Blochmann, *Briefwechsel, 1918–1969,* ed. Joachim W. Storck (Marbach am Neckar: Deutsche Schillergesellschaft, 1989).

ASSISTANT TO EDMUND HUSSERL

January 7, 1919. Edmund Husserl submits a letter of request to the Ministry of Education that Martin Heidegger be appointed to a salaried assistantship to the chair of philosophy that he had been occupying since 1916 at the University of Freiburg. Request granted the following year.

† January 9, 1919. Letter to Father Engelbert Krebs. Bernhard Casper first discovered and published this letter in his article "Martin Heidegger und die Theologische Fakultät Freiburg, 1909–1923," *Freiburger Diözesan-Archiv* 100 (1980): 541; Hugo Ott then published a slightly corrected version in Ott 1988/1993, pp. 106–107/106–107. Translated by John van Buren as "Letter to Engelbert Krebs (January 9, 1919)" in John van Buren, "The Young Heidegger," Ph.D. dissertation, McMaster University, 1989, pp. 573–74; presented in revised form in chapter 6 of this volume with the permission of Hermann Heidegger, executor of his father's literary estate.

KNS 1919. Lecture course. "Die Idee der Philosophie und das Weltanschauungsproblem" (The Idea of Philosophy and the Problem of Worldviews), two hours. In GA56/57: *Zur Bestimmung der Philosophie,* ed. Bernd Heimbüchel (1987), pp. 1–117. GA56/57 translated by E. H. Sadler as *Toward the Definition of Philosophy* (London: Athlone Press, 2001).

SS1919. Lecture course. "Phänomenologie und transzendentale Wertphilosophie" (Phenomenology and Transcendental Philosophy of Value), one hour. In GA56/57 119–203.

SS1919. Lecture course. "Über das Wesen der Universität und des akademischen Studiums" (On the Essence of the University and Academic Studies), one hour. In GA56/57 205–14.

SS1919. Seminar. "Einführung in die Phänomenologie im Anschluß an Descartes, *Meditationes*" (Introduction to Phenomenology in Connection with Descartes' *Meditations*). No publication announced.

WS1919–20. Lecture course. "Grundprobleme der Phänomenologie" (Basic Problems in Phenomenology), two hours. Published as GA58: *Grundprobleme der Phänomenologie*, ed. Hans-Helmuth Gander (1992).

WS1919–20. Seminar. "Übungen im Anschluß an Natorp, *Allgemeine Psychologie*" (Exercises in Connection with Natorp's *General Psychology*). No publication announced.

April 1920. Talk on Oswald Spengler in Wiesbaden. No publication announced.

† 1920. Book review essay. "Anmerkungen zu Karl Jaspers *Psychologie der Weltanschauungen*" in Hans Sahner, ed., *Karl Jaspers in der Diskussion* (Munich: R. Piper & Co. Verlag, 1973), pp. 70–100. Reprinted in GA9: *Wegmarken*, ed. Friedrich-Wilhelm von Herrmann (1976), pp. 1–44. Translated by John van Buren as "Comments on Karl Jaspers' *Psychology of Worldviews*" in Martin Heidegger, *Pathmarks*, ed. Will McNeill (New York: Cambridge University Press, 1998); reprinted in revised form in chapter 7 of this volume. The permissions of the German publisher, Klostermann, and Cambridge University Press for the roughly simultaneous appearance of this translation in *Pathmarks* and the present volume are gratefully acknowledged.

April 21, 1920ff. Correspondence with Karl Jaspers. Martin Heidegger and Karl Jaspers, *Briefwechsel 1920–1963*, ed. Walter Biemel and Hans Saner (Frankfurt: Klostermann, 1990).

SS1920. Lecture course. "Phänomenologie der Anschauung und des Ausdrucks. Theorie der philosophischen Begriffsbildung" (Phenomenology of Intuition and Expression: Theory of Philosophical Concept-Formation), two hours. Published as GA59: *Phänomenologie der Anschauung und des Ausdrucks. Theorie der philosophischen Begriffsbildung*, ed. Claudius Strube (1993). Translated by E. H. Sadler as *Phenomenology of Intuition and Expression* (London: Athlone Press, forthcoming).

SS1920. Seminar. "Kolloquium im Anschluß an die Vorlesung" (Colloquium in Connection with the Lecture Course). No publication announced.

WS1920–21. Lecture course. "Einleitung in die Phänomenologie der Religion" (Introduction to the Phenomenology of Religion), two hours. In GA60 1–156.

WS1920–21. Seminar. "Phänomenologische Übungen für Anfänger im Anschluß an Descartes, *Meditationes*" (Phenomenological Exercises for Beginners in Connection with Descartes' *Meditations*). No publication announced.

SS1921. Lecture course. "Augustinus und der Neuplatonismus" (Augustine and neo-Platonism), three hours. In GA60 157–299.

SS1921. Seminar. "Phänomenologische Übungen für Anfänger im Anschluß an Aristoteles, *de anima*" (Phenomenological Exercises for Beginners in Connection with Aristotle's *De anima*). No publication announced.

August 19, 1921. Letter to Karl Löwith. In Dietrich Papenfuss and Otto Pöggeler, eds., *Zur philosophischen Aktualität Heideggers*, vol. 2: *Im Gespräch der Zeit* (Frankfurt: Klostermann, 1990), pp. 27–32. Translated by Gary Steiner in Richard Wolin, ed., *Martin Heidegger and European Nihilism* (New York: Columbia University Press, 1995), pp. 235–39.

WS1921–22. Lecture course. "Phänomenologische Interpretationen zu Aristoteles. Einführung in die Phänomenologische Forschung. Einleitung" (Phenomenological Interpretations in Connection with Aristotle: Introduction to Phenomenological Research. Lead-in), two hours. Published as GA61: *Phänomenologische Interpretationen zu Aristoteles. Einführung in die Phänomenologische Forschung,* ed. Walter Bröcker and Käte Bröcker-Oltmanns (1985, 2d ed., 1994).

WS1921–22. Seminar. "Phänomenologische Übungen für Anfänger im Anschluß an Husserl, *Logische Untersuchungen* II" (Phenomenological Exercises for Beginners in Connection with Husser's *Logical Investigations,* vol. 2). No publication announced.

SS1922. Lecture course. "Phänomenologische Interpretationen zu Aristoteles. Ontologie und Logik" (Phenomenological Interpretations in Connection with Aristotle: Ontology and Logic), four hours. To be published as GA62: *Phänomenologische Interpretation ausgewählter Abhandlungen des Aristoteles zu Ontologie und Logik,* ed. Günther Neumann (forthcoming).

SS1922. Seminar. "Phänomenologische Übungen für Anfänger im Anschluß an Husserl, *Logische Untersuchungen* II, 2. Untersuchung" (Phenomenological Exercises in Connection with Husserl's *Logical Investigations,* vol. 2, 2nd Investigation). No publication announced.

June 30, 1922. Curriculum vitae sent to Georg Misch. In GA16 41–45.

† Autumn 1922. Introduction to a planned book on Aristotle. "Phänomenologische Interpretationen zu Aristoteles (Anzeige der hermeneutischen Situation)." First published and edited by Hans-Ulrich Lessing with an introduction by Hans-Georg Gadamer in *Dilthey Jahrbuch* 6 (1989): 229–74. Translated by John van Buren as "Phenomenological Interpretations in Connection with Aristotle: An Indication of the Hermeneutical Situation" in chapter 9 of this volume. The permissions of the editor of the *Dilthey Jahrbuch,* Frithjof Rodi, and Heidegger's literary executor, his son Herman Heidegger, are gratefully acknowledged, as

are valuable translation suggestions by Michael Baur in his earlier translation of this text in *Man and World* 25 (1992): 355–93.

October 20, 1922 to November 18, 1924. Correspondence with Erich
Rothacker. In "Martin Heidegger und die Anfänge der 'Deutschen
Vierteljahrsschrift für Literaturwissenschaft und Geistesgeschichte':
Eine Dokumentation," ed. Joachim W. Storck and Theodore Kisiel,
Dilthey Jahrbuch 8 (1992): 192–218.

WS1922–23. Seminar. "Übungen über: Phänomenologische Interpretationen zu Aristoteles *(Nikomachische Ethik* VI; De anima; *Metaphysik* VII)
(privatissime)" (Exercises: Phenomenological Interpretations in Connection with Aristotle [*Nicomachean Ethics* 6; *De anima; Metaphysics* 7]
[private]), two hours. No publication announced.

WS1922–23. Seminar. "Phänomenologische Übungen für Anfänger im
Anschluß an Husserl, *Ideen* I" (Phenomenological Exercises for Beginners
in Connection with Husserl's *Ideas,* vol. 1). No publication announced.

SS1923. Lecture course. "Ontologie (Hermeneutik der Faktizität)," one
hour. Published as GA63: *Ontologie. Hermeneutik der Faktizität,* ed.
Käte Bröcker-Oltmanns (1988, 2d ed., 1995). Translated by John van
Buren as *Ontology—The Hermeneutics of Facticity* (Bloomington: Indiana University Press, 1999).

SS1923. Seminar. "Phänomenologische Übungen für Anfänger im
Anschluß an Aristoteles, *Ethica Nicomachea*" (Phenomenological Exer-
cises for Beginners in Connection with Aristotle's *Nicomachean Ethics*).
No publication announced.

SS1923. Seminar. "Kolloquium über die theologischen Grundlagen von
Kant, *Religion innerhalb der Grenzen der bloßen Vernunft,* nach aus-
gewählte Texten, für Fortgeschrittene (mit Ebbinghaus)" (Colloquium
for Advanced Students on the Theological Foundations of Kant's *Religion within the Limits of Reason Alone,* Selected Texts [co-taught with
Ebbinghaus]). No publication announced.

SS1923. Seminar. Continuation of "Übungen über: Phänomenologische Interpretationen zu Aristoteles" from WS1922–23. No publication announced.

MARBURG PERIOD

Associate Professor, University of Marburg

WS1923–24. Lecture course. "Einführung in die phänomenologische
Forschung" (Introduction to Phenomenological Research), four hours.
Published as GA17: *Einführung in die Phänomenologische Forschung,* ed.
Friedrich-Wilhelm von Herrmann (1994).

WS1923–24. Seminar. "Phänomenologische Übung für Anfänger: Husserl, *Logische Untersuchungen* II.1" (Phenomenological Exercises for Beginners: Husserl's *Logical Investigations*, vol. 2, Investigation I). No publication announced.

WS1923–24. Seminar. "Phänomenologische Übung für Fortgeschrittene: Aristoteles, Physik B" (Phenomenological Exercise for Advanced Students: Aristotle's *Physics* B). No publication announced.

WS1923–24. Essay. "Wahrsein und Dasein (Aristoteles, Ethica Nicomachea Z)" (Being-True and the Being-There of Dasein [Aristotle, *Nicomachean Ethics* Z]). In GA80 (forthcoming).

December 7, 1923. Talk at the Kant Society in Hamburg. "Aufgaben und Wege der phänomenologischen Forschung" (The Tasks and Paths of Phenomenological Research). Not announced for publication.

† February 14 and 21, 1924. Two-part talk in Rudolf Bultmann's theology seminar, "The Ethics of St. Paul," at the University of Marburg (preceded by Heidegger's shorter discussion on January 10 of the topic of living in faith in connection with Romans 6). "Das Problem der Sünde bei Luther." Heidegger's manuscript not scheduled for publication and presumably lost. Student transcript first published in Bernd Jaspert, ed., *Sachgemäße Exegese: Die Protokolle aus Rudolf Bultmanns Neutestamentlichen Seminaren 1921–1951* (Marburg: N. G. Elwert, 1996), pp. 28–33. Translated by John van Buren as "The Problem of Sin in Luther" in chapter 8 of this volume, with the permission of the publisher.

SS1924. Lecture course. "Grundbegriffe der aristotelischen Philosophie" (Basic Concepts in Aristotelian Philosophy), four hours. In GA18: *Grundbegriffe der aristotelischen Philosophie,* ed. Mark Michalski (2001).

SS1924. Seminar. "Fortgeschrittene: Die Hochscholastik und Aristoteles (Thomas, *de ente et essentia;* Cajetan, *de nominum analogia*)" (Advanced Students: Late Scholasticism and Aristotle [Thomas, *On Being and Essence;* Cajetan, *On the Analogy of Names*]). No publication announced.

July 25, 1924. Talk for the Department of Theology at the University of Marburg. "Der Begriff der Zeit." Published as *Der Begriff der Zeit: Vortrag vor der Marburger Theologenschaft Juli 1924,* ed. Hartmut Tietjen (Tübingen: Max Niemeyer, 1989). Also in GA64: *Der Begriff der Zeit,* ed. Friedrich-Wilhelm von Herrmann (forthcoming). Translated by Will McNeill as *The Concept of Time* (New York: Basil Blackwell, 1992).

1924. Essay composed in connection with the above talk. "Der Begriff der Zeit." In GA64 (forthcoming).

WS1924–25. Lecture course. "Interpretation Platonischer Dialoge (Σοφιστής, Φίληβος)" (Interpretations of Plato's Dialogues [*Sophist, Philebus*]), four hours. Published as GA19: *Platon: Sophistes,* ed.

Ingeborg Schüßler (1992). Translated by Richard Rojcewicz and André Schuwer as *Plato's Sophist* (Bloomington: Indiana University Press, 1997).

WS1924–25. Seminar. "Übungen zur Ontologie des Mittelalters (Thomas, *de ente et essentia, summa contra gentiles*)" (Exercises on the Ontology of the Middle Ages [Thomas, *On Being and Essence, Summa contra gentiles*]). No publication announced.

December 1–8, 1924. Lecture series for the Kant Society in Elberfeld-Barmen, Cologne, and Dortmund based on the above similarly titled essay in WS1923–24. "Dasein und Wahrsein nach Aristoteles (Interpretationen von Buch VI der *Nikomach. Ethik*)" (The Being-There of Dasein and Being-True in Aristotle [Interpretations of Book VI of the *Nicomachean Ethics*]). In GA80 (forthcoming).

† April 16–21, 1925. A series of lectures at the Hessian Society for Art and Science in Kassel. "Wilhelm Diltheys Forschungsarbeit und der Kampf um eine historische Weltanschauung." Heidegger's manuscript not announced for publication and presumably lost. Walter Bröcker's transcript, first discovered, edited, and introduced by Frithjof Rodi, is published in *Dilthey-Jahrbuch* 8 (1992–1993): 123–30, 143–80. Also in GA80 (forthcoming). Translated by Charles Bambach as "Wilhelm Dilthey's Research and the Struggle for a Historical Worldview" in chapter 10 of this volume with the permission of the journal's editor, Frithjof Rodi. On April 15, Heidegger's announcement of and introduction to the lecture series were published in the *Kassler Post* and have been reprinted in GA16 49–51.

SS1925. Lecture course. "Geschichte des Zeitbegriffs. Prolegomena zur Phänomenologie von Geschichte und Natur," four hours. Published as GA20: *Prolegomena zur Geschichte des Zeitbegriffs*, ed. Petra Jaeger (1979, 3rd ed., 1994). Translated by Theodore Kisiel as *History of the Concept of Time: Prolegomena* (Bloomington: Indiana University Press, 1985).

SS1925. Seminar. "Anfangsübungen im Anschluß an Descartes, *Meditationes*" (Exercises for Beginners in Connection with Descartes' *Meditations*). No publication announced.

October 15, 1925. Informal talk. "Zum Hochzeitstag von Fritz und Liesel Heidegger" (On the Wedding Day of Fritz and Liesel Heidgger). In GA16 52–54.

1925ff. Correspondence with Hannah Arendt. Martin Heidegger and Hannah Arendt, *Briefe 1925 bis 1975 und andere Zeugnisse*, ed. Ursula Ludz (Frankfurt: Klostermann, 1988, 2d ed., 1999).

1925–1927. Notes. "Aufzeichnungen zur Temporalität (Aus den Jahren 1925 bis 1927)" (Notes on Temporality [From the Years 1925 to 1927]), *Heidegger Studies* 14 (1998): 11–26.

WS1925–26. Lecture course. "Logik" (Logic), four hours. Published as GA21: *Logik. Die Frage nach der Wahrheit,* ed. Walter Biemel (1976, 2d ed., 1995).

WS1925–26. Seminar. "Anfänger: Phänomenologische Übungen (Kant, *Kritik der reinen Vernunft*)" (For Beginners: Phenomenological Exercises *[Kant's Critique of Pure Reason]*). No publication announced.

WS1925–26. Seminar. "Fortgeschrittene: Phänomenologische Übungen (Hegel, *Logik,* I. Buch)" (Advanced Students: Phenomenological Exercises [Hegel's *Logic,* Book 1). No publication announced.

March–November 1926. First draft of Divisions I and II of part 1 of *Sein und Zeit,*[18] these divisions appearing in print with revisions in April of the following year under the title *Sein und Zeit. Erste Hälfte* (*Being and Time.* First Half) in *Jahrbuch für Philosophie und phänomenologische Forschung,* vol. 8 (Halle: Max Niemeyer, 1927), pp. xi–438. Reprinted as GA2: *Sein und Zeit,* ed. Friedrich-Wilhelm von Herrmann (1977). Translated by John Macquarrie and Edward Robinson as *Being and Time* (New York: Harper & Row, 1962). Also translated by Joan Stambaugh as *Being and Time: A Translation of Sein und Zeit* (Albany: State University of New York Press, 1997).

Chapter Two

PER MORTEM AD VITAM

Thoughts on Johannes Jörgensen's
Lies of Life and Truth of Life (1910)

JOHN PROTEVI AND JOHN VAN BUREN, TRANSLATORS

In our day, everyone talks much about "personality," and the philosophers find new concepts of value. Apart from critical, moral, and aesthetic evaluation, they operate also with "evaluation of personality," especially in literature. The person of the artist moves into the foreground. Thus one hears much about interesting people. Oscar Wilde the dandy, Paul Verlaine the "brilliant drunkard," Maxim Gorky the great vagabond, the Overman Nietzsche—all interesting people. And when in the hour of grace one of these interesting people becomes conscious of the great lie of his gypsy's life, smashes the altars of false gods, and becomes a Christian, then they call this "tasteless, revolting."

Johannes Jörgensen took this step. It was not the urge for sensation that drove him to conversion—no, it was a deeper, more bitter seriousness.

This powerful struggle to free himself from a perverted and deceitful philosophy, tireless searching and building, the ultimate step to the summit of truth:

For bibliographic and other background information on this 1910 book review essay from the first theological phase of Heidegger's Student Period, when he was studying for the priesthood in the Department of Theology at the University of Freiburg, see pp. 3–4, 21.

these mark the moodful vitality of the sixty-eight small pages of this inconspicuous little book *Lies of Life and Truth of Life*.[1]

At age 18, Jörgensen was an atheist, and soon he swam in the currents of free thinking, which around the seventies Georg Brandes—Denmark's Heine—had put into motion: free research and free thinking had become the battle cry of the modern Danish literati. The spirit of Nietzsche and Zola became all-powerful. Denmark's greatest atheist, J. P. Jakobsen, too weak for life and not sick enough for death, dragged himself through his wretched existence, and with this model of decadence Jörgensen set about his learning.

In beauty the artist has his heart, and there also is his art. But what did they find beautiful, those who knew only one law, one aim? The unhappy author of *Niels Lyhne* gives the answer: "*What is wild I find beautiful, untamed and untamable nature, the ardent,* never-satisfied passion of men of the Renaissance." The purest Cesara Borgia enthusiasm of a Nietzsche. They praise to the skies the graven images of horror and sin. The Golden Calf Fama and the Babylonian Venus stood on the alters.

And what's the point of their poetry? To flatter the lusts of the people. "Consider," says the stranger in the profound parable of "The Shadow" in *Parables*,[2] "consider that we others live as you write . . . we are as you form us. . . . We are chaste if you are, immoral if you will it." Such were the men who shrugged off "supernaturalism." The enemies of obscurantism, the great "personalities," who wildly brought their egos to full development, their life was an intoxication. And further and further they drifted downward to the point where they loved death and despair and "called decay holy."

Among those who sacrificed happiness for truth—so they said—stood Jörgensen. Often in balmy summer nights he had looked up longingly at the white, pure stars. And now and then, when the mad frenzy faded, the call came from afar out of the deepest depths of his tortured inner life: "Oh, tired soul, come here!"

And again the night sank in, leaden, without stars, the night of death. "My life would be chaotic, as the life of my comrades—a chain riveted together with one link of joy and ten links of sorrow, one ring of gold and ten rings of lead. . . ."

Until that morning came, when God had to help. A strong hand struck him. He saw. The Darwinist was shaken. With iron consistency he marched onward, upward. His extremely sharp, almost caustic criticism made the long, arduous path to life easier for him.

Happiness is possible only through a life of deceit. Will Ibsen be proven right in this statement? No, he contradicts a fundamental biological law. Truth must naturally lead to happiness, deceit to destruction. That is the fertile ultimate principle. Depart from truth, and it will punish you for your violation. And yet who had more rigorously sought truth, who had indeed thrown all prejudices overboard, smashed all chains, who had indeed created their convictions with the "spiritual and moral sovereignty of the ego"? As we saw above, did the great "personalities" find happiness? No, despair and death. See that line of witnesses as though they had gone astray and held a revolver to their heads. So none of them had the truth. So individualism is the false standard of life. Therefore banish the will of the flesh, the teachings of the world, of paganism.

And again a biological prerequisite.

Higher life is conditioned by the destruction of lower forms. For growth, the plant needs inorganic matter. The animal can live only through the death of the plant, and so on up the ladder. If you want to live spiritually, to gain your salvation, then die, kill the baseness in yourself, work with supernatural grace, and you will be resurrected. And thus he rests now in the shadow of the cross, this strong-willed, joyously hopeful poet-philosopher: a modern Augustine.

This thin book about conversion provides an interesting contribution to the psychology of the free thinker. He does not *want* to believe, he *wants* to trample down truth, he *wants* his moods and passions.

Unfortunately, space does not permit me to represent *in extenso* the phases of conversion of the great Dane, to look into the first waking seeds in his earlier writings, beginning with the *Travelogue.*[3] One more word from a literary point of view. The composition of his works lacks rigor. But they are all the more deeper on account of this. Moodful dreaminess, muted impressionism, seriousness, stateliness, restrained summoning, and admonition is entirely his style, just as generally the writings of those from the northern countries—I recall Selma Lagerlöf—show something ponderous, quiet, fabulous. Something else characterizes Jörgensen: he uncovers again and again our great indestructible connections to the past. With the *mystics* of the Middle Ages he gladly tarries. For the *Poverello,* his peace-filled poet's heart glows. Let us love this frank Dane, let us immerse ourselves and live in his lovely books.

Chapter Three

THE PROBLEM OF REALITY
IN MODERN PHILOSOPHY (1912)

PHILIP J. BOSSERT AND JOHN VAN BUREN, TRANSLATORS

In his characteristic manner, the witty Frenchman Brunetière writes concerning the problem of the external world: *"Je voudrais bien savoir, quel est le malade ou le mauvais plaisant, et je devrais dire le fou, qui s'est avisé le premier de mettre en doute 'la réalité du monde extérieur,' et d'en faire une question pour les philosophes. Car la question a-t-elle même un sens?"* ["I should very much like to know which sick person or sorry jokester—and I must also say fool—it was who first got it into his head to doubt the reality of the external world and make it a question for philosophers. Does such a question even make any sense?"][1] In this case, the critical thinker who coined the phrase "the bankruptcy of science" did not look deep enough. His appeal to "common sense," a subject about which Kant recorded some rather pointed views,[2] lags far behind any methodically scientific treatment of our question. If one distinguishes the naive (though, for practical life, fully adequate) view that presumes to grasp the "real" at a single glance from the reflective, methodically executed positing and definition of realities in science, one is faced with a certain

---

For bibliographic and other background information on this 1912 journal article from the second neo-Scholastic philosophical phase of Heidegger's Student Period, when he abandoned plans for the priesthood and transfered to the Department of Natural Sciences and Mathematics at the University of Freiburg, see pp. 4–5, 22.

problem. The necessary precondition for developing a deeper understanding of a problem that cries out to be resolved is precisely that one make an all-out effort to free oneself from the leaden weight of allegedly self-evident truth.

I

In order to gain a historical basis for the discussion of this problem, I might briefly note that the thought of Greek philosophy was oriented toward a critical realism.[3] The Neoplatonists, the philosophers in the Middle Ages, and those in the modern era thought in a realist manner as well. Though a wide variety of views concerning the *definition* of the real can be found, there was agreement concerning the positing of something trans-subjective. It was not until Berkeley[4] that the position of realism became shaky. With his formula of *esse-percipi,* that is, the identification of being and being-perceived, he asserted the identity of the physical and psychical. The existence of an independent world of physical bodies transcendent to consciousness was nullified. From a psychological standpoint, Berkeley was indeed still a realist in that, along with the substance of the soul, he also assumed the existence of a multitude of minds. His successor, Hume, then thought this sensationalism through to its final consequences. The basic concepts of substance and causality were stripped of their objective, real characteristics in that each was reduced to a "bundle of perceptions," which was in turn traced back to a subjectively felt force on the basis of which the associatively conjoined reproductions of certain simultaneous perceptions are thought of as being in an objective relation. Kant, who sought to overcome the dangerous one-sidedness of English empiricism and wanted to safeguard a universal and necessary kind of knowledge that would within certain limits be valid for all human beings, could do no better than to posit a mysterious "thing in itself." And when one realizes that ultimately Kant applied his transcendental method only to formal sciences in that he investigated how pure mathematics, the natural sciences, and metaphysics (in a rationalist sense) were at all possible,[5] it becomes clear that the problem of reality simply had no place in his epistemology. While Kant toward the end of his life did try to bridge the gap between metaphysics and physics, it was no longer possible for him to find a solution. And it is quite evident that philosophy immediately after Kant, eventually culminating in the extravagant idealism of Hegel, moved further and further away from reality and an understanding of how it can be posited and defined. When, after the downfall of Hegelian philosophy, the individual sciences forcefully tore themselves away from the tutelage of philosophy and threatened to completely stifle it (one need only consider the precarious position and dependent function of philosophy in positivism), the only salvation seemed to be "back to Kant." Thus it is that philosophy today lives in the spirit of Kant but is no less influenced by the English and French empiricist movements. There is good reason to see the true *spiritus rector* of contemporary philosophy in Hume.[6] Hence, the dominant epistemological trends are characterized by *conscientialism* (immanentism) and *phenomenalism,* views that attempt to show that a definition of the real or, for that matter, according to the first view, even the mere positing of an external world independent of consciousness, is inadmissible and impossible. Simultaneously with this flourishing of modern philosophy, the empirical research of the natural sciences has undauntedly continued its work in the spirit of a healthy realism that has brought splendid achievements.

Is the conflict confronting us here between philosophical theory and the praxis of the natural sciences a real one? Or is it perhaps the case that, as "disciplines which mull over formalistic notions," the "standpoint of actuality"[7] and phenomenalism have perhaps outlived their time? An epistemological investigation seeing its task to be the application of the transcendental method to already established sciences—that is, in our case, attempting to answer the question, how are empirical natural sciences possible?—will have to give, on the basis of its results, an affirmative answer to the above question. In light of what has been said thus far, it is understandable how O. Külpe could write in the conclusion of his *The Philosophy of the Present in Germany* that "at the threshold of this philosophy of the future . . . stands the *problem of reality.*"[8] It is this professor of philosophy in Bonn who seems more than any other to have dedicated his distinctive research to the above problem. In his more recent works, he touches upon it time and again. At the philosophical congress this year in Bologna, he delivered a paper on the history of the concept of reality.[9] And in a work appearing last year, *Epistemology and the Natural Sciences,* he provides a positive discussion of the problem of reality with particular reference to the natural sciences.[10]

As already noted, the undeniable, epoch-making state of affairs of the natural sciences has brought our problem to the focus of interest. When the morphologist defines the structure of plants and animals, when the anatomist explains the internal structure of living creatures and their organs, when the cellular biologist undertakes the study of the cell, its construction, and development, when the chemist delves into the elements and combinations of chemical compounds, and when the astronomer calculates the position and orbit of the celestial bodies, the researchers in all of these various individual sciences are convinced that they are not analyzing mere sense data or working on pure concepts but rather positing and defining real objects that exist independently of them and their scientific research.

How is this understanding of reality *[Realisierung]* or, more precisely, this positing and defining of trans-subjective objects, possible? The positive solution to this problem that has been raised will have to be preceded by a critical investigation that lays down foundations and determines if it is at all justifiable to attempt to transcend the actuality of consciousness, i.e., to posit and define realities, and such an investigation comes down to a debate with conscientialism and phenomenalism. Consequently, the whole problem can be condensed into the following four precisely defined questions (EN 9ff.):

1. Is positing the real justifiable?

2. How is positing the real possible?

3. Is defining the real justifiable?

4. How is such defining possible?

In order to proceed in a methodical manner, we will begin with a consideration of the first and third questions, and in treating the other two, we will return to Külpe's above-mentioned work.

II

1. By way of introduction, we mentioned Hume's significance in the development of modern epistemology. In our own time, English empiricism has undergone a diversity of modifications. Richard von Schubert-Soldern has worked out a theory of *solipsism* and considers it a self-evident fact requiring no additional proof. The consciousness of the knower, and this alone, is the object of knowledge. This *philosophy of immanence* finds its chief representative in Schuppe. He explains his position and attempts to justify it in his *The Logic of Epistemology*.[11] All being *[Sein]* is being-conscious *[Bewußt-Sein]*. The concept of consciousness includes both the conscious subject and the object of consciousness, but these two moments are only separable by abstraction. The result of this is the inextricable concatenation of thought and being. Related to this philosophy of immanence is the empirio-criticism of Avenarius who, in his three major works,[12] sets himself the goal of determining the one true concept of the world. Finally, note must be taken of E. Mach,[13] the founder of so-called *sense-data monism*. He has best developed his ideas in the work, *Essays on the Analysis of Sense Data*. A thing, a body, and matter are nothing other than a context of elements (sense data), that is, nothing other than colors, tones, and so on in addition to the so-called distinguishing features that are perceived.[14]

With the refutation of conscientialism, realism would at least represent a possible position. This refutation would go the surest route if it turned its attention primarily to an emphasis on the core of conscientialist thought, namely, the *principle of immanence*.[15] The negative arguments for the "standpoint of actuality," which are supposed to undermine the positive arguments usually brought forth in support of realism (e.g., the application of causal laws to the contents of consciousness as such), all suffer from the same logical mistake, namely, they are based upon a principle of immanence that is in fact what first needs to be proven. Closer consideration is warranted for the direct, positive arguments that Klimke narrows down to three: the a priori argument, the empirical argument, and the methodological argument.[16]

The first argument attempts to see a contradiction in the concept of being as something independent of thought. When one thinks about this kind of reality, it becomes dependent on thought and thus on the actuality of consciousness.

However, a being that is thought is in no way identical with being in thought. What is in being here (in the phenomenal sense) is a concept whose content is intentionally referred to transcendent being. The psychical existence of a concept and the ideal being of the content of this concept are completely different things. Real being is thought by means of a concept, but this in no way means that such being is taken inside the subject and transformed into psychical being. In my opinion, Geyser is not wrong when he writes: "The whole alleged difficulty is nothing but the dazzling sophism of dialectical pseudo-logic."[17] One need only draw out the consequences of this procedure in which one identifies the act and the content of a concept, and it then becomes clear that, given the correctness of the above assumption, all intellectual life would be condemned to come to a standstill. If the act were essential to the content, then for this content to be repeatedly thinkable in an identical manner it would require that at each partic-ular time the same act and also the same accompanying milieu of consciousness should appear. However, the fact of the continuous flux of psychical happenings shows this to be an impossible demand, in that each moment of time presents us experientially with a different picture of our psychical life.

The *empirical* argument contains the claim that only the facts of con-sciousness are in fact given, and that out of these facts all knowledge is imma-nently constructed without a moment of transcendence in one direction or another. However, the simple summation of the data of consciousness (who is supposed to be doing the summation and recognizing the summation for what it is?) produces no knowledge. Simply stringing together perceptions and ideas one after another according to no particular principle can only lead to a chaotic pic-ture. Rather, we find it to be the case that certain fundamental principles for all knowing, namely, basic principles of logic, steer our knowledge along immutable and absolutely valid courses of thought. But, say the conscientialists in order to block our way, these real laws in the connection of our acts of thought also are psychical matters of fact, i.e., causal laws of psychical events, and hence no argu-ment against our position. It is here that once again the erroneous identification of the psychical act and the logical content comes to the surface. The funda-mental principles of logic are not inductively based and thus are not valid only as the causal laws of subjective psychical events. Rather, we see in them immediately evident, objective, ideal principles "whose content exhibits the most general rela-tions between intentional thought and objects [in the logical sense]."[18] Finally, this empirical argument comes into conflict with psychological experience, for the awareness involved in having the contents of consciousness present to oneself already implies that one goes beyond the given sphere of one's consciousness per se. Moreover, this given sphere of consciousness can never provide one with the primordial fund of experience. The latter can only be uncovered by an abstract-ing activity of thought that transcends what is immediately given.[19] And besides, how can the degree of certitude required for scientific knowledge be reached merely by having facts of consciousness at one's disposal?

Certainly, says the *third methodological* argument, the goal of science is the absolute certitude and universal validity of its propositions. It is, however, impossible for these propositions to be based on arbitrary presuppositions and hypotheses that have been brought into play. The only certain unshakeable foundation can be provided solely by what is immediately and irrefutably given in consciousness. In reply to this, it need only be remarked that certitude cannot be predicated of simple facts (nor of judgements considered as psychical acts). Facts simply *are* or are not. Only knowledge can be certain and, as we saw above, knowledge cannot be obtained from the data of consciousness alone. Concerning this kind of certitude postulated especially by Mach, Külpe writes, "Certainty of this kind is, of course, unshakeable; however, this is not because it proves itself in argumentation, not because it withstands and prevails over opposition to it, but because argumentation and opposition are in no way possible for it."[20]

2. For conscientialism, whose attempted justification we have just shown to be unsound, our problem basically does not even exist. Not quite so radical, however, is the epistemological position of phenomenalism. It considers the positing of the real to be both possible and necessary, but only that much. Any *definition* of this reality is *forbidden* in the rule book of phenomenalism. An unknown X, i.e., a mysterious thing in itself, functions as the substrate for the sense data aroused in the subject from the outside. The classic representative of phenomenalism is Kant. According to him, the transcendental conditions of the knowledge found in intuition and understanding have the kind of genetically a priori, subjective character he attempted to demonstrate in his "Transcendental Doctrine of Elements."[21] Consequently, we know things only in terms of the subjective veils of their appearance to us. Quite apart from the fact that, as would indeed seem to be the case with just a cursory glance at the problem, the inference from the a priori character and subjectivity of the pure forms of intuition and understandings to the position adopted by phenomenalism is not valid, the claim that these forms have a modifying function in a subjectivistic sense remains nothing but an utterly *dogmatic assumption*. It will be ever impossible to provide justification for this presupposition. Kant himself gave up his thesis that only what is intuited can be an object of thought, and that consequently the understanding has no specific object, when he made the pure concepts of the understanding and their deduction the object of his investigations. When he writes, "We shall therefore follow up the pure concepts to their first seeds and dispositions in the human understanding, in which they lie prepared, till at last, on the occasion of experience, they are developed, and by the same understanding are exhibited in their purity, freed from the empirical conditions attaching to them,"[22] this intellectual labor can only be realized on the presupposition that what is not intuited, namely, "pure concepts," also can be an object of thought. And it is just as possible, contrary to Kant's position, to think without categories. Külpe rightly notes: "Even the unordered, chaotic matter of sensory impressions, which is presupposed by Kant as the stuff of sensory knowledge, can in fact be thought, although definitely not represented and

certainly not experienced. If thought was necessarily tied to the use of categories, then such chaos could in no way be thought" (K 85). Furthermore, concepts, judgments, and conclusions are raised to the level of objects of thought in logic, and thus here, as in the case of the formulation of general laws, one thinks objects that are not intuited. Hence, the empiricist contention of Kant concerning the intuitive nature of all objects of thought is not tenable. The "given," what we find in our experience, no doubt provides the material foundation for thinking about the reality that manifests itself in this "given," and it is the definition of this reality, and not merely of its appearance, that is the goal of science. When, in Kant, experiential material is worked on by the understanding, this actually operates in a manner that runs opposite to any understanding of reality. Instead of the subjective additions to the object of knowledge being eliminated, this object undergoes an increased subjectification by means of the categories. Knowing distances itself even further from its true object.

It is not difficult to see that a correct explanation of the *relation between experience and thought* is of fundamental importance for the possibility of defining the realities one has posited. The sensationalism of modern psychology has stripped thought of its independent status. In actuality, however, what is proper to thought is an activity independent of the activity of sensation and the process of association. It rules over the fund of empirical material by taking it up and working on it in accordance with objective, universally valid, and ideal principles. It stands over this material as an activity that analyzes it and adds to it. Külpe is in agreement with us when he writes: "If one asks what constitutes the lawfulness of thought if it does not affect its object in any way, it can be answered that thought is directed toward, and accommodates itself to, its objects. The laws of thought are the laws of its objects, and therefore the Copernican revolution Kant claims for his theory of knowledge [namely, that objects are supposed to accommodate themselves to thought] does not hold for thought." "One can indeed define thought in terms of the fact that it has the possibility of thinking something whose existence and essence is independent of this thinking and of the thinking subject" (K, 98, 97).[23]

With the repudiation of conscientialism and phenomenalism, the positing and defining of realities is shown to be possible. However much these two epistemological movements are seen to exclude an understanding of reality, they have nonetheless indirectly impelled us toward a deeper grasp of our problem and to a more securely founded solution for it. Two questions now come to the fore that will be considered for a positive treatment of our problem: How is the positing of real objects possible? How is defining them possible?

3. The goal of understanding reality is to take the given, i.e., what we find in our experience, and define it as it is in itself by eliminating from it the knowing subject's modes of understanding and additions that modify it. The spatio-temporal conditions of the objects of experience, their coexistence and succession, the gaps in perception, and the relations among the contents of consciousness that

force themselves upon us and are not determinable by our will—all of this reveals indisputably a lawfulness independent of the experiencing subject. The positing of realities transcendent to consciousness is demanded above all by the fact that one and the same object is immediately communicable to different individuals. Geyser, who devoted a detailed and penetrating investigation to our topic, although doing so in a different context, writes appropriately: "This communication is a fact, and it is utterly basic to the possibility of any universally valid science of experience."[24]

It would be a hasty move to assert, after the manner of naive realism, that the contents of perception in the form in which they present themselves to us are objective realities. The organs of sensation—more particularly, the peripheral fibers into which the sensory nerves branch out—are stimulated by mechanical, physical, and chemical influences. The sensory nerve fibers then convey the produced stimuli to certain nerve centers and thereby make us conscious of events in the external world. Facts such as the presence of a stimulus threshold and limit or disturbances in the physiological organization of the senses (e.g., total or partial color blindness, differences in visual acuity) clearly indicate that not only the existence of perceptions but also their contents are essentially dependent upon subjective factors, and that in the contents of perception we thus have before us *phenomenal formations* produced with help of the subject. Even if the *relata* between which the lawful relations of perceptions hover undergo subjective modifications on the basis of the laws bound up with the characteristic energy of our senses, the relations themselves must nevertheless be posited as objectively real laws. The abstraction of subjective moments, in which the negative task that belongs to the special act of understanding reality consists, and the extraction of objective states of affairs from the world of the actuality of our consciousness can only be accomplished by experience *and thought*. Pure thought is not a competent court for decisions about ideal and real being. Only experience can give us information about whether real objects exist, though not in such a way as to be the sole, absolute authority for deciding this question. Sense impressions as such are not themselves reality. They cannot without further ado be used for defining reality. Hence, it is only where empirical and rational moments work together that our experience rings true. If the external world is posited as the cause of our sensations, then there is a mixed criterion at work. Külpe does not believe that this particular criterion, which has acquired such special significance since Schopenhauer, is completely appropriate, in that "the true motive of scientific realism would remain unrecognized and the impression would be given that the nature of the objective causes could be inferred from the subjective effects" (EN 24). A causal relation between the external world and sense impressions must undeniably exist, but this says nothing at all about the qualities of the causes that stimulate our senses. As scientific experience has shown, sensory stimuli (occurrences of motion) are not comparable to such perceived objects as color, tone, smell, and taste. Clearly, in order to stave off a mistaken view, Külpe has given expression to the above criterion in a different, obviously more precise form when he sees the external world as "the basis of the externally determined, lawful relations of our sense impressions." Using an analogy to a physical phenomenon (forced motion), he defines these relations as something compelling and "forced upon us." That this is still a causal relation is clear.

4. The following special question now emerges: How is it possible to define these realities, i.e., the compelling factors? Such defining is regulated in its content by the observed relations, i.e., it must be such that the *relata* are presented as capable of bringing about real events. Külpe explains the idea succinctly: "Natural substances are perfect examples of capacities which allow the real relations, states, and changes bound up with them to occur" (EN 27). A conclusive, adequate definition of the realities that have been posited as existing will always remain an ideal goal for sciences of reality. Even if all experienceable relations could be exhibited, it still must be kept in mind that there are dependent realities that, even with the most refined instruments to aid our sense organs, we can never reach in our sensory knowledge. And can the true nature of realities be unambiguously defined? Nonetheless, there still remains a broad field to be cultivated by science. In addition to material progress, the history of sciences unambiguously exhibits an advancement in the regulative definition of its objects.

However, must not the kind of definition of reality pursued in the spirit of critical realism come to a halt before that barrier which is apparently thrown up by the principle of the subjectivity of sensory qualities? It is true that, when we heed this principle, realities lose their intuitive character, but this does not eliminate these realities as such. It does mean, however, that a break must be made with the epistemological dogma of sensationalism, which states that all knowledge remains tied to what can be intuited. The actual practice of sciences of reality does not know this prejudice.[25]

In view of the contemporary trend of thought that is already permeated with pragmatist concepts (scientifically quite shallow ones), Külpe also is looking for an answer to the question about whether critical realism has noteworthy significance from this point of view as well, though for science this is by itself admittedly not the decisive point of view. Justifiably, the answer turns out to be affirmative. Külpe shows in his exceedingly vivid manner of presentation that in the last analysis the opposing viewpoints of conscientialism and phenomenalism shunt the tasks of sciences of reality and their fulfillment onto a dead-end track. He writes: "There is nothing more unproductive than the overly restrictive accounts of those researchers of nature who continually assure us in the spirit of this [conscientialistic] theory of knowledge that they obviously do not want to associate any realist views with their adoption of realist expressions. They import into their accounts a viewpoint foreign to the very field they are investigating, and forget that caution is the mother not only of wisdom but of inaction as well. Only those who believe that a real nature can be defined will devote their energies to gaining knowledge of it" (EN 38).

Even if one cannot agree with Külpe throughout, and above all not concerning his concept of "inductive" metaphysics, its hypothetical character, and its justification, his merit will remain in having placed epistemology once again before its authentic task after it had strayed so far off its proper path.[26] Aristotelian–Scholastic philosophy, which has always thought in a realist manner, will not lose sight of this new epistemological movement. Positive, progressive work must be its main concern.

Chapter Four

THE CONCEPT OF TIME IN THE
SCIENCE OF HISTORY (1915)

HARRY S. TAYLOR, HANS W. UFFELMANN,
AND JOHN VAN BUREN, TRANSLATORS

Motto: Time is what changes and diversifies itself, eternity remains simple.

—Meister Eckhart

For some time a certain "metaphysical drive" has awoken in academic philosophy. Remaining with simple epistemology will no longer suffice. The persistence in epistemological problems, which is born of a legitimate, energetic awareness of the necessity and value of critique, does not allow the ultimate questions about the goal of philosophy to arrive at their immanent meaning. Hence, the tendency toward metaphysics, which is one moment covered over and the next manifestly seeing the light of day. One will have to interpret that as a deeper

---

See pp. 5, 20–21, 25 for bibliographic and other background information on this lecture from Heidegger's Student Period, which was presented to the Department of Philosophy at the University of Freiburg in 1915 and then published the following year as a journal article. Heidegger's subsequent marginalia in the latter have been included in endnotes marked in the body of the essay by superscripted letters in lower case and presented at the end under the title "Marginalia" so as to distinguish them from the notes in the original publication.

grasp of philosophy and its problems and see therein the will of philosophy to power, though certainly not to power in the sense of the violent intellectual forces of the so-called "worldview of natural science."

Critical consciousness is too tenaciously alive in modern science and philosophy for them to want to master our culture with ungrounded or poorly based claims to power—so tenaciously alive that while recognizing the indispensability of an ultimate metaphysical grounding (the Platonic ὑπόθεσις [hypothesis]), they indeed still apply a major part of their energy to dealing with epistemological problems, i.e., logical problems in the wider sense. For there can be no mistake that numerous problems in theory of science still await a solution, despite the fruitful research precisely in this field during the last decades. The natural sciences, like the cultural sciences, have been rendered problematic with regard to their logical structure. In fact, one of the main results of this research is precisely their sharp demarcation over against each other and the logical grounding of their autonomy. But there are still enough particular problems that must be solved before the comprehensive task of establishing a general theory of science can be tackled in the future. One such particular problem will be made an object of investigation in what follows.

Some brief general indications regarding science and the theory of science should be given in advance so that the goal and peculiar character of such investigations remain at all times present.

Science is a context of kinds of theoretical knowledge that is ordered and grounded through principles. Such knowledge is set down in judgments; these judgments are true, they are valid. Strictly speaking, what is valid is not the *act* of judgment carried out by the individual researcher in the acquisition of knowledge but rather the *sense* of the judgment—its content. Conceived of in terms of the idea of its completion, each science is a self-subsisting context of valid sense. As temporally conditioned cultural facts, the particular concrete sciences are never complete but rather always on the way in their discovery of truth.

The manner in which knowledge in the individual sciences is discovered, i.e., the method of research, is determined by the object of the respective science and the points of view under which it is examined. The methods of research in the different sciences work with certain basic concepts, and it is the *logical structure* of these concepts that theory of science has to reflect on. The formulation of this question in theory of science leads from the particular sciences into the domain of the ultimate basic elements of logic: the categories. For the researcher in a particular science, such investigations in theory of science easily give the impression of a certain self-evidence and thus unproductivity. However, this happens only insofar as he expects from such investigations *new subject matter* for *his* particular scientific field. The investigations cannot, of course, provide this because they move in a completely new dimension. Consequently, they become meaningful for the researcher in a particular science if and only if he forgets himself as this kind of researcher—and philosophizes.

Bringing into relief the logical foundations of methods of research in the particular sciences is thus the concern of logic as theory of science. This cannot be developed in its entirety in what follows; rather, a certain particular category (a basic logical element)—the concept of time—will be singled out and its structure clarified. What will ultimately be shown is that a central concept is made a problem here, and that its solution also should shed light on the whole logical character of the particular sciences that apply this category. The question now is, on what path can we be most certain of arriving at knowledge of the logical structure of the concept of time in the science of history? When we speak of a special logical structure that belongs to this concept of time, we mean that its content is determined in a peculiar manner by very specific ultimate categorial elements. This determination of the concept "time in general" into the concept of "historical time" is what must be brought into relief. It will be presented through the fact that the science of history applies the concept of time in a manner corresponding to its tasks. Accordingly, we will be able to read off the *structure* of the concept of time in history from its *function* in the science of history; this peculiar function should in turn be able to be understood on the basis of the goal of the science of history. Therefore, the path we will follow in solving our problem of a logical characterization of the concept of time in the science of history proceeds from the goal of the science of history via the resulting function of the concept of time and to the structure of this concept. The problem can be formulated in the following summary manner: *What structure must the concept of time in the science of history have in order for it to be able to begin to function as a concept of time in a manner corresponding to the goal of this science?* Thus we will not be presupposing a particular philosophical theory about the science of history and investigating what structure of the concept of time fits in with it but rather proceeding from the science of history as a fact, studying the *factual* function of the concept of time in it, and from this defining the logical structure of the concept. Should we arrive at a solution to this problem as so formulated, then if we have recognized the concept of time in the science of history as one of its central concepts, it should be possible to determine something general about the logical structure of history as a science.

The peculiarity of the structure of the concept of time in the science of history will undoubtedly emerge more clearly if it can be brought into relief in contrast to a different structure of time. In order to make this possible, we shall, before dealing with our actual problem, briefly characterize the concept of time in the natural sciences—and, more precisely, in physics. With respect to the concept of time in physics, we now formulate the problem in the same manner as we did in relation to the concept of time in the science of history and ask: *What structure must the concept of time in physics have in order for it to be able to begin to function as a concept of time in a manner corresponding to the goal of physics?*

I

We first need to clarify the goal of physics as science. The best way to do this is by bringing into relief the basic trend of physics that has come to light ever more clearly in the course of its history from Galileo to the present.

Ancient and medieval philosophy of nature[1] sought to investigate the metaphysical essence and hidden causes of the appearances that impose themselves on us in immediate reality. In contrast to this metaphysical speculation about nature, Galileo's science signifies something fundamentally new in its *method*. It seeks to gain mastery over the diversity of appearances by means of laws, and *how* it arrives at laws—this is its strangely new accomplishment. Because the basic tendency of physics can be seen most clearly in this method of gaining knowledge of laws, this method can be explained by using a classic example, namely, Galileo's discovery of the law of gravity. The old way of examining nature would have proceeded by attempting, through the observation of the individual instances of the appearance of gravity, to draw out what was common to all appearances of gravity, in order then to infer from this the essence of gravity. Galileo did not begin with observation of individual instances of the appearance of gravity but rather with a general assumption (hypothesis) that runs: Bodies—having lost their support—fall in such a way that their velocity increases in proportion to time ($v = g \cdot t$), that is, bodies fall with equally accelerated motion. The initial velocity is 0, the final velocity $v = g \cdot t$. If we use the mean velocity $\frac{g}{2} \cdot t$, then we have a uniform motion. The basic definitional formula for this is $s = c \cdot t$: the distance travelled is equal to the product of velocity and time. In our case $c = \frac{g}{2} \cdot t$. The insertion of this value into the last formula yields $s = \frac{g}{2} \cdot t^2$. Galileo tested this equation against concrete instances, and it was confirmed by them. Thus the above assumption, from which the law was obtained in a purely deductive manner and subsequently experimentally confirmed, is valid. The entire train of thought was intentionally depicted in detail in order to demonstrate that nowhere in the whole examination was there talk of this or that particular body, this or that duration of time, this or that space of a falling body. The assumption $v = g \cdot t$, which subsequently becomes a law by way of a conclusion drawn on the basis of the experiment that verifies it, is a general one about *all* bodies.

Thus two peculiar features are found in this new method: (1) An assumption is set up that makes it possible to grasp conceptually appearances in a particular field—here this means appearances of motion. (2) The assumption does not posit a hidden quality as the cause that explains the appearances but rather contains mathematically understandable—i.e., measurable—relations between the ideally conceived moments of the appearances. This manner of formulating problems that Galileo for the first time consciously used has in time gained dominance in the individual branches of physics (mechanics, acoustics, theory of heat, optics, magnetic theory, theory of electricity). In each of these fields of physics, one seeks equations in which the most general lawful relations regarding processes can be applied to the respective fields.

But modern physics has not stopped here. It has discovered basic laws that permit, on the one hand, the inclusion of parts of acoustics and theory of heat in mechanics and, on the other, optics, magnetism, and the theory of radiant heat in the theory of electricity. Today, the numerous special fields of physics have been reduced to two: mechanics and electrodynamics or, as it also is put, the physics of matter and the physics of ether. As hotly as the battle between the mechanical and the electrodynamic "worldviews" (!) has raged, the two fields will, as Planck says, "in the long term not at all be able to be sharply demarcated."[2] "Mechanics requires for its foundation in principle only the concepts of space, time, and that which moves, whether one considers this as substance or state. And neither can electrodynamics do without these same concepts. This is why a sufficiently generalized mechanics could also well include electrodynamics, and there are in fact many favorable signs that these already partially overlapping fields will eventually be unified into a single field—that of a general dynamics."[3]

It is with this that the goal of physics as a science must be brought into relief. Its goal is the unity of its picture of the physical world, tracing all appearances back to the basic mathematically definable laws of a general dynamics, to the laws of motion of a still undetermined mass. Now that we know what the goal of physics is, we can formulate our second question: *What function is appropriate for the concept of time in this science?*

Stated briefly, the object of physics is the lawfulness of motion. Motions run their course in time. What exactly does this mean? "In" time has a spatial meaning; however, time is obviously nothing spatial—indeed, we always contrast space and time. But it is just as clear that motion and time are somehow related. In a passage from his *Discorsi,* Galileo speaks precisely of an "affinity between the concepts of time and motion." "For just as the uniformity of motion is determined and comprehended through the equality of the times and spaces . . . , so through this same equality of the segments of time we can also comprehend increase in velocity (acceleration) which has come about in a plain and simple manner."[4] In the relation between motion and time, what is clearly at issue is *measurement* of motion by means of time. As a quantitative determination, measurement is the concern of mathematics. Theoretical, i.e., mathematical, physics forms the foundation of experimental physics. Thus if we wish to obtain precise concepts of motion and time, we must examine them in their mathematical form.

The position of a material point in space is determined by the spatial point with which it coincides. Let us assume now that space is empty except for the material point whose position is to be determined. But space is infinite—each point in space is equal to every other and likewise each direction to every other. Thus it is impossible to determine the position of the material point in question without another point in relation to which its position can be determined. Such a reference point must always be presupposed. All determinations of position are valid relative to it and therefore never absolute. The determination of a position results from our thinking of three straight lines placed through the reference point and running perpendicular to each other—the x, y, and z axes. The position of point P is now determined by the distances from the coordinate axes—the coordinates x, y, and z. Let us assume a point P lying on a spatial curve. We now examine it in terms of its motion, i.e., we study its positions, how they follow after each other temporally. At each second we read off the clock, we can take three measurements, i.e., register the determinate values of x, y, and z, which determine the position of point P at time t. The values of x, y, and z are *dependent* on the particular time t, that is, they are functions of time [$x = x(t)$; $y = y(t)$; $z = z(t)$]. If the value of time t changes by an infinitesimally small value, the values of the coordinates are likewise changed. If we now assign all possible sequential values for t, then the coordinates as constant functions of t mark out the inclusive concept of all temporally sequential positions of point P. We call this inclusive concept of all positions *motion*.

"If we want to describe the motion of a material point," says Einstein, "then we give the values of its coordinates as functions of time."[5]

All other basic concepts in the theory of motion, such as velocity, uniform motion, acceleration, and irregular motion, are defined by particular relationships between quantities of space and time. The concrete sensible qualities of the defined phenomenon in question are dissolved and elevated entirely into the realm of mathematics.

As objects of physics, motions are thus measured by means of time. *It is the function of time to make measurement possible.* Because motions are always treated in physics with respect to *measurability,* it is not the case that they are only occasionally brought into relation with time, and that there are kinds of knowledge in physics where consideration of time as such is held in suspension. Rather, as the equations of motion have shown above, time forms a necessary moment in the *definition* of motion. It is in this necessary connection with time that motion is first able to be grasped conceptually in mathematical physics. Since we now know that time is a condition of the possibility of defining the object of physics, i.e., motions, we can forthwith answer our last question about the structure of this concept of time. In the equations of motion $x = x(t)$, $y = y(t)$, and $z = z(t)$, time is presupposed as an independent variable in such a way that it is constantly changing, i.e., flows uniformly from one point to the next with no jumps. Time presents a series with a single direction in which each point of time differs only through its place as measured from the initial point. Because the one point of time differs from the preceding one only in that it follows after it, it is possible to measure time and thereby motion. As soon as time is measured—and only as time that is measurable and to be measured does it have a meaningful function in physics—we determine a "so many." The registering of the "so many" gathers into one the points of time that have until then flowed by. We as it were make a cut in the time scale, thereby destroying authentic time in its flow and allowing it to harden. The flow freezes, becomes a flat surface, and only as a flat surface can it be measured. Time becomes a homogeneous arrangement of places, a scale, a parameter.

Before we conclude our examination of the concept of time in the natural sciences, an objection still needs to be considered. One could point out that in the discussion so far the newest theory in physics—the theory of relativity—has not been taken into account. The conception of time resulting from it "surpasses in boldness everything previously achieved in speculative natural science and even in philosophical theories of knowledge."[6]

But we usually overlook the following: As a *theory in physics,* the theory of relativity is concerned with the problem of *measuring time,* not with time itself. The theory of relativity leaves the concept of time untouched and in fact only confirms to a greater extent the character of the concept of time in the natural sciences which was brought into relief above, i.e., its homogeneous, quantitatively determinable character. Nothing more clearly expresses the mathematical character of the concept of time in physics than the fact that it can be placed alongside three-dimensional space as a fourth dimension and can, along with this space, be treated with non-Euclidean geometry, i.e., one with more than three dimensions.

If we now wish to proceed to a description of the structure of the concept of time in the science of history, it at first glance seems quite doubtful whether a new problem can in any way be formulated here. For in the science of history, time is likewise an arrangement of places in relation to which the events in question are assigned their particular places in time and thereby *historically* established. Frischeisen-Köhler has recently written that "in certain circumstances it is sufficient to record an event in time to turn a concept formed on principles in the natural sciences into a historical one."[7] Thus the concept of "the famine in Fulda in the year 750" designates a quite definite individual event and is accordingly[a] a historical concept.

Here we face an alternative: either the above-mentioned concept is not a historical concept insofar as it is not understandable why the mere determination of the time should turn a universal concept into a historical one, since even processes of motion in physics are determined as to their time; or, we do have before us a historical concept—which is in fact the case. But then the determination of time found in it must be a quite peculiar one that can be understood only from out of the essence of the science of history.

At least this much has become clear: a problem lies hidden in the concept of time used by the science of history. It thus makes sense and is legitimate for us to question after the structure of the historical concept of time. This structure can only be read off from its function in the science of history, and in turn this function can only be understood on the basis of the goal and object of the science of history.

II

In dealing with the science of history, it may seem that this path from the goal of the science to the function of its concept of time and from there to the structure of this concept of time is a detour. We can reach our goal much easier and quicker in the science of history if we remember that there exists in the method-ology of the science of history a special auxiliary discipline that deals specifically with determining time in the science of history: historical chronology. Here the peculiar character of the historical concept of time would immediately come to light. Why this course is not being taken can be explained only at the end of our analysis. We will then also be in a position to understand the only essential moment in chronology that is of relevance for the historical concept of time. We will thus follow the path already mapped out and first attempt to find out some-thing about the goal of the science of history.

Here we are immediately confronted with a difficulty insofar as complete agreement among historians about the goal and object of the science of history has not been reached. Thus whatever we determine here about this problem can-not claim to be conclusive and complete. However, this fact cannot put our actual problem in jeopardy if we are identifying only *those* moments in the con-cept of the science of history that will allow us to understand the function of the concept of time in it.

The object of the science of history is human beings—not as biological objects but rather to the extent that their achievements in the realms of mind and body actualize the idea of culture. This creation of culture in its fullness and mul-tiformity runs its course temporally, undergoes development, is subject to the most diverse transformations and reorganizations, takes hold of what is in the past in order to work with it further or combat it. The creation of culture by human beings within and in unison with the associations and organizations (the state) created by them is basically the objectification[b] of the human spirit. This objectification of spirit that actualizes itself in the course of time is of interest to the historian not in its entirety at each particular time, as though the historian wanted in each case to record everything that in any sense happened at the time. It has been said that it is only what is historically effective that interests the his-torian. Eduard Meyer, who has given this qualification, elaborates on it and cor-rectly explains it as follows: "The selection depends on the historical interest the present has in some effect, in the result of a development."[8]

An interest is, however, always determined on the basis of a point of view, guided by a norm. The selection of the historical from the fullness of what is given is thus based on a relation to values. Accordingly, the goal of the science of history is to depict the context of the effects and development of the objectifica-tions of human life in the singularity and uniqueness of these objectifications, which are able to be understood through a relation to cultural values. But one essential characteristic of every historical object still has not been touched on.

The historical object is, as historical, always past—strictly speaking, it no longer exists. Between it and the historian stands a temporal distance. The past always has meaning only when seen from a present. What is past *is* not only no longer when viewed by us—it *was* also something *other* than us and our context of life today in the present. So much is already clear: time has an utterly original meaning in history. Only where this qualitative otherness of past times presses forth into the consciousness of the present does a historical sense awaken. Insofar as the historical past is always an otherness of objectifications of human life, and we ourselves always live in such an objectification and create such objectifications, the possibility is always in advance given for us to understand the past, since it cannot be something *incomparably* other. However, the temporal gulf remains between the historian and his object. If he wishes to depict this gulf, he must in some way have the object before him. It is necessary to overcome time—by crossing over the temporal gulf, to move from the present into the past, immerse oneself in it, and live in it. The requirement of overcoming time and depicting a past—a requirement necessarily co-given in the goal and object of the science of history—will for its part be possible only insofar as time itself begins to function here in some manner. John Bodin, already in 1607, included a separate chapter on time in his *Methodus ad facilem historiarum cognitionem.* We find there the sentence: "Those who think they can understand histories [the plural case is noteworthy] without chronology are as much in error as those who wish to escape the windings of a labyrinth without a guide."[9]

We can most reliably study the function of time involved in the overcoming of time necessary for the science of history if we direct our attention to the *methodology* of the science of history with which it gains access to the past and depicts it historically. It would take us too far afield to investigate all of the details of the function of time within the methodology of the science of history, uncovering the relations of its basic concepts to the main concept guiding it. Rather, we only need to characterize a few especially noticeable concepts and procedures of the method of the science of history that illustrate the function of the concept of time here. Thus a moment will be provided that is at least *adequate* for analyzing the structure of the concept of time.

The initial foundational task of the science of history is that it must first of all guarantee the factuality of the events it is to depict. "Perhaps the greatest service of the critical school in our science, at least the one most important with respect to its method," writes Droysen, "is to have achieved the insight that the foundation of our studies is the testing of the 'sources' from which we draw. *It is in this way that history's relation to the past is brought to its scientifically definitive stage.*"[10]

Thus the "source" makes possible scientific access to historical reality. It is from it that this reality is in the first place built up. But this is possible only if the source is secured in its value as a source, i.e., if its authenticity is demonstrated. And that happens through criticism. Let us suppose, for example, that the authenticity of a document is to be demonstrated. This might happen by seeking a decision about its "official" character. "Documentary testimonies from an office functioning in an orderly manner will at *particular times* display definite characteristics. The inclusive concept of all these characteristics *at a particular time* constitutes what is meant by official character."[11] Thus the concept of time lies hidden in the concept of official character.

But to the demonstration of the official character of a document, i.e., diplomatic criticism, must be added legal-historical criticism and general historical criticism, i.e., the document in question must be compared to the legal and general cultural circumstances of *the time* to which it is supposed to belong. For example, the pseudo-Isidorian decrees were proved fraudulent by showing the individual papal letters to be anachronisms. We know that it was Pope Gregory the Great who for the first time used the title "servus servorum Dei" at the start of his letters. Previous popes already refer to themselves by the same title in the letters in question in the Isidorian collection. We know further that up until the end of the fourth century, popes did not date their letters according to the Roman consuls, yet this happens in the Isidorian letters in question. The decrees supposedly stemming from the first centuries presuppose certain ecclesiastical-legal circumstances that emerged only later. Thus criticism shows that, with respect to their form and content, the letters do not at all display the *stamp of the time* in which they are supposed to have emerged but rather that of a *later time*. The scientific use of a source demands that the time of its emergence be determined, because its value as evidence depends on how far it is *temporally* removed from the historical fact to which it is supposed to be a testimony. "The method most commonly used is a comparative investigation into what *epoch* it is to which the source in question initially corresponds in its form, style, and content—in short, in its total character . . . for each time displays in all its creations and expressions a character which is different from that of other times and which we may well recognize."[12] In written sources it is above all handwriting and language—"these most malleable expressions of the spirit of the time"—that make it possible for us to determine the time.

The concept of time plays a no less essential role in the second main task of the method of history: bringing into relief *the context* of the facts which are at first individually established. What is initially necessary here is to understand correctly the significance of the particular facts within their context, i.e., to interpret correctly the relevant content of the sources.

An interesting example of this comprehensive function of the concept of time in history is offered by Troeltsch's recent study of Augustine.[13] Troeltsch shows that Augustine was "in fact the conclusion and culmination of Christian antiquity, its last and greatest thinker, its intellectual practitioner and people's tribune. It is from this point of view that he must in the first place be understood."[14] On the other hand, Troeltsch characterizes Christian antiquity in its conclusion from the point of view of Augustine. This characterization then makes it possible for him to demarcate the second period in the history of Christianity from the first. Here Troeltsch writes regarding differentiations of the great periods of Christianity: ". . . they must be made according to the fact that the Christian Church belongs to general cultural contexts at particular times."[15]

These examples should suffice for us to be able to see right away the essential element in the historical concept of time. *Historical times differ qualitatively.* It is the "guiding tendencies" (Ranke) of a *time,* an *age,* that direct us regarding how it is to be demarcated over against another.

Thus the concept of time in the science of history has nothing of the homogeneous character of the concept of time in the natural sciences. This is why historical time cannot be expressed mathematically by a series, since there is no law that determines how the *times* follow after each other. In the time of physics, temporal moments differ only in terms of their place in the series. Historical times do indeed come after one another—otherwise, they would not in any sense be times—yet in the structure of its content, each is[d] a time that is other. *The qualitative element in the historical concept of time means nothing other than the condensation—crystallization—of an objectification of life given in history.* Thus the science of history does not work with quantities. Yet what else are historical dates? In the concept of "the famine in Fulda in the year 750," the number 750 by itself means nothing to the historian. He is not interested in the number *as a quantity,* as an element that has its particular place in the series of numbers from one to infinity, is dividable by 50, and so on. The number 750, and every other historical date, has meaning and value in the science of history only by considering the content in question that is historically significant.[16] Trecento, quattrocento could not be further from being quantitative concepts. The question of "when" has entirely different meanings in physics and in history. In *physics,* I would ask when the weight on the Atwood gravity machine would reach a certain place on the scale, i.e., after *how many* beats of the seconds pendulum. If I ask about the "when" of a *historical* event, then I am asking about its place[e] in a *qualitative historical* context, not about a "how many." But, on occasion, the historian does also pose the question of "how many." Thus it will later be of interest to military history to know *how long* the Mackensen army needed to push its offensive from the Carpathian Mountains right up to the Russian-Polish quadrant. However, the *quantitative* determination—about 12 weeks—does not *by itself* have value and meaning for the historian but rather only insofar as from it we can judge the tremendous combat strength of our allied troops, the sureness of the whole operation in reaching its goal, and on the other side the Russian army's power of resistance. Historical dates are convenient numerical markers, but they are without meaning when considered by themselves, since for any number another could equally be substituted by simply shifting the starting point of counting. And precisely the beginning of the time-reckoning in calendars shows that this reckoning always starts at a historically significant event (founding of Rome, birth of Christ, Hedschra).

Historical chronology, an auxiliary discipline in the science of history, is of significance for a theory of the historical concept of time only from the point of view of *the beginning* of its time-reckoning. For example, it is said that establishing the beginning of the year on January 1 was at first displeasing to the Christians, "because January 1 had no relation to the Christian religion whatsoever."[17] Therefore, the Church moved the Feast of Circumcision to this day in order to give it a religious *significance.* It was always on significant holidays—Easter, Christmas—that the beginning of the year was established. This shows that in the science of history anything to do with numbers and counting regarding time is *determined qualitatively* through the way in which the beginning of the counting is established. It can be said that the principle of concept-formation in history shows itself even in the beginning of time-reckoning: a relation to values.[18]

Recognizing the fundamental meaning of the concept of time in history and its complete otherness vis-à-vis the concept of time in physics will make it possible for theory of science to penetrate further into the authentic character of the science of history and to ground it in theory as an original, intellectual approach that is irreducible to other sciences.

MARGINALIA

a. In what sense is individual = historical?

b. Means what? Are "associations" objectifications?

c. This is not "ascertaining facts."

d. What does "is" mean here? It does not have to do with *objective* qualities.

e. What does "place" mean here?

Chapter Five

THE THEORY OF CATEGORIES
AND MEANING IN DUNS SCOTUS

AUTHOR'S BOOK NOTICE (1917)

John van Buren, translator

This investigation into the history of *problems* ultimately has a *systematic* goal: the theory of categories, whose fundamental establishment and organic development has today been made one of the clearly recognized tasks of philosophy. As an investigation into the *history* of problems, it takes as its theme the philosophy of the Scholastic Duns Scotus, so that through one of the most intellectually complete and rich models of medieval Scholastic thought, a deeper understanding of this thought itself can be gained from the point of view of the *general* problem of categories *and of logic* and the common evaluation of medieval Scholasticism and its logic opposed. In doing this, the major emphasis in Part I (the theory of categories) is laid on what is a basic requirement for any treatment of the problem of categories: demarcating different domains within objects in general. In the first place, the most general determinations of objects in any sense and the individual domains (logical, mathematical, physical, psychical, and metaphysical reality)

See pp. 5–6, 20–21, 25–26 for bibliographic and other background information on the following two texts at the end of Heidegger's Student Period: "Author's Book Notice," which summarizes the published contents of Heidegger's 1915 postdoctoral dissertation, "The Theory of Categories and Meaning in Duns Scotus"; and "Conclusion: The Problem of Categories," which was "written as a supplement" for the publication of the dissertation.

had to be subjected to a description that read them off. Part II (the theory of meaning[1]) provided the opportunity to present in more detail a particular sphere of objects, that of meanings, and thereby to draw out basic theses about acts and the sense of acts of meaning and knowledge in their interrelation and furthermore about the basic forms of meaning in general (the "categories of meaning"). The concluding chapter attempts, in a forward-looking manner, to lay out the structure of the problem of categories and the potential path to its solution.

CONCLUSION: THE PROBLEM OF CATEGORIES (1916)

Roderick M. Stewart and John van Buren, translators

Motto: We seek the unconditioned *[Unbedingte]* everywhere and only ever find conditioned things *[Dinge]*."

—Novalis, *Fragments*[2]

The authentic goal of this investigation as an investigation into the history of a *problem* requires with systematic necessity as a conclusion—in addition to a look back at the main points having resulted and an overview of them in which they are reworked and evaluated—a look forward at the *systematic* structure of the problem of categories. However, what we are able to deal with here is not much more than bringing into relief *essential potencies of this problem and their contexts,* the *fundamental* setting in motion and actualization of which has not yet been realized in the treatment of the problem up to this point. This is also the reason why the systems of categories having been attempted until now have been unable to avoid the impression of a certain deathly emptiness.

In the preceding, where the task was at first to present a certain *historical* shaping of the problem of categories while at the same time lifting it up to the systematic level, it was not feasible to put forth at the beginning fundamental theses with definite content, for their being more penetratingly related to a special formation of the problem would surely have been questionable without a prior acquaintance with this special formation. Moreover, the kind of problem necessarily involving taking up a fundamental position and often ranging broadly would have heavily burdened the above presentation that aimed at a simple systematic understanding and would have disagreeably interfered with it by constantly introducing open questions. In contrast, this is now the appropriate place to give the intellectual *unrest* a chance to speak that until now has remained suppressed and that the philosopher must experience each time he studies the historical formations of his world of problems.

But bringing into relief the essential potencies of the problem of categories can be carried out only to the extent that these potencies are analyzed in isolation and one after another. Thus it is all the more crucial to emphasize from the outset that these potencies reciprocally condition one another and that what is apparently immediate and unmediated is always something mediated. What we establish individually in the following receives its full sense only within the totality.

If we conceive of the categories as elements and means for interpreting the sense of what is experienceable—of what is an object in any sense—then what ensues as a basic requirement for a theory of categories is *characterizing and demarcating the different domains of objects into spheres that are categorially irreducible to one another*. We attached importance to the fulfillment of this task already in the whole *structure* of the preceding investigation.[3] Thus what we needed to achieve at the same time was destroying the impoverished and unproblematic appearance up to now of the logic of medieval Scholasticism. This was done by bringing into relief the elements of definition that foundationally characterize individual domains of objects. The fact that these elements extend to the ultimate categorial sphere of objects (the transcendentals) then provided the regions being separated with a fundamental unifying integration. What was required here was a rigorously *conceptual* and in a certain sense one-sided presentation with conscious suspension of more deeply ranging contexts of metaphysical problems.

These contexts of problems can be understood to be ultimately decisive for the problem of categories only if we recognize a second basic task of any theory of categories: *situating the problem of categories within the problems of judgment and the subject*. Even this side of the problem of categories was at the very least touched on in Scholastic logic. Admittedly, our presentation of Duns Scotus' theory of judgment tended in a different direction: it was supposed to characterize the domain of the logical, and here the essential relation of judgment to the categories remained for the time being completely shrouded in darkness. Nonetheless, the theory of meaning in Duns Scotus did permit an avenue of access to subjectivity (by which not individuality but the *subject in itself* is meant). Duns Scotus' task, i.e., the analysis of a certain stratum of acts—the *modus significandi* [mode of meaning]—forced him to enter into the sphere of *acts in general* and to establish certain fundamental things about the individual strata of acts (*modus significandi, intelligendi, essendi* [modes of meaning, understanding, and being]) and their relations to one another.

Precisely the existence of a theory of meaning within medieval Scholasticism reveals a refined disposition for attentively listening in on the immediate life of subjectivity and its immanent contexts of sense without having acquired a precise concept of the subject. We might be tempted to "explain" the existence of such "grammars" by making reference to the industry of medieval schools and their traditions. This kind of "explanation," generally preferred in the science of history but highly dubious for problems in intellectual history, does indeed have *a certain degree* of justification, even in our case. However, when we are concerned with a living understanding of a "time" and the effective intellectual accomplishments in it, what becomes necessary is an *interpretation of its sense that is guided by concepts of ultimate goals*. Usually employing the facile label "construction," one is in the habit of superciliously dismissing this kind of forehaving and plan *[Vorhaben]* with a wave of the hand as unhistorical and thus worthless, failing to see—in consequence of a fundamental ignorance about the essence of historical knowing and of concept-formation in history—how much merely piling up as many "facts" as possible on top of one other actually leads away from the living life of the historical past and in a curious manner comes close to being a leveling construction which suspends the kind of sense that unifies and provides goals.

Because of its regress to a fundamental sphere of problems having to do with subjectivity (the strata of acts), the theory of meaning is, in spite of its immediate schematic character, especially significant for a philosophical interpretation of medieval Scholasticism in connection with the problem of categories. The investigation of the relation between the *modus essendi* [mode of being] and the "subjective" *modi significandi* [modes of meaning] and *intelligendi* [understanding] leads to the principle of the *material determination* of every form, which for its part includes in itself the fundamental correlation of object and subject.[4] The essential interconnection between the object of knowledge and knowledge of the object is expressed most clearly in the concept of *"verum"* [true] as one of the *transcendentals,* i.e., the determinations of objects *in general.* Nevertheless, there are still two things missing here that are intrinsically bound up with understanding the problem of knowledge: first, consciously incorporating the problem of judgment into the subject-object relation and, second, bringing categories into relation with judgment.

Because these contexts of problems have not yet received a basic clarification even today when realism is embraced, we need to provide a deeper discussion of this task which, besides that of demarcating domains of objects, is a fundamental one for a theory of categories. In doing so, we also are given the opportunity to point at least in very general outline to the necessity of a metaphysical solution of the problem of knowledge.

A category is the most general determination of objects. Objects and objectivity *[Gegenständlichkeit]* have, as such, sense only *for* a subject. In this subject, objectivity *[Objektivität]* is built up through judgments. Consequently, if we want to conceive of categories in a decisive manner as determinations *of objects,* then we must establish their essential relations to the forms that build up objectivity *[Gegenständlichkeit]*. Thus it was no "accident" but rather grounded in the innermost core of the problem of categories that this problem arose in both Aristotle and Kant in some sort of connection with predication, i.e., with judgment. This might mean that the categories would have to be reduced to mere *functions of thinking,* but the possibility of such a move does not make any sense at all for a philosophy that has acknowledged *problems having to do with sense.* And precisely transcendental idealism, which in its present form should not without further ado be identified with Kantian epistemology and the way it is formulated, emphasizes from the outset that all thinking and knowing is always thinking and knowing *of an object.* It is then with reference to this that we ought to gauge what is involved in explaining categories as mere "forms of thinking."[5]

Even the most general determinations of objects, which in terms of their content are *faded*, i.e., reflexive categories, cannot be fully understood without reference to the *judgments* that constitute objectivity *[Objektivität]*, i.e., a universal theory of objects that is *only* "objective" and does not include the "subjective" side necessarily remains incomplete. All differences are certainly differences in objects but, indeed, on the other hand, only *as differences that are known and judged to be such*. The reason for a multiplicity of *domains of validity* within the totality of categories lies *primarily* though not *exclusively* in the multiplicity of regions of objects, in each case conditioning a corresponding structured form of fashioning judgments, and it is from the latter that the categories can be "read off" for the first time in their *full content*.

It is then only by starting from judgment that even the problem of the "immanent and transeunt [lying 'outside of thinking'] validity" of the categories can be solved. It does not make any sense to speak of *immanent and transeunt* validity without taking into consideration "subjective logic." Immanence and transcendence are relational concepts that acquire a clear meaning only by establishing that *with reference to which* something is thought of as immanent or transcendent. It is indisputable "that all transeunt validity stands or falls with the recognition of objects,"[6] only it is precisely *a problem what kind of objectivity [Gegenständlichkeit] this can only be* if we take into consideration that objectivity has sense only for a judging subject and that without this subject we could never manage to bring out the full sense of what we designate by the term "validity." Whether validity means a peculiar kind of "being" or an "ought" or *neither of these but can only be understood through deeper groups of problems contained in the concept of living spirit* [7] *and doubtlessly closely connected with the problem of value is something we will not decide here.*

The close connection between the problem of the categories and that of judgment permits us then once again to make the *form-matter relation* and the meaning-differentiating function of matter into a problem. The form-matter duality is today such a crucial means of treating epistemological problems that a *fundamental* investigation into the value and limits of this duality has become unavoidable.

Of course, a definitive clarification of this question can in no way be attained by remaining within the logical sphere of sense and the structure of this sense. At best we are led to an exponential growth (Lask's theory of levels of forms) that undeniably accomplishes the important task of illuminating the structural multiplicity of the logical itself, but nevertheless precisely compounds still more the problem of the meaning-differentiating function of matter and shifts it into a new sphere without adequately taking into account the fundamental difference between sensory and nonsensory matter.

We cannot at all see logic and its problems in their true light if the context *from* which they are interpreted is not a translogical one. *Philosophy cannot for long do without its authentic optics: metaphysics.* This signifies for theory of truth

the task of an ultimate metaphysically teleological interpretation of consciousness. Value already lives in consciousness in a primordially original manner insofar as consciousness is a living deed that is filled with sense and actualizes this
sense. One has not in the least understood consciousness if it is neutralized into
the concept of a blind, biological factuality.

Within the wealth of directions of the formation of living spirit, the theoretical attitude is only *one* kind of approach, and for this reason it is a fundamental and fatal error of philosophy as "worldview" if it contents itself with a
spelling out of actuality and does not—and this is its most authentic vocation—
aim beyond an always provisional synopsis that gathers up the whole of what is
knowable and at a *breakthrough* to true actuality and actual truth. It is only with
this orientation to the concept of living spirit and its "eternal affirmations" (F.
Schlegel) that epistemological logic will be protected from becoming limited
exclusively to the study of structures and will make logical sense *even in its ontic
meaning into a problem.* A satisfactory answer will then for the first time become
possible as to how nonactual and "unreal" "transcendent" sense ensures us true
actuality and objectivity.

As radically as Lask has brought into relief structural problems in theory of
judgment and that of categories, he himself was just as inexorably brought from
the context of his problems to metaphysical problems without his perhaps being
fully conscious of these latter problems. And precisely in his concept of objects
"characterized by being beyond oppositions" lies a fruitful element in which epistemological theories that are in many respects divergent can now be brought
together. But here we should not overlook the difficulties involved with the problems of opposition and value, i.e., overlook the problem of the ontic interpretation and logical understanding of "objects."[8]

In this kind of *transcendental-ontic* understanding of the concept of an
object, the problem of the "application" of categories no longer makes sense, and
this becomes more certain the more resolutely one takes seriously the fundamental meaning of the *principle of immanence* (not to be understood "individu-
alistically"), whose necessary *ultimate* grounding—which can only be carried out
metaphysically—will in my opinion have to be provided from out of the concept
of living spirit we have roughly indicated. Provided that one even acknowledges
the problem of the *application* of categories as a *possible* problem, it is surely here
if anywhere that the *merely* objective manner of treating the problem of categories
in logic must be seen to be one-sided.[9]

The epistemological subject does not signify the metaphysically most
meaningful sense of spirit, to say nothing of its full content. And only if it is situated within this full content will the problem of categories attain its authentic
depth dimension and enrichment. *Living spirit is as such essentially historical spirit
in the widest sense of the word.* The true worldview is far removed from the merely
fragmentary existence of a theory detached from life. Spirit can be conceptually
grasped only when the total fullness of its accomplishments, i.e., *its history,* is

lifted up within it, and with this constantly burgeoning fullness that is in the process of being philosophically conceptualized a continually developing means for gaining a living conceptual grasp of the absolute spirit of God is provided. History and its teleological interpretation in philosophy of culture *must become a determining element for the meaning of the problem of categories* if we want to think differently about working out the *cosmos* of categories in order to go beyond an impoverished schematic table of categories. This is, in addition to demarcating the domains of objects and including the problem of judgment, a third basic requirement for a promising solution to the problem of categories. Looking at the matter the other way round, it is from the point of view of such a broadly oriented theory of categories that the conceptual means and goals can for the very first time be supplied for conceptually grasping the individual epochs of the intellectual history of spirit in a living manner. To the extent that it is going to be more deeply treated, the problem of the "medieval worldview," touched on in the Introduction and of special interest in connection with the present investigation, lacks to this day the *proper conceptual foundation in philosophy of culture* which can for the first time provide clarity, certainty, and unity concerning the whole. The peculiar will-to-life and refined spiritual composure of such a period call for the *openness* of an empathetic understanding in conformity with it and of a broadly—i.e., philosophically—oriented evaluation. For example, the concept of *analogy* discussed in this investigation[10] in regard to the problem of metaphysical reality appears at first glance to be an utterly faded and no longer meaningful schoolbook concept. However, as the dominant principle in the categorial sphere of sensible and supersensible reality, it contains the conceptual expression of the *qualitatively* filled and value-laden experiential world of medieval man that is related to transcendence. It is the conceptual expression of the particular form of inner Dasein that is anchored in a primordial, transcendent relation of the soul to God and lived precisely in the Middle Ages with an unusual reserve. The multiplicity of relations in life between God and soul, between the here-and-now and the beyond, are subject to change in virtue of the increasing distance or proximity (in a qualitatively intensive sense) between them at particular times. The metaphysical linkage accomplished through transcendence is at the same time a source of manifold oppositions and thus the source of the most abundant thriving of the immanent personal lives of individuals.

Transcendence does not mean a radical distancing from and loss of self—rather, there is here precisely a life-relation that is built on a certain correlativity and as such does not have a *single* inflexible directional sense but is to be compared to the flow of experience running back and forth between mutually attracted spiritual individuals, though here we have of course not taken into consideration the absolute superior value of the one term of the relation. The scale of values does not therefore gravitate exclusively toward the transcendent but rather is as it were reflected back from the fullness and absoluteness of the transcendent and comes to rest in the individual.

Thus what also is found throughout the whole of the medieval worldview—just because it is so radical in its conscious *teleological* orientation—is a whole world of multifarious differentiations of value. The possibilities of experience and the fullness of experience resulting from this for subjectivity are accordingly conditioned by that dimension of spiritual life that stretches *into the transcendent* and not like today by the *breadth of its fleeting content.* In this attitude of life running its course broadly on the surface of things, the possibilities of mounting uncertainty and complete disorientation are much greater and almost limitless, whereas in contrast the basic development of the form of life of medieval man from the outset did not in any way lose itself in the breadth of content of sensible reality and anchor itself there. Rather, it subordinated this very sensible reality—*as something in need of being anchored*—to the necessity of a transcendent goal.

What is opened up in the concept of living spirit and its relation to the metaphysical "origin" is an insight into its basic metaphysical structure in which the uniqueness, the individuality, of its *acts* is joined together in a living unity with the universal validity, the subsisting-in-itself, of *sense*. Looking at this from the side of the objects involved, what stands before us is the problem of the relation between time and eternity, change and absolute validity, world and God, a problem that in terms of theory of science finds itself reflected in *history* (formation of values) and philosophy (validity of values).[11]

If we keep in mind the deeper essence of philosophy as worldview, then even the conception of the Christian philosophy of the Middle Ages as a Scholasticism that stood in conflict with the *mysticism* of this period must be exposed as a fundamental error. Scholasticism and mysticism belong together essentially in the medieval worldview. The two pairs of "opposites"—rationalism-irrationalism and Scholasticism-mysticism—*do not coincide with one another.* And when one attempts to equate them, such an attempt is based on an extreme rationalization of philosophy. Philosophy as a rationalistic construction detached from life is *powerless*—mysticism as irrational experience is *without a goal.*

The philosophy of living spirit, of active love, of reverent intimacy with God, the most general directions of which we were only able to indicate roughly, and especially a theory of categories guided by the basic tendencies of this philosophy, stand before the great task of a fundamental critical discussion of that system of historical worldview that is the most powerful one regarding fullness as well as depth, wealth of experience and concept-formation and as such lifted up into itself all of the fundamental motives previously at work in philosophical problems—that is, a critical discussion of Hegel.

Chapter Six

LETTER TO FATHER ENGELBERT KREBS (1919)

JOHN VAN BUREN, TRANSLATOR

January 9, 1919

Dear Professor,

The past two years in which I struggled for a fundamental clarification of my philosophical position and put aside all specialized academic tasks have led to conclusions I would not be able to hold and teach freely, were I bound to a position outside of philosophy.

Epistemological insights extending to a theory of historical knowledge have made the *system* of Catholicism problematic and unacceptable to me, but not Christianity and metaphysics—these, though, in a new sense.

I firmly believe that I—perhaps more than your colleagues who officially work in this field—have experienced what the Catholic Middle Ages bears within itself regarding values and that we are still a long way off from a true appreciation of them. My investigations in the phenomenology of religion, which will draw heavily on the Middle Ages, should show beyond a doubt that in transforming my basic philosophical position I have not been driven to replacing

See pp. 6–8, 27 for bibliographic and other background information on this letter announcing Heidegger's confessional and philosophical turn at the start of his Early Freiburg Period.

objective appreciative judgment of and deep respect for the life-world of Catholicism with the angry and coarse polemics of an apostate.

Thus it will in the future be important for me to remain in contact with Catholic scholars who understand and acknowledge the problems in this field and are able to sympathize with those with different convictions.

It is therefore especially important to me that I not lose the benefit of your invaluable friendship—and I would like to thank you deeply for it. My wife, who first talked with you, and I too would like to keep the very special trust we have shared with you. It is difficult to live as a philosopher—inner truthfulness regarding oneself and in relation to those for whom one is supposed to be a teacher demands sacrifices, renunciation, and struggles which ever remain unknown to the academic technician.

I believe that I have the inner calling to philosophy and, through my research and teaching, to do what stands in my power for the sake of the eternal vocation of the inner man, and *to do it for this alone,* and so justify my existence *[Dasein]* and work ultimately before God.

Sincerely and gratefully yours,
Martin Heidegger

P.S. My wife sends her warmest regards.

Chapter Seven

COMMENTS ON KARL JASPERS'
PSYCHOLOGY OF WORLDVIEWS (1920)

JOHN VAN BUREN, TRANSLATOR

A "fitting" orientation for a positive and illuminating critical review of this work published by Jaspers is *not* available in the current inventory of our scientific and philosophical knowledge. Making such an admission right at the outset may serve as an appropriate indication of the originality and significance of Jaspers' achievement. This critical review will attempt to orient itself in a fitting manner to the immanent intentions of Jaspers' work and follow up on them. Some preliminary reflections on the scope of this course of inquiry and on the range of its claims also will help us characterize the actual object to be dealt with in the following comments and will thus be far from an otiose discussion of possible methods.

Jaspers' work developed out of a concern with psychology as a whole (5), and psychology is supposed to allow us to see "what the human being is" (ibid.). The psychology of worldviews, which is a "part" of the whole of psychology with its own specific nature and function, attempts to mark out the "limits of our psychical life,"[1] and thereby provide a clear and comprehensive horizon for our psychical life. Marking out such limits is more precisely a type of observation in

---

See pp. 8, 28 for bibliographic and other background information on this book review essay from the first part of Heidegger's Early Freiburg Period.

which we comprehensively examine the being of the human mind in its sub-
stantial totality and classify its ultimate positions. And this means "marking out
that domain of which we already possess a conceptual understanding at present"
(6). Psychology of worldviews is only *one* way of acquiring a "basis" for understanding the whole of our psychical life, the other way being given in "general
psychology" (a doctrine of principles and categories, a methodology for gaining
knowledge in psychology). According to the way it is undertaken by Jaspers, this
type of observation giving us an understanding and overview of the basic capacities and tendencies of the psychical life of the mind as a whole already in itself
has—apart from being evaluated in terms of its primary purpose—a positive significance for knowledge in psychiatry as well as in the human sciences. For it
expands our "natural" psychological understanding, rendering it more receptive
and versatile, i.e., more perceptive regarding the nuances, dimensions, and different levels of our psychical being.

But the concrete tendency of Jaspers' work—its concern with the whole of
psychology, with acquiring the fundamental domain of psychology and its horizon of *principles*—should in fact already be seen as "philosophical." Psychology
of worldviews is not supposed to develop a positive worldview and impose it on
others. Rather, by understanding and classifying the positions, processes, and
stages of our psychical life, this type of observation is meant to provide us with
"clarifications and possibilities which can serve as means to our self-reflection (in
our worldviews)" (Foreword). It is in this way that the aforementioned direction
of Jaspers' inquiry, namely, gaining access to psychology as a whole, is assigned
its ultimate goal. The way the first set of tasks gets carried out is simultaneously
the way to fulfill the second set of real, philosophical tasks. In turn, this orientation to the goal of philosophizing, which is described by Jaspers in a particular
manner, provides fundamental guidance for his preoccupation with the problem
of psychology.

This review intends to deal with the principles at work in Jaspers' book.
Thus we will not be focusing on particularities in the content of this text, or on
the individual components of Jaspers' classificatory schemata, so that we can, for
instance, modify these and replace them with others. Our goal is not to add supplementary content or insert missing "types." Rather, what is important is to
characterize the "how" of this philosophical review in regard to its basic approach
and in relation to the problems it intends to broach. In providing this characterization, we will simultaneously be limiting the range of claims we can make.

The basic approach of this review lies in its attempt to free up the real tendencies of Jaspers' work. In doing so, it seeks to bring into sharper focus both the
primary direction in which Jaspers' problems tend and the basic motivations for
this direction. Here we will determine to what extent Jaspers' approach to his
tasks, his choice of methods, and his way of employing these methodological
means to carry out his tasks are really in keeping with the underlying tendencies
of his inquiry and the directions in which these tendencies discernibly point us.

We also will examine whether the motivations and tendencies of Jaspers' inquiry have themselves been shaped radically enough in line with the tentative orientation to philosophizing lying at the basis of his inquiry. Accordingly, every type of review oriented to fixed standards will remain out of play for us. Jaspers' observations will not be confronted with the aid of a finished philosophy established on some secure foundation or evaluated in terms of their distance from a consummate objective systematics in the field of philosophical problems. Nor are they to be assessed in relation to a fixed ideal of scientific and philosophical rigor in methodology. Where such standards have become available in one's philosophizing, a type of review oriented to fixed standards is not only justifiable but may also even be urgently needed, and all the more so when the work under discussion is experienced as unsettling, provocative, and challenging. But this kind of review has been ruled out at present insofar as Jaspers' investigation will not be judged with the help of such ideas as the "the absolute validity of truth," "relativism," and "skepticism." This type of assessment will be avoided precisely because the following comments endeavor to sharpen our consciences regarding the need to inquire into the genuine sense of "intellectual history" and return radically to the original genetic motivations in this history having led to the establishment of such epistemological ideals in philosophy. We need to determine anew whether these ideals satisfy the fundamental sense of philosophizing, or whether they do not rather lead a shadowy life that has hardened into a long, degenerate, and spurious tradition and has never been appropriated in an original manner. It is certain that such sharpening of the conscience cannot be taken care of, or approached in any genuine manner whatsoever, by "creating" a "new" philosophical program; rather, it must be actualized in a very concrete manner in the form of a destruction directed precisely to what has been handed down to us in intellectual history. This task is tantamount to explicating the original motivational situations in which the fundamental experiences of philosophy have arisen. And these experiences are to be understood as having undergone theoretical development and refinement in the establishment of the aforementioned epistemological ideals. In this regard, the meaning of the term "theory" is itself geared precisely to its origin (cf. Plato, Aristotle). The "idea" we have of the meaning and scope of this task is such that it can scarcely be overestimated. On the contrary, we will come to see *what* is concretely "necessary" in philosophy precisely *by restricting ourselves to this task* and consciously abandoning aspirations to "creative" philosophizing that are in fact traditional, even if somewhat historically open-ended.

If this review emphatically rules out any intention of assessing Jaspers' work with fixed, highly refined points of reference that have demonstrably not, however, been appropriated in any radical sense, it is likewise very suspicious of all indulgent "philosophies of life" making claims to free thinking and an apparent primordiality. "Philosophy of life" will be called into question by analyzing it to show that the basic philosophical motive coming to expression in it does so in a hidden manner, is hardly able to be grasped with the meager inventory of concepts available to philosophy of life, and in fact manifests itself in a degenerate form.

Refraining from the type of review that brings into play fixed standards to orient itself means anything but an uncritical approach advocating an ambivalent syncretism that is blind to differences and subjects everything to mediation. A definite orientation also is to be found in the basic approach we will be working out and actualizing in this review, and the essential character of this approach is expressed precisely in the "how" of our persisting in it. This "how" of a critical approach always remains subject to a type of appropriation that must constantly renew itself in the form of a destruction. Our review is phenomenological in the genuine sense, but it is not "without presuppositions" in the bad sense. Here one turns what is immediately "on hand" in one's objective historical, intellectual situation into the in-itself of the "things themselves." One fails to see what is characteristic of all intuition, namely, that it actualizes itself in the context of a definite orientation and an anticipatory foreconception of the respective region of experience. Thus when one shuns constructivistic points of view foreign to the subject matter and is concerned with immediacy only in this respect, one's intuition can all too easily fall prey to a certain blindness regarding the fact that its own motivational basis is itself in the end not primordial. The meaning of primordiality does not lie in the idea of something outside of history or beyond it; rather, it shows itself in the fact that thinking without presuppositions can itself be achieved only in a self-critique that is historically oriented in a factical manner. An incessant actualizing of a certain worry[2] about achieving primordiality is what constitutes primordiality. (The term "historical"[3] is used here in a sense that will become somewhat more explicit in the course of the following reflections.) Thinking without presuppositions is here intended to be taken in a philosophical sense and not in a specifically scientific sense. The path leading to the "things themselves" treated in philosophy is a long one. Thus the excessive liberties taken recently by many phenomenologists in their use of essential intuition appear in a very dubious light and are hardly in line with the "openness" and "devotion" to the things themselves preached by these phenomenologists. It might just be the case that even the directions of inquiry in which we could find access to the things themselves of philosophy lie covered over for us, and that what is thus necessary is a radical deconstruction and reconstruction, i.e., a genuine confrontation with the history we ourselves "are." And this confrontation would be something actualized within the very meaning of philosophizing. In the end, it is just this precisely oriented detour and the type of roundabout understanding actualized in it that make up *the* path to the things themselves. In connection with the fundamental question of the sense of the "I am," we need to ask ourselves if it is not high time to determine whether we have really so thoroughly come to terms with that which we ourselves purportedly "have" and "are." Are we, rather than taking firm hold of the most important questions in a philosophically rigorous manner, generating an unspeakable hustle and bustle in our care for the preservation of culture, though we never actually get around to applying ourselves to this task? Are we today troubling ourselves with peripheral matters that were transformed into fundamental problems by an earlier form of intellectual industriousness that searched too *broadly* for all objects of philosophical investigation? Thinking phenomenologically without presuppositions denotes a certain approach and orientation, and this is neither mere sport nor prophetic pageantry promising the salvation of the world. In a review guided by this type of thinking, it involves exploring the nature of the intuitive experiences lying at the basis of the author's initial approach to the respective problems and the conceptual explication of such an approach (experience is to be understood here in a phenomenological sense). This "intuition" grounding the author's approach is interrogated in a critical fashion regarding its primordiality, its motivation, its tendencies, and the extent to which it is genuinely actualized and seen through to the end.

In adopting this kind of basic critical approach to free up the respective work under investigation, to explore its internal features, and finally to examine these features with regard to the way their intrinsic meaning actually shows itself, one constantly runs the risk of missing the mark, i.e., being led down unintended paths, or singling out and highlighting tendencies of thought that were treated at random. The more we go wrong in this respect, the less value there is in communicating a positive review to others, and the more the value of such communication is limited to the function of clarifying for oneself what one has ventured to do. But whatever the plight of this communication may be, its claims must be restricted to *calling something to the attention of others.* This is ultimately the predicament of all philosophizing regarding its intention of having an effect in the world of others.

The "positive" side of this review consists simply in formulating problems and understanding what is intended in Jaspers' work in a more "precise" manner. And it might just be the case that "more precise" means something other than simply achieving a progressively clearer conceptual presentation of what is intended in this work. Though always guided by a fundamental orientation, the "preliminary work" we need to do is radically destructive, and in our opinion it involves such great difficulties and perhaps even prolonged tediousness that we will not be able to venture putting forth any finished results in this review. It will suffice if we can call attention to and discuss one or another decisive experiential motivation for Jaspers' explication of the phenomena with which he deals.

An explication of both aforementioned directions in which Jaspers' book moves, namely, the preliminary one (establishing the science of psychology as a whole) and the real one (providing clarifications and possibilities that can serve as a means to self-reflection), will allow us to proceed in the direction of those problems to be highlighted in this review. Psychology of worldviews marks out the limits of the human soul. The movement of our lives in worldviews is supposed to be understood from the standpoint of "limit-situations" (246). "An influence on all aspects of our psychical life must occur in the experience of these limits, and here everything will in one way or another presumably be a determining factor for the worldview of a human being" (6). Marking out such limits allows us to gain a "clear horizon" for the whole of our psychical life. Here we find a preoccupation with providing a regional definition of the whole of our psychical life, which has never before been accomplished along such paths and with such breadth, and in fact it has never once been attempted in this manner. In its initial approach, it works with a certain basic aspect of psychical life, namely, that it has limits. In psychical life, there are "limit-situations" to which certain "reactions" are possible, and these reactions to the structural antinomies of limit-situations take place in the "vital process" of psychical life, which functions as their medium (247). The Dasein of our mental life, i.e., its "being-there," arises through antinomies (304).[4] In this way of formulating the problem of psychical life in psychology of worldviews, we find a certain understanding of psychical life. Prior to Jaspers' initial approach to the problem of psychical life, this psychical life is for its part implicitly seen from the point of view of a certain traditionally expressed foreconception of it: namely, the soul has limits, i.e., limit-situations, in the experience of which an "influence" *must* occur on the play of mental forces making up our Dasein. From the point of view of the underlying tendency that actually guides Jaspers' problem of psychical life, is it at all feasible for him to adopt this foreconception about what the basic aspect of psychical life is? In other words, is this foreconception really in keeping with the underlying tendency of Jaspers' problem of psychical life? Are not unexamined pre*suppositions* introduced here in an illegitimate manner? Is the task of gaining access to psychology as a whole promoted in a radical fashion? Can this task be posed at all in such an isolated manner? Such questions must be confronted and dealt with by fundamental reflection. To begin with, we need to see but one thing, namely, *a foreconception of psychical life, expressed in a particular manner, is already given and at work in Jaspers' initial approach to the problem of psychical life.*

Psychology of worldviews is not supposed to work out a doctrine of life and impose it on others; rather, its goal is "to give clarifications and possibilities which can serve as means to self-reflection." This work of clarification means clarification *of* "life," and here "life" is seen in some manner. In Jaspers' initial approach to this clarification, in the techniques he uses for it, and in the nature and scope of his goals here, life itself is *forced to appear under a certain aspect* for those who are appropriating such clarifications. If possibilities are disclosed, they are possibilities *under* a certain articulated aspect of our life and psychical Dasein and *for the sake of* it. A notion of the essential meaning of the "how" of life itself is expressed in this aspect. However much Jaspers made the attempt to undertake everything in the nonprejudicial attitude of mere observation, it is nonetheless the case that when we attempt to understand what he has presented in his observations and to use it in our own self-reflection, what is demanded of us is that we adopt and acquiesce in certain basic approaches to the way life and the self are to be intended. If genuine psychology is supposed to allow us to see "what the human being is" (5), then the initial manner in which it actually formulates the problem must from the start harbor within it certain foreconceptions about the sense of being belonging to this whole of the psychical Dasein of our mental life, and then again foreconceptions about the possible "how" in accordance with which this life, having now been clarified, is supposed to be lived, i.e., foreconceptions about the basic sense of that in which such things as "possibilities" can in any sense be brought to light.

However, in seeing these particular foreconceptions that accompany Jaspers' investigations, we should not be tempted to undertake a philosophically feeble and sterile type of sham critique in which we would now reproach Jaspers for having *contradicted* his own intentions, maintaining on the basis of this charge that his intentions could never be realized in the concrete and arguing that his whole project is thus "refuted in principle" and "dealt with." This type of criticism always claims a formal type of superiority in argumentation, but it thereby fails to take up the productive possibility of returning in a positive fashion to the thoughts in question and understanding them in a deeper sense. What our review of Jaspers' work really needs to do is to highlight his foreconceptions in a *still more* precise manner, delve into the motivation, the sense, and the scope of the direction of inquiry that led to such foreconceptions, and become aware of what is *demanded* by the very sense of these foreconceptions, even though the author himself may not have actually understood these demands in an explicit manner. In other words, we must ultimately evaluate Jaspers' foreconceptions with regard to the philosophical relevance and primordiality of their immanent intentions.

What these problems indicate and lead us to acknowledge is that foreconceptions "are" at work "everywhere" in the factical experience of life (and therefore also in the sciences and in philosophizing), and that what we need to do is simply as it were to join in the experience of these foreconceptions wherever they operate, as they do, for example, in providing direction for any fundamental type of knowledge about something. Moreover, we need simply to proceed in light of how such foreconceptions themselves call for their own clarification. It is by proceeding in this manner that the concrete context in which we actualize some form of understanding (e.g., a particular science) can be made genuinely transparent. In other words, our method can be made more appropriate. All problems of foreconception are ones of "method," and such problems differ in each case according to the primordiality, the tendencies, the regional orientation, and the theoretical level of the foreconceptions in question. We cannot but give ourselves an initial understanding of method along with our foreconceptions of the subject matter. Method arises along with these foreconceptions and out of the same source. A definition of the concept of "method" must work with a formally indicative meaning (e.g., "path") and thereby remain open to being shaped concretely in actual research. In obtaining these concrete definitions of method, we must at the same time also get rid of any prejudices that may have found their way into them by means of the formally indicative meaning of method we have been working with. If method is from the start cut to the measure of specific, isolated problems in the subject matter of a particular science and is nonetheless taken to be a technique that can be applied anywhere, one loses the possibility of understanding method in a primordial manner in each particular case of research. One becomes blind to the fact that one's own way of proceeding is loaded down with this particular approach. When objects are approached by way of a specifically oriented mode of apprehension and this mode of apprehension is, whether explicitly or not, understood and used as a technique, i.e., basically as a means of defining these objects that is not, however, restricted to them, it might turn out that these objects become lost for good by being forced to conform to a particular type of apprehension alien to them. And, consequently, the copious use of "methods" and possible variants of these methods would only continue to miss the very objects one actually intends to gain knowledge of.

Our investigation of the aforementioned problem of foreconception in Jaspers' work endeavors to demonstrate that his approach to the problems in question *requires* a more radical type of reflection on method. This is the case not only because it should be possible for the underlying tendency of these problems to be realized in a more consistent and genuine manner but also and primarily because the object apprehended in these foreconceptions is in fact what it is only by virtue of a primordially immanent "method." This method is part of the object's very makeup and is not something merely foisted on the object from the outside. If one is not aware of this problem of explication in a "rigorous" enough manner, one can, to be sure, nonetheless still wind up actually intending the object in some manner, but a surrogate will, without further explanation, have been inserted into one's intuition and concepts. This surrogate will then henceforth constantly make demands on us to treat it from different sides in order to master it in knowledge (we are motivated to do this on the basis of real acts of intending the object, but these intentions do not get involved with the object and grasp it). The surrogate finally becomes so intrusive that it passes itself off as the genuine phenomenon, whereas the possibility of a genuine experience of the real phenomenon vanishes and continues to exist merely in words. "We have no dominant method, but rather now this one, now that one" (11), and according to Jaspers, this is supposed to be the case within the basic approach of "mere observation."

The object actually investigated in Jaspers' work can be defined in formal indication as our *existence* [Existenz]. Having such a formally indicated meaning, this concept is intended to point to the phenomenon of the "I am," i.e., to the sense of being in this "I am" that forms the starting point of an approach to a context of fundamental phenomena and the problems involved there. In formal indication (which should be seen to make up the fundamental methodological sense of all philosophical concepts and their relationships, though this will not be explained in more detail here), any uncritical lapse into a particular interpretation of existence—for example, Kierkegaard's or Nietzsche's—ought to be avoided from the start, so that we can free up the possibility of pursuing a genuine sense of the phenomenon of existence and explicate what comes to the fore in this pursuit. In an exegesis of Kierkegaard's thought, Jaspers writes: "The consciousness of our existence arises precisely through our consciousness of situations of antinomy" (217). Limit-situations shed light on our vital Dasein. "It is in limit-situations that the most intense consciousness of existence flares up, and this consciousness is a consciousness of something absolute" (245). "Limit-situations are experienced as something ultimate for human life" (274). With this critical analysis of limit-situations (202–47), we come to the solid core that sustains the whole of Jaspers' work. It should be possible to develop the previously outlined problems of foreconception and method to some extent in connection with this concrete and indeed most powerful section of Jaspers' investigation. (Though a student of Kierkegaard and Nietzsche, Jaspers displays in this section a very rare talent and energy, giving these free play in his breakdown and treatment of "psychical states" and compiling the respective phenomena in a valuable, even if only classificatory, manner.)

There are certain crucial situations "bound up with our very humanity and unavoidably given for our finite Dasein" (202). As soon as human beings attempt to attain certainty about the totality of the world and life, they find themselves faced with ultimate forms of incompatibility. "We and our world are split apart in the form of an antinomy" (203). "The structural antinomy of our Dasein [the world and we ourselves, i.e., the objective and subjective sides of this split] poses a limit for any objective worldview" (?), and the "subjective" (?) counterpart of this limit is a type of "suffering bound up with all human life" (204). "Struggle, death, chance, and guilt" are "particular instances" of this "universal" nature of limit-situations (ibid.). Certain reactions to these situations of antinomy are possible, i.e., particular ways human beings attempt to cope with these situations and find some security in the face of them. "When human beings advance beyond their finite situations in order to see them within the whole," they see "oppositions" and "processes of destruction" everywhere. "Insofar as everything objective is able to be conceptually expressed, [these oppositions] can be thought of as contradictions" (203f.). Here destruction means a type of destruction that lies in the rationality of contradiction. "As antinomies, contradictions remain at the limit of our knowledge about the infinite. Thus the concepts of infinity, limit, and antinomy belong together" (205). The concepts of antinomy and limit derive their meaning from a definite or, we should rather say, an indefinite aspect of the infinite. It is from our experience of antinomy that there arises in us a vital will to unity (213). "We see experiences of 'unity' again and again, and it is precisely the most intense thinkers of antinomy who in their paradoxical expressions readily teach us about such mystical and vital unity" (215). The life of the mind is itself life oriented to unity (213). Human beings "always finds themselves on paths leading to the infinite or the whole" (204).

It should by now be sufficiently clear that it is from this initial foreconception of "the whole" ("unity," "totality") that all talk of "destruction," "division,"

and "opposition" derives its sense. Human beings stand within antinomies insofar as they see themselves in the "whole" and thus have a foreconception of *this*
aspect of life, seeing themselves essentially to be inserted into this whole as something ultimate and experiencing their Dasein as something "surrounded" by this
unbroken "medium." Antinomies destroy and bifurcate, and our experience of
them amounts to standing within limit-situations, only because all of this is initially viewed from the vantage point of our approach to the flowing stream of life
as a whole. Regarding the genesis of their meaning, even concepts have their origin in the whole of life. "And if antinomy, infinity, limit, and the Absolute are
concepts which revolve around the same thing" (245), this is likewise the case
with the concept of totality. These concepts not only revolve around the same
thing but also derive their meaning from it, i.e., their conceptual structure or perhaps lack thereof, as well as their appropriateness or perhaps inappropriateness
for promoting a conceptual understanding of what they are supposed to grasp
and express. We are told nothing definite about what this "seeing within the
whole" and this experience of antinomies within an infinite reflection are supposed to mean. At any rate, this is a type of "thinking" or "seeing" that gets its
motivation from the above-mentioned foreconception of the whole, and its
approach, tendencies, and scope are oriented to this foreconception. It is only on
the basis of *this* particular foreconception that the notion of "attaining certainty
about the totality" has any meaning.

It might seem as though the point of our exposition of Jaspers' central,
guiding foreconception is to demonstrate that his position belongs under the
rubric of "philosophy of life." This kind of approach is indeed possible, and it
could possibly draw upon the *particular focus* H. Rickert has used in his recently
published critical review of various philosophies of life. This review and others
like it cannot but meet with approval whenever they, in principle, affirm the need
for the rigorous "formation" of concepts, i.e., whenever they approach this from
the vantage point of an ideal of philosophical knowledge that is incontestable in
the formal sense that it stresses the importance of rigorous conceptuality, while
the concrete approach one should take to this ideal is left open for discussion. But
Rickert tells us nothing about the "how" of this concept-formation, about the
way philosophical concepts get their structure, and about the basic intention of
conceptual explication in philosophy. Assuming that all one's talk about concept-
formation and all of the structural characteristics of concepts one has extracted
from the workings of concept-formation in particular sciences have a validity that
is nonprejudicial in more than a simply formal sense, and this is something that
needs to be investigated, it might turn out to be the case that in rightly stressing
the importance of concept-formation, one nonetheless has failed to give due
attention precisely to *the real* problem, namely, the one arising from the fact that
the work of "differentiating the meaning of forms" begins with the "material" one
is dealing with. How is the material in question actually there for us, how do we
actually "have" it there before us, and what does gaining access to it really mean?

When our conceptualization of the material takes its motivation from this access to and having of the material and persists in them, how is it constituted? Here the *positive* tendencies of philosophy of life need to be examined to see if a certain radical tendency toward philosophizing is not indeed ventured in it, even if this happens in a covert manner and with the help of a means of expression borrowed from tradition rather than fashioned in an original manner. Here we would have to examine above all the high point of philosophy of life in Dilthey, to whom all those who came later are indebted for their important insights, though these inferior offspring actually misunderstood his real intuitions, and he himself was not even able to achieve real insight into them. In this regard, it is with an eye to the radical tendency toward philosophizing in philosophy of life that our review is pursuing its course of analysis. It is important to see that philosophy of life, which developed out of a genuine orientation to intellectual history, tends—whether explicitly or not—in the direction of the phenomenon of existence, though the same cannot be said for the type of philosophy of life found in specialized literati. (Because this point is of importance for a positive evaluation of philosophy of life, it can be formulated and indicated in rough fashion by defining the "vague" concept of life with reference to two principal tendencies in its meaning, though these themselves are ambiguous. However, regarding the need for a radical treatment of the problem of life, we run the risk here of expecting too much from individual philosophies of life when considered separately. We find in contemporary philosophy of life a widespread, vociferous but nebulous emphasis on orienting our Dasein to the immediate reality of life and the need for enriching, fostering, and intensifying life. That is, we encounter the now common and extensively cultivated way of speaking about life, a feeling for life, lived experience, and experiencing. All of this is a symptom of a certain intellectual situation that involves a tangled interplay of motives deriving from intellectual history and arising from the most varied types of experience. It is this interplay of motives that has led to the predominance of the current interest in the reality of mental life and to the interpretation of life primarily from the point of view of the human sciences, even though biological concepts of life have not been completely eradicated here. The characteristic feature of this intellectual situation is perhaps precisely a muddled interplay of biological, psychological, social-scientific, aesthetic-ethical, and religious concepts of life. It is in this muddled fashion that problems in contemporary philosophy are predominantly centered on "life" as the "primordial phenomenon" in one of two ways. Either life is approached as the fundamental reality, and all phenomena are seen to lead back to it, so that everything and anything is understood as an objectification and manifestation "of life," or life is seen as the formation of culture, and this formation is thought to be carried out with reference to normative principles and values. The meaning of this watchword "life" should be allowed to remain ambiguous, so it is able to indicate for us all of the different phenomena intended in it. Here we need to single out two directions in the sense of this term which have led the way in shaping its meaning and in which we find expressed a tendency toward the phenomenon of existence.

(1) Life is understood as objectifying in the widest sense, as an act of creative formation and achievement, as an act of going out of itself, and thus—though this is not clearly spelled out—as something like our *"be-ing there"*[5] *in* this life and *as* this life.

(2) Life is understood as experiencing, as having an experience, understanding, appropriating, and thus—though again the connection is left unexplained—as something like our *"be-ing there" in* such experiencing.)

The progress Jaspers' work makes lies in the fact that his classification of the phenomena, not previously made available in this manner, has called our attention to the problem of existence in a much more concentrated fashion and has in connection with this moved the problems of psychology into more fundamental domains. Its philosophical shortcoming with respect to the need for actually getting down to work and delving into the problems it broaches is clearly visible in the fact that Jaspers persists in a certain untested opinion. He thinks that the foreconception of "the whole," highlighted above, can help him get a handle on the phenomenon of existence, and that he can understand this phenomenon precisely by means of those concepts already available to him in his intellectual milieu.

Keeping in mind the positive tendency of Jaspers' work directed toward the phenomenon of existence, we now need to discuss the above-mentioned foreconception of this work with regard to the methodological consequences of its structure for making the phenomenon of existence visible and conceptually understanding it. How does the meaning of this phenomenon get articulated when such a foreconception forms the starting point of one's inquiry?

It is only with reference to the infinite whole of life that the particular framework of such concepts as the "limits of life," "limit-situations," "structural antinomies," "reactions," and "vital process" can be understood to have the function it does in Jaspers' scheme of classification. The very meaning of this conceptual framework somehow depends on an initial approach to the whole of life, and the contexts of meaning Jaspers describes are always ultimately related back to this whole.

The way this foreconception of the whole of life functions in conceptually articulating the basic meaning of the phenomenon of "existence" can be brought into relief in the following manner. In its teleological contexts, the biological life of the body is an intensive infinity, i.e., "things never come . . . to an end" here (289). This infinity stands in contrast to the limitlessness found in the possible data able to be gathered about an individual being (e.g., a stone). "The *life of the mind* possesses the same kind of infinity that the life of the body does" (ibid.). Here, too, we never come to an end when we attempt to understand the contexts in which the human mind lives. "The medium here is the psychical. But in this psychical realm we find not only the *life* of the mind but also a mere *limitlessness* of phenomena similar to the limitlessness of facts available in the individual forms of lifeless matter. The infinity of this life of the mind is there for us, whether we deal with this life in general terms or deal with it in the concrete and unique form of an individual person. This intensive infinity of the mind, i.e., this infinity in which it lives, stands in contrast to the limitlessness of the mind in which it has a chaotic character" (289). When we attempt to understand life, we find only the finite and the particular. But we can see that behind all of this something is astir as its driving force, namely, a movement oriented in the direction of the infinite. Since life is "motion," the essence of mental life lies in the fact that it is always "on a path leading to the actualization of its qualities" (290).

Our examination of these claims is not meant to be focused on the question of whether the different aspects of the meaning of infinity gleaned from the reality of *bodily* life can be so freely applied to the "life of the mind." For (understood on the level of the distinctions Jaspers himself works with) the limitlessness of data about an individual being (or limitless progression in knowing and defining it) and the limitlessness of teleological contexts in the organic world (or never coming to an end in defining the organic world) do not in any sense differ with respect to the meaning of infinity. They tell us absolutely nothing about the meaning of the infinity belonging to life as such. The objective "concept" of infinity apparently obtained specifically from the unity of *biological* objects is claimed for the life of the mind as well, but in such a way that when Jaspers goes on to define the life of the mind further, a different notion of life intervenes. In looking at the life of the mind, one notices a movement toward the infinite "behind it." Does "infinite" mean here limitless progression in our attempt to understand actual human lives, i.e., their purposeful contexts, or is a completely different sense of infinity introduced here? What is meant by "infinite" here is certainly not the limitlessness of the individual "products and appearances" of the human mind. In connection with the notion of infinity, the essence of the mind is characterized as a "path." Here the direction toward the infinite experienced "behind" the life of the mind clearly means a type of infinity that lies in the sense of the actualizing of acts and their relational tendency. This type of infinity is then somehow equated with the sense of "infinity" obtained from the objective, external observation of biological unities of life. However, this objective concept of infinity (i.e., the infinity related to a type of objectifying, *theoretical understanding* concerned with material or organic objects) is not sufficiently explained, and regarding the new sense of infinity (i.e., an infinity relative to the immanent sense of tendencies found in the context of the actualizing of acts that have a certain direction), no attempt is made to obtain it from the "movement of life" itself and define it conceptually on the basis of this movement. Nor has it been shown that these two fundamentally different concepts of infinity can be equated with each other in such a cursory manner, for in establishing this connection between them, one presumably decides an issue of crucial importance. If the "mere observation" of Jaspers' investigations can proceed along these lines, this is only because of the foreconception involved here, which initially takes an objectifying approach to "life" itself as a whole. Both concepts of infinity, each of which is already vague on its own, are made to reflect each other in a muddled fashion when the talk comes around to the notions of "infinite whole" and "infinite process." Jaspers in fact approaches life as a whole by means of a foreconception in which life is, with respect to the intentional sense of its relational tendency, thought of as a thing-like object: i.e., "it is there," a process in motion (motion means intentionally directed, and process means "taking place" in the manner of an occurrence). Life is *something given* in the objective medium of psychical being, it occurs there, and it is a process that takes place there before itself. Life as a whole is the "encompassing" region in which processes of composition and decomposition run their course. That a certain "direction" is ascribed to the driving forces, processes, and phenomena of movement generally does not change the slightest thing in the basic aspect of life described here as an encompassing realm and as a flowing "stream" that bears all movements within itself. Even if one professes to reject metaphysics, one still owes it to oneself—if it is indeed true that "dodging the issues" should have no place in philosophy—to give some explanation of the objective sense and the mode of being on the basis of which this whole, or psychical stream, is intended. When one talks about how every attempt to understand life or a "part" of it is able to grasp only finite aspects, this is only an expression of the fact that life is initially approached as an undivided realm which, in conformity with the idea we have of it, can eventually be grasped in its totality.

Every attempt to understand life is forced to turn the surge and flux of the aforementioned process into a static concept and thereby *destroy* the essence of life, i.e., the restlessness and movement (again understood more as an occurrence than as a directedness to something) that characterize life's actualization of its ownmost qualities. Such argumentation works with the objective concept of infinity related to *theoretical understanding*. In putting forth its poorly grounded demonstration that a stilling of the psychical stream "takes place" objectively in this manner, it believes itself to have thereby ascertained something of importance about the possibility of understanding "life" with respect to the precise sense of the actualizing of its acts. But, in fact, one has here forgotten to begin one's investigation by first of all taking a close look at the sense of these contexts of actualizing. Instead, one at the same time takes a "concept" to be an objective, thing-like apparatus that inevitably breaks apart the unbroken psychical medium it is applied to. This characteristically Bergsonian line of argumentation suffers from a certain paralysis in a twofold sense. Apart from the fact that problems concerning meaning, concepts, and language are approached only from a very narrow perspective focusing on objective, reifying concepts, these problems are allowed to remain on the level of a very crude and vague treatment that contributes nothing to that type of treatment in which one would attempt to define the fundamental sense of life and lived experience as a whole. And instead of using this "glut on the market" to provide oneself with an air of profound philosophy (such talk about ineffability easily gives the impression that one has actually gazed upon ineffable realms), it is high time that we found genuine problems to deal with. When one has actually succeeded in discovering new contexts of phenomena, as is the case in Jaspers' investigation, such a backward theory of expression is unnecessary. However little Jaspers has defined the concept of life as a whole with precision, we can nonetheless glean from it what is decisive for the context of problems under discussion, namely, the function that "life" has. It is *the* realm, *the* fundamental reality, and the one, all-encompassing domain into which Jaspers inserts all phenomena he examines.

Since the point of this review is to discuss the central, guiding foreconception in Jaspers' work with respect to *what* is intended in it and *how* it is intended, as well as to examine this foreconception more specifically with regard to whether it is appropriate for conceptually demarcating the phenomenon of existence and providing us with the fundamental kind of objectivity in which this conceptual demarcation ought to be carried out, we now need to understand the functional sense of this foreconception more concretely than we have up until this point.

"Understood from the standpoint of its worldviews, life is played out within the subject-object split" (248). "The primal phenomenon of experience lies in the fact that objects stand opposite the subject." "Where no objects stand opposite us, so that every content of our experience disappears and cannot be spoken about, and yet something is still experienced, here we speak of the mystical in the broadest possible sense" (19). Insofar as the life of the mind lies in the restlessness and movement of taking up different positions and then abandoning them, "it is also, as something infinite, beyond the subject-object split." "The mystical is both alpha and omega" for the human mind (305). Due to all of the movement involved with it, the mystical is the only thing in which the Absolute can be grasped without being an object. "From those limits which *encompass* all spheres of the subject-object split as the mystical (and here the mind does not flee into the mystical as a refuge, but rather constantly undergoes it and thereby finds that its proper sphere lies in movement), there falls an ineffable light on all *particulars* within the subject-object split, an indefinable meaning constantly pressing forth into form" (305, emphases added). The various types of mental life include kinds of movements that do not merely take place "between subject and object" but rather "stand at the same time beyond both of them and form the basis of the split between them" (307 n.; 388ff.). "Whereas most of the psychical phenomena we are able to describe are described within a subject-object split as properties of the subjective side or the objective side of this split, there are other kinds of psychical experiences in which the subject-object split either has not yet appeared or has been superseded" (392). What comes to be experienced in this supersession of the subject-object split is not something objectively marked off and removed from us; rather, it is characterized by a certain infinity from which arise driving forces that give direction to life (action, thinking, and artistic creation) (393). The subject-object split is itself "the very essence of human understanding" (426). "It is essentially within the form of this subject-object split that human beings live, and they never come to rest here, but are always striving after some kind of goal, purpose, value, or good" (202).

The whole of life is that from which all forms break forth into the light of day, and it is *what* "splits" itself asunder in this way. If we are to understand how the foreconception guiding Jaspers' work basically gets worked out in concrete terms, the main thing we need to consider is that he always describes this "splitting asunder" precisely as the *primal phenomenon of psychical life.* It constitutes the fundamental meaning of the relation between subject and object (and here the concepts of subject and object each contain a whole multiplicity of phenomena, so that in the former, for example, we find the soul, the ego, lived experience, personality, the psycho-physical individual [cf. 21]). This splitting asunder makes sense only insofar as we begin with the notion of that which is not split asunder and approach it as the underlying reality. To avoid misunderstandings about the methodological intentions of our examination of the foreconception guiding Jaspers' work, it should be clearly noted that the question as to whether one understands this whole in a metaphysical sense or avoids this kind of interpretation, as Jaspers himself wants to do, is irrelevant in the present context.

Our examination is not focused on the question of whether and in what way one could prove that this whole really exists in this or that sense of reality, or on what grounds its reality might possibly be posited as an idea. The really important thing here is much rather the functional sense of that which is initially put forth in Jaspers' foreconception. He intends it to be the realm in which everything takes place or occurs, and it is accordingly an object that ultimately demands a theoretical, observational "attitude" as the correlative way of understanding it and as the basic sense in which it comes to be experienced by us. This means that the fundamental character of the objective correlate of this theoretical attitude lies in the fact that it is an objective *thing.* Everything split asunder, all movements, and all actions and reactions break forth into the light of day from out of this whole, pass through it, and return to it. It is from this context that the subject, one of the two basic components of the primal split, essentially derives its meaning. The subject is that in which life itself and its "driving forces" are "anchored" (24), i.e., it is basically characterized as a limited individuation of life itself, which always comes to expression only imperfectly in such individuations. "Life nowhere produces a concrete individual without remainder" (290).

The central, guiding foreconception supporting everything in Jaspers' work will now be discussed on a fundamental level as a foreconception. If such an adjudication of this foreconception is to be what we intend it to be, then it can only mean that we must pursue and actualize a type of examination that is demanded by the very sense of this foreconception, and our examination must accordingly focus on the question of whether the motivation that leads to the formation of the full sense of this foreconception actually enjoys the level of primordiality claimed for it. The full sense of any phenomenon includes the following intentional characteristics: the intentional relation, the intentional content, and the intentional actualizing (here "intentional" must be understood in a completely formal sense, to avoid any special emphasis on a *theoretical* sense of the intentional relation, and it is this specific meaning of "intentional" that is so easily suggested when one understands intentionality as "thinking about" *[Meinen von]* or correlatively as "being-thought"). Our treatment of these intentional characteristics making up the sense of any phenomenon should not consist of arranging them as an aggregate or succession of moments tallied up. Rather, their sense derives from a structural context of relationships that varies in each case according to the levels and directions of experience involved. This context of relationships and the shifts of emphasis occurring here should not be understood as a "result" or as a momentary "addendum" but as the authentic factor that comes to light in the phenomenological articulation of the above-mentioned intentional characteristics. In turn, this authentic factor itself is to be understood precisely as a kind of "prestruction" of one's own existence. Such prestruction is in each case actualized in the current facticity of one's life in the form of a self-appropriation. It discloses and holds open a concrete horizon of expectation that is characterized by worry and is developed and worked out in each particular context of actualizing it.

Whence and in what way does the foreconception under discussion make its appearance? Which motives would lead one to make it the starting point of one's inquiry and see it through to the end? What is the nature of these motives? Jaspers does not formulate such questions. Were he to call to mind his own guiding foreconception, he would find these questions about it empty and inconsequential. However, an attempt will not be made here to persuade him of their importance. It is up to him to decide whether he can "go on" without raising these questions and to what extent these questions might not arise precisely from the "infinite reflection" that constitutes the "genuine" sense of mental life and thus also scientific life. As is, Jaspers works more with what he has taken over from the intellectual history of his own present, doing this in part unconsciously and in part through reflective appropriation. He has his eye specifically on what is of importance in this intellectual history for his special project of endeavoring to establish the science of psychology as a whole. Regarding the approach he initially takes in his foreconception, Jaspers would be able to say the following: Life as a whole is a central, guiding idea for me, and I need only look around to see that this life is somehow or other simply there for me wherever I go. This uniform and unbroken whole, this ultimate harmony, which transcends all oppositions, encompasses all life, and is free of all fragmentation and destruction—this is what guides my experience. I see all particulars in its light, all genuine illumination comes from it, and it marks out in advance the fundamental domain of sense on the basis of which everything I encounter comes to be understood as something that develops and breaks forth out of this life, eventually sinking back into it again. This whole provides me with the essential articulation of those objects I have attempted to observe and classify in my work.

The actual motivational basis from which this foreconception thus arises is a fundamental experience of the whole of life in which we keep this whole before our gaze in the form of an idea. In a very formal sense, this experience can be defined as a "fundamental aesthetic experience." This means that the relational sense belonging to the primary type of experience that initially gives us the object called "life" actually consists of gazing upon something, observing it, and striving after it. We are not saying here that Jaspers "subscribes" to an "aesthetic" worldview. I know nothing about this. His worldview could just as well be an essentially moral one, supposing that such hackneyed philosophical coinage still means anything. Yet it is possible here that without allowing himself to be placed before an antimony, Jaspers does indeed gain access to the essential thing for him, i.e., the Absolute, within a fundamental aesthetic attitude and sets about classifying it in the same manner. It is likewise possible that his view of life focusing on the full "vehemence" and "force" of the "vital process" is an aesthetic one, even if the content of this "process" is understood to be of an ethical nature. Life "is there" as something we have by means of looking at it, and it is by means of this kind of having that we gain possession of it in the sense of a whole encompassing everything. Here Jaspers would perhaps, on principle, make the following reply: For me, it is indeed precisely a matter of mere observation, and what is observed must then be an object in the basic sense of being an observed object. There is no other way of proceeding here. In response, the following needs to be said: This formal type of argumentation remains from the start empty as long as we have not answered an important question, namely, does not the formal sense of theoretical understanding allow itself to be deformalized into very individual and concrete ways of understanding? And this question cannot be answered in a formally deductive manner but rather only by starting from particular contexts of phenomena and allowing ourselves to be guided by them. Observation *can,* in accord with its sense, always have a theorizing character, but this does not necessarily entail that the sense of being belonging to what is observed must as such become accessible primarily within observation. And it is this simple point we have been stressing in our examination of Jaspers' foreconception. The relational sense of the *initial giving* of the object is not also the relational sense of the explication that has come across this pregiven object. Accordingly, the mere observation used throughout Jaspers' work and extending all the way to the foreconception in which the actual object of investigation is given has in no way been justified by Jaspers as the appropriate method of explication. The basic experience in which the actual object is initially given needs to be examined regarding its full sense, and it must prescribe for us the genuine structure of explication. "Observation" in Jaspers' sense might be a fitting approach, but it also might not be. An answer to this question will be obtained in the following discussion, but for the time being it will take the form of making visible the problems involved here. To this end, what Jaspers has taken up in the foreconception of his work must be discussed in more concrete terms.

The whole of life, i.e., life *itself,* is something about which we can say nothing directly (288), but it must indeed be intended by us somehow, since the consciousness of our existence arises precisely from the fact that we look *to* the whole of life. When human beings "see [their finite situations] within the whole," when they "want to attain certainty about the totality of things," they have the experience that the objective world and their subjective action are split apart in the form of an antinomy. "Insofar as the driving forces in worldviews move human beings," and insofar as human beings are somehow "concerned about something essential," "they always find themselves on paths leading to the infinite or the whole." It is "*in view of* the infinite" that human beings find themselves in antinomies. Antinomies are oppositions, but they are oppositions "*from* the *point of view* of the Absolute and value." Antinomy is "destruction." When this destruction is experienced, it is experienced along with the "unity" or whole that is breaking apart in one way or another. The essence of the human mind is "the will to unity." Insofar as all processes of destruction are able to be formulated in a rational manner, they can be thought of as contradictions: for example, death contradicts life, whereas chance contradicts necessity as well as meaning (203ff.). But struggle, death, and chance are at the same time described also as limit-situations, i.e., we can experience struggle and death as limits in our consciousness of that whole that somehow exceeds life. "Struggle is a fundamental form of all existence" (227). "No existence is whole" (229), and that is why human beings must struggle if they want to live. This struggle "never lets a particular individual come to rest in any state of wholeness." "The process of life would cease without struggle" (227). Moreover, transitoriness holds for all *reality.* Every experience and all of our current conditions fade away into the past. Human beings are constantly changing (229). Experiences, individual human beings, a people, a culture—all of these fall prey to death. "The relation human beings have to their own deaths is different than their relations to all other forms of transitoriness. Only the absolute non-being of the world is a comparable notion." "Only the perishing of their own being or of the world in general has a *total* character for human beings" (230). A "lived relation to death" is not to be confused with "universal knowledge about death." This lived relation is there in one's life only "when death has appeared as a limit-situation in one's experience," i.e., only when one's possible "consciousness of limit and infinity" (231) has not been left undeveloped.

We shall not at this point enter into a critical commentary on the various limit-situations Jaspers has listed as concrete instances of the universal concept of a limit-situation. We also can put aside for now the question of whether the concepts of "finite situation," "limit-situation," and "situation" have been explained in such a way that they accomplish something of significance for a real philosophical understanding of them. The following related questions may be left out of consideration as well. Do all of the concrete limit-situations mentioned above satisfy the "universal concept" of a limit-situation in the same sense? Do universal concepts that can be applied to such concrete situations exist in any sense? To what extent is concrete knowledge of antinomies different from a "lived relation" to oppositions? How does the one arise from the other? Can these *experienced* antinomies—antinomies experienced *as* limit-situations or antinomies experienced *in* limit-situations (this distinction has not been clearly worked out)—really be "rationally formulated" and thought of as "contradictions" without further ado? Do they not thereby lose their genuine sense? And, on the other hand, is it not precisely this theorizing reinterpretation that initially makes it possible for Jaspers to treat the concrete instances as contradictions that can be, as it were, lined up in a row for observation? We also will leave undiscussed the question of whether the concrete limit-situations stand in particular relations to each other when they are experienced, and to what extent it is precisely these concrete limit-situations that should properly be spoken of as limit-situations. Even if it is supposed to be "mere observation," I consider what Jaspers puts forth about concrete limit-situations (in line with their fundamental significance within the total sphere of phenomena he intends to deal with, and to have emphasized this is precisely his main contribution) to be not in the least worked out in a fitting conceptual manner. That is the reason a critical commentary focused on the particulars of Jaspers' work would all too easily run the risk of imputing to him views and meanings he would not be willing to see as his own. In pursuing this type of critical commentary, we always move around in uncertainties as long as the basic context from which the phenomena and concepts in question have arisen is not more clearly visible. That is why critical observations always find themselves referred back to the problem of foreconception.

Where are the intellectual motives to be found in a factical sense for the initial approach Jaspers takes in his foreconception? It is not difficult to recognize the historically "contingent" origin of the concept of the Absolute he uses in his "observations." This concept represents a syncretism in which the Kantian doctrine of antinomies and its guiding concept of infinity are combined with Kierkegaard's concept of the Absolute, which has been "cleansed" of its specifically Lutheran religious sense and its particular theological meaning in this regard. Furthermore, these two components, which derive from very different basic foreconceptions, are transplanted into that vagueness arising from the concept of life we described above. More precisely, they are in fact viewed primarily on the basis of this vagueness. In the course of his general discussion of limit-situations, Jaspers at one point suddenly makes the comment about his "observations" that they amount to "only a presupposition for understanding a psychology of types of mental life and are not yet themselves psychology" (204). What, then, are they? Logic or sociology? (2f.) What is it that we strive after in these "observations" that are supposed to provide us with the fundamental presuppositions, and how do we strive after it?

It is possible that Jaspers wants these observations to be understood in a very formal sense, but then what is really needed is a discussion of the meaning of this "formal" factor, and here we need to raise the following questions. To what extent does this formal factor prejudice the observations that deal with concrete material? To what extent does it not do this? In what way can prejudice be avoided? In turn, to what extent can we obtain this formal sense only by means of beginning in a distinctive manner with that which is factically, concretely, and historically available to us and then explicating this experiential point of departure in a particular way? To what extent does the conceptual expression found in actual understanding revoke the formal, and do this in such a manner that here concept-formation does not mean that we bring to light a theoretical theme for some merely theoretical purpose, but rather that our experience itself is illuminated through interpretation and that we call attention to this experience in communication with others?

Jaspers' foreconception has now been described in terms of its functional sense (its initial objective, factual approach to an intended realm), as well as in terms of the sense of its basic attitude (its aesthetic point of view) and its origin (its undiscussed adoption from the intellectual history of Jaspers' present situation). At this point, we need to examine Jaspers' foreconception with regard to the question of whether it does in fact intend or even *can* intend that which it really wants to bring into view and understand, namely, phenomena of our existence. We need to ask whether it can in any sense simply put us into the situation of *being able* to actualize questioning about our existence and the sense of the phenomena found there. Or does the most proper and full sense of Jaspers' foreconception actually move us away from this situation? Might it be the case that if this foreconception dominates our thinking, *it will never be possible for us even to "circle round" the phenomenon of existence?*

What kind of explanation is required for our "existence"? From what was noted in our introductory comments on this problem, it should be obvious that we are not of the opinion that one can approach the problem of existence directly. This problem is characterized precisely by the fact that it is lost sight of when approached in this way (i.e., when one attempts to avoid all detours in a purportedly superior fashion). Even laying out the very specific *problem of our initial approach,* which belongs precisely to the problem of existence, and doing this in a way that satisfies the most rigorous conceptual requirements, is out of the question here, given especially the restricted context of our approach in this review. But we should make the preliminary remark that the meaning of this problem of our initial approach is such that it cannot be settled through empty, formalistic reflections. And it is just as pressing to underscore that this problem should not be considered something "out of the ordinary" and "novel," which allows us to raise a new commotion in philosophy and to curry favor with the hustle and bustle of an avant-garde culture at bottom really hungry for other things, even if it does display wonderful religious antics.

In line with the specific aim of this commentary, we wish only to call the reader's attention to a few themes and thereby to point to *the persistence of a problem*.

Using formal indication (a particular methodological level of phenomenological explication that will not be dealt with further here, though some understanding of it will be gained in what follows), we can make the following remarks in order to provide an initial approach to this problem (an approach that, according to its very meaning, must in turn be deconstructed).

"Existence" is a determination of something. If one wants to characterize it in a regional fashion, though in the end this characterization actually proves to be a misinterpretation that leads us away from the real sense of existence, it can be understood as a certain manner of being and thus as a particular sense of "is," that "is," it has the essential sense of the (I) "am." And we have this (I) "am" in a genuine sense not through thinking about it in a theoretical manner, but rather by actualizing the "am," which is a way of being belonging to the be-ing of the "I." Understood in this way, the be-ing of the self has the formally indicative meaning of existence. Here we are given a clue about where we must find the sense of existence as the particular "how" of the self (of the I). What turns out to be important here is accordingly the fact that I *have myself*, i.e., the basic experience in which I encounter myself as a self. Living in this experience and gearing myself to *its* very sense, I am able to question after the sense of my "I am." This having-myself is ambiguous in many different respects, and this diversity found in its meaning must be understood specifically with reference to *historical* contexts rather than to contexts of classification that have been elevated to the stature of regions within an autonomous system. In the archontic sense belonging to the actualizing of our basic experience of the "I am," an experience that concerns precisely me myself in a radical manner, we find that this experience does not experience the "I" as something located in a region, as an individuation of a "universal," or as an *instance* of something. Rather, this experience is the experience of the "I" as a self. When we keep purely to this actualizing of our experience, it becomes clear that the notion of a region or an objective realm is quite foreign to the "I." We see that each time we attempt to give a regional definition of the "I" (a definition that arises from a foreconception about such things as a stream of consciousness, a context of experience), we thereby "efface" the sense of the "am" and turn the "I" into an object able to be ascertained and *classified* by inserting it into a region. *Consequently, there is a need for radical suspicion* (and the appropriate investigations as well) *about all foreconceptions that objectify by means of regions, about the networks of concepts that arise from such foreconceptions, and about the various avenues through which these concepts arise.*

When it has the sense of "is," the sense of being has developed from objectively oriented experiences which have been explicated in "theoretical" knowledge, and in which we always somehow or other say of *something* that it "is something." The object here need not be classified expressly within a particular scientific realm that has been worked out through the special logic of the science in question. Rather, it usually takes the form of the nontheoretical "objectivity" that belongs to *what is of significance to us*[6] in our experience of the environing world, the with-world of others, and also the self-world. In factical life, I have dealings of one sort or another with what is of significance to me, and to these "dealings with" there corresponds a unique sense of objectivity that can be understood phenomenologically. When the sense of existence is investigated in terms of its origin and our genuine basic experience of it, we see that it is precisely *that* sense of being which cannot be obtained from the "is" we use to explicate and objectify our experience in one way or another when we acquire knowledge about it. The sense of human existence is to be obtained rather from its own basic experience of having itself in a certain *worried* manner. This having is actualized *prior to* whatever knowledge about it we might later acquire by objectifying it with the "is," and such knowledge is in fact inconsequential for this actualization. If I seek this objectifying knowledge, the attitude of observation will become central for me. All of my explications will then have an objectifying nature, but they will put me at a remove from existence and from a genuine having of it (worry).

The "I" should be understood here as the full, concrete, and historically factical self that is accessible to itself in its historically concrete experience of itself. It is not synonymous with the notion of the empirical subject as the possible subject matter of theoretical observation in psychology. In this kind of objectivity, which is understood more or less as a realm of "physical" processes that occur, the "soul" has been eclipsed in a fundamental sense. That is, whenever *this* kind of psychology has begun with *this* kind of object, it has never once brought the "soul" experientially into view, so that it could be given in a preliminary way as an object for further investigation.

Insofar as the "I am" is *something* that can be articulated into "he, she, it is" (or further, "is something"), existence can be spoken of in a formal manner as a particular sense of being and as a particular "how" of being. Here we also should take note of the fact that the "is" in "he, she, it is" (each of which must be understood in the concrete at any particular time) can in turn have different meanings, and these differences mark out a multiplicity of contexts of life and realms of objects. For example, "he is" can be taken in the sense of being-present-to-hand and occurring in nature as it is represented objectively (a multiplicity of objects and relations). Or, "he is" can have the sense that he plays a certain role in the environment of the with-world. This sense is expressed, for example, in the trivial question, "what does X do in Y?" The "was" and the "will," which belong to this "is" in connection with the "he," have their own meanings that are crucial for the "is."

But the basic experience of having-myself is not available to one without further ado, nor is it a kind of experience aimed at the "I" in such general terms. Rather, if one is to be at all capable of experiencing the specific sense of the "am" and appropriating it in a genuine manner, the actualizing of one's experience must have its origin in the full concreteness of the "I," and it must be directed back to this "I" by way of a particular kind of "how." Such experience is not a type of immanent perception that is pursued with a theoretical purpose in mind and is intent on observing the qualities of present-to-hand "psychical" processes and acts. On the contrary, the experience of having-myself in fact extends historically into the past of the "I." This past is not like an appendage that the "I" drags along with itself; rather, it is experienced as the past of an "I" that experiences it historically within a horizon of expectations placed in advance of itself and for itself. And here the "I" also has itself in the form of a self. To explicate phenomenologically the "how" of this actualizing of experience according to its basic *historical* sense is the task that is most important for us in the whole complex set of problems we face concerning phenomena of existence. Little is to be gained by an external view of the psychical in which one emphasizes that past and future act in conjunction with each other within *"consciousness,"* if past and future are understood here as effective states of affairs. In dealing appropriately with this task, we need to understand that the nature of explication lies in the actualizing of interpretation. The essential character of the *explicata* involved here is found in the fact that they are *hermeneutical* concepts to which we have access only in a continual renewal of interpretation that constantly begins anew. It is in this way that we must bring these *explicata* to their genuine level of "precision" and maintain them in it, though such precision cannot be compared to other kinds of conceptual refinement with a different orientation.

In the above-mentioned basic experience that is relationally directed to the I, the facticity of this I is decisive. Lived *hic et nunc* and actualized accordingly in a situation within intellectual history, one's own factical experience of life also actualizes the basic experience of one's I that arises from it, remains within it, and ever returns to the factical. But this factical experience of life, in which I can have myself in different ways, is itself not anything like a region in which I am located, or a universal that gets individuated in my self. According to the "how" of its own actualizing, this experience is rather an essentially "historical" phenomenon. However, it is not primarily an objective historical phenomenon (my life happening as something that takes place in the present) but rather a phenomenon of *historical actualization* that experiences itself in such actualization. When, in accord with the relational sense of one's experience, one is directed historically to one's self, the context of this experience also has a historical nature in accord with the sense of its actualizing. The "historical" is here not the correlate of theoretical and objective historical observation; rather, it is both the content *and* the "how" of the self's worry about itself, from which the former certainly cannot as such be detached. Having-oneself arises from such *worry,* is maintained in it, and tends toward it. And in this worry, the specific past, present, and future of the self are not experienced as temporal schemata for objectively classifying facts; rather, they are experienced within a nonschematic sense of worry having to do with the actualizing of experience in its "how." Accordingly, the phenomenon of existence discloses itself only in a radically historical manner of actualizing our experience and striving after such actualization. This actualization of experience is not oriented to the attitude of observation and does not aim at that classification which objectifies the phenomenon of existence within a region but rather is itself essentially characterized by a certain worry about the self. It is itself not something extraordinary and removed; rather, it is something to be actualized in our factical experience of life as such and appropriated from out of such factical experience. And this is supposed to happen not merely once in a momentary, isolated fashion but rather again and again in a constant renewal of worry, which is necessarily motivated by the self's worry about itself and is moreover oriented in a historical manner. In accord with its fundamental sense, "conscience" is understood here as the actualizing of conscience and not merely in the sense of occasionally having a conscience about something *(conscientia)*. Conscience is a historically defined "how" of experiencing the self (the history of this "concept" needs to be examined in connection with the problem of existence, and this is not just an academic problem, even if it is already a pressing problem when approached in such a way). In indicating this connection between the sense of historical experience and the sense of the phenomenon of conscience, we are not giving the concept of the historical a broader meaning; rather, we are understanding it in such a way that it is being returned to the authentic source of its sense. And this also is the factical though concealed source from which historical experience in the sense of the development of objective historical knowledge (the historical human sciences) arises. The historical is today almost exclusively something objective, i.e, an object of knowledge and curiosity, a locus providing the opportunity to glean instructions for future action, an object for objective critique and rejection as something antiquated, a fund of materials and examples to be collected, a conglomeration of "instances" for systematic observations dealing with the universal. Since we are unable to see phenomena of existence today in an authentic manner, we no longer experience the meaning of conscience and responsibility lying in the historical itself (the historical is not merely something of which we have knowledge and about which we write books; rather, we ourselves are it and have it as a task). Thus even the motives for returning to the historical via our own history are inactive and hidden from us.

In its relation to what it experiences, our concrete and factical life-experience has of itself a characteristic tendency to fall away into the "objective" kinds of significance in the experienceable world around it. This falling away is the reason the sense of being belonging to these objective kinds of significance becomes predominant for us. Thus it is understandable that regarding its sense of being, the self quickly becomes experienced as having an objectified kind of significance (personality, ideal type of humanity) and within this experiential orientation comes to be understood theoretically and takes on meaning in philosophy. The more the experienced and known past works its way into our own present situation in the form of an objective tradition, the more the self is understood in this objectified manner. As soon as we see that factical life is characteristically loaded down with tradition in this way (tradition can be understood here in many different senses), and that the most pernicious effects of this loading down are mainly to be found precisely in the resulting experiences of having-oneself in the self-world, we are led to the insight that the concrete possibility of bringing phenomena of existence into view and explicating them in a genuine kind of conceptuality can be opened up for us *only when* the concrete tradition experienced as still at work in one form or another has been subjected to a destruction with an eye to the question of the ways and means of explicating our actual experience of the self, and when as a result of this destruction, the basic experiences that have become the effective motives of our thought have been brought into relief and discussed regarding their primordiality. According to its very sense, this kind of destruction always remains inseparable from the concrete, fully historical worry of the self about itself.

The self is what it is in its relations in the self-world, the with-world of others, and the environing world. The sense of these directions of experience is ultimately historical and inseparable from the self-world. When phenomenology first burst onto the scene with its specific aim of appropriating the phenomena of *theoretical* experience and knowledge in a new and primordial manner (the *Logical Investigations,* i.e., a phenomenology of theoretical *logos*), the goal of its research was to win back an unspoiled seeing of both the sense of those objects experienced in such theoretical experiences and correlatively the sense of "how" these objects become experienced. But if we are to understand the philosophical sense of the tendencies of phenomenology in a radical manner and appropriate them genuinely, we must not merely carry out research in an "analogical" fashion on the "other" "domains of experience" (the aesthetic, ethical, and religious domains) which we, following one philosophical tradition or another, have partitioned off from one another. Rather, we need to see that experiencing in its fullest sense is to be found in its authentically factical context of actualization in the historically existing self, and this self is in one way or another the ultimate question of philosophy. It will not do to bring in the notion of the person on occasion and *apply* to it philosophical results that were arrived at under the guidance of one philosophical tradition or another. On the contrary, the concrete self should be taken up into the starting point of our approach to philosophical problems and brought to "givenness" at the genuinely fundamental level of phenomenological interpretation, namely, that level of interpretation related to the factical experience of life as such. From these unavoidably terse remarks, one thing should have become clear: namely, the authentic phenomenon of existence refers us to the actualizing of that way of access to it that is appropriate for it. We come to have the phenomenon of existence only within a certain "how" of experiencing it, and this "how" is something that has to be achieved in a specific manner. It is precisely this *"how"* of appropriation and moreover the "how" of our *initial approach* to the actualizing of such appropriation that are decisive.

That our factical, historically actualized life is at work right within "how" we factically approach the problem of "how" the self, in its worry about itself, appropriates itself—this is something that belongs originally to the very sense of the factical "I am."

Insofar as the phenomenon of existence and the problem it poses are intended in this form, the question of how we should actualize our initial approach and access will *constantly* stand before us in the starting point of our approach to this problem of existence whenever we have understood it in a genuine way. Our question about this "how" is the problem of method, though not the method for a knowledge of objects that defines them with reference to regions, or for a classification of diverse kinds of objects that are given in advance for us and can likewise be given in advance throughout our classifying. Rather, method means here the method belonging to our interpretive, historically actualized explication of concrete and fundamental experiential modes of having-oneself in a factically worried manner.

We are here able to give only a rough indication of the questions phenomenology urgently needs to address in order to clarify its philosophical sense and work out its position today. These questions, as listed below, must be answered not through abstract formal reflections but rather in the course of concrete research.

1. In regard to the problem of existence we have touched on, to what extent does the basic phenomenological attitude—which first burst onto the scene with Husserl and is a philosophical attitude unable to be learned by rote as a technique—preserve the most radical origin that can be assigned to the meaning of philosophy? To what extent does it explicitly preserve the decisive direction of worry that essentially pervades all problems?

2. To what extent does "history" get appropriated here in such a way that it is seen to be more than just a discipline in philosophy? To what extent do we gain an understanding of the fact that the historical is, according to its very sense, originally already there for us right within our philosophical problems and that accordingly the problem of the relationship between the history of philosophy and systematic philosophy is at bottom a pseudo problem, even if one believes oneself to have "solved" it with formalistic ruses?

3. If we have appropriated the basic sense of the phenomenological attitude in a genuine way, to what extent would we sooner have it misused in any other type of intellectual and literary nonsense than have it misused to supply a forced orthodox dogmatics with its apologetic principles, a "perversion" for which a desire has recently begun to stir in phenomenology (and be this dogmatics in its tenets ever so praiseworthy and today still ever so misunderstood as the dogmatics of the Middle Ages, which was according to *its own* sense a genuine type of dogmatics)?

Returning to our central problem of foreconception, it now becomes clear that insofar as it aims at the phenomenon of existence, Jaspers' foreconception is unsuitable for realizing its own underlying intention. Such is the case both in regard to the functional sense of this foreconception (it initially posits that on the basis of which and within which we are to *observe* our existence as concrete life, and it posits it as a whole with an essentially regional character) and in regard to the sense of the basic experience that motivates the foreconception (the attitude of looking ultimately upon this whole, harmony, and unity of life, inserting phenomena into it in a businesslike fashion and remaining all the while unworried about the self-world).

However, the full sense of Jaspers' foreconception is not only unsuitable for realizing its own underlying intention at work in it; rather, it actually *runs counter to* this intention. For regarding the intentional relational sense of its understanding, this orientation toward a region puts us at a remove from the phenomenon of existence which, according to its sense, cannot be formulated and classified in regional terms. And regarding the sense of the actualization of its fundamental (formally) aesthetic attitude, this orientation does not let the self's worry about itself emerge in a crucial sense as that which first gives direction to and characterizes all problems, their objectivity, and their explication.

If we can now show concretely that in Jaspers' work "method" remains essentially at the level of a technical managing and classifying which, according to its relational sense, is characterized by the businesslike insertion of phenomena into a region, and if we also can show here that "method" is thus from the start not raised as a problem, it will become clear to us from this that Jaspers' method is indeed in keeping with the structure of his foreconception, only that it thereby places itself *in opposition to* its very own intention of penetrating to phenomena of existence.

Jaspers characterizes the attitude of his method as mere observation. What is it supposed to accomplish? "The object of all observation is simply that which exists and is there for us so far in human experience. All observation has the tendency to take this as the whole" (329). Do "that which exists and is there for us so far," "being-there," and "so far" have the same meaning for any and every type of observing? Jaspers wants to observe "what life is" (250). This is what observation is supposed to teach us about. Observation stands "in the service of burgeoning life" (ibid.). The object that observation pursues is that whole initially approached in Jaspers' foreconception, as well as the variety of concrete forms belonging to this whole. As observation, which is in itself not creative, it looks only to what is there before it. But how exactly is "life" there for us? And how do we obtain that which exists and is there for us so far? Phenomena of life are after all not like the pieces on a checkerboard that we now need to rearrange. That which is there for us so far, i.e., that which exists in life as something available and knowable, always exists and is "there" in various types of understanding and conceptual expression that have brought about this "being-there." After taking up what is given in this interpretive understanding of life and adopting it as that which actually exists and is really there for us, Jaspers in turn proceeds to organize and classify it in the specific context of understanding with which he works. This should already be clear to us from our previous attempts to make Jaspers' underlying foreconception explicit. If our pursuit of phenomena of life merely looks at "what is there," is it at all capable of taking a single step without treating what is there for us so far in a specific context of understanding? Even if we expressly relinquish the claim that our observation is observation *per se,* or the only possible kind of observation, our observing of phenomena of life is *historical,* insofar as it must inevitably be interpretive. It is "historical" not merely in the superficial sense of being valid only for a particular age; rather, according to the characteristic sense of its ownmost actualization, it has something essentially historical for its object. One needs to become clear on the nature of this interpretation if one wants to understand "observation" as a method and recommend it as such.

The fact that today we live in a quite peculiar manner from, in, and with history is surely at the very least something that also exists and "is *there*" for us, if it is not indeed an essential factor of our times. This is the case even if "psychology" has not at all noticed it yet, and if philosophy has taken note of it only within an objective, external orientation. However, any use of observation that intends to get at phenomena of existence must regard precisely this fact of our times as something needing to be "understood."

It might just be the case that phenomena of life, which are "historical" in accord with their own basic sense, can themselves become accessible to us only in a "historical" manner. And here we need to answer the following question: Does the objectifying kind of understanding in the science of history represent the most authentic and radical way of formulating our historical experience in theory? Or is it not the case that when this question is seen in its inseparable connection with the problem of existence, we are confronted by the problem of finding a method of interpreting our existence in a primordially historical manner? Thus another question arises here. In actualizing and explicating this type of interpretation that aims at phenomena of our existence, would we in any sense be calling for anything like the setting up of types? Would this not rather be quite unsuitable for interpreting our existence? Whenever this approach is brought into play, does it not result in essentially skewing the real direction in which understanding should move, since all work with types and any esteem for them always remains within a surreptitious, aesthetic attitude? In the present context, it is only important for us to see here how two things *go together:* on the one hand, Jaspers' supposed intention of pursuing *observation,* one that treats phenomena of life as a variety of types and forms, or concretions and instances, which have been stripped of their proper historical provenance; and on the other hand, his *previously described foreconception.* What this shows us is that Jaspers does not see that the historical is a fundamental character of the sense of our existence. Consequently, neither has the problem of method, with respect to its basic meaning and the nature of its point of departure, been geared to the historical in his work.

The other features exhibited by Jaspers' method, namely, the treatment of the question of conceptual expression and the question of "systematics," also are

based on his underlying foreconception (i.e., on the initial approach to life as a
region and the observational attitude toward this region). Life is an infinite flowing whole, but since concepts are forms that bring life to a standstill, it is impossible to grasp life and truly understand it.

The inexpressibility of the soul has often and enthusiastically been asserted
in connection with the impossibility of fully grasping the individual. However, it
is of crucial importance here to ask which concept of the individual lies at the
basis of this problem of conceptual expression. Instead of constantly reformulat-
ing the well-worn saying *"individuum est ineffabile"* [the individual is inexpress-
ible] in new ways, it might be about time to ask the following questions: What
exactly is *"fari"* [expressing] supposed to mean here? What kind of understanding is supposed to come to expression? Is it not the case that what lies at the basis
of this dictum is a particular way of understanding the individual that is ultimately based on an aesthetic, external observation of the "whole person"? Does
not this kind of observation still remain in effect even when personality is "understood" immanently in psychology, since the objective, pictorial point of view
remains operative here (cf. Dilthey, for example)?

The manner in which Jaspers selects his "method" and interprets it finds
its motivation in the first place in his foreconception, but it goes back in particular to that influence of Max Weber and Kierkegaard which Jaspers himself
expressly mentions. However, in both cases, this happens via a fundamental misunderstanding of the real intentions of these thinkers, a misunderstanding that
gets its motivation from Jaspers' own preconception. What turned out to be
important for Jaspers in Weber's work was, firstly, his distinction between scientific observation and the promotion of values in worldviews and, secondly, the
connection he made between the most concrete kind of historical research and
systematic thinking (13). I can only understand what Jaspers means here by "systematic" thinking to be Weber's attempt to develop a genuine type of rigorous
conceptual expression appropriate to the meaning of his own science. But this
means that for Weber the problem of method was *an urgent problem* specifically
in the domain of his very own science, and in fact only here. That he himself ben-
efited in an essential way from subscribing to the particular theory of science and
conceptuality that he did reveals only how clearly he saw the importance of the
following two things: on the one hand, the fact that his science is a historical
human science of culture ("sociology" is "an empirical science of human action")
and, on the other hand, the fact that Rickert's investigations provide the theoretical and scientific foundations particularly for the historical sciences of culture.
This is why Weber had a certain right simply to adopt Rickert's investigations.
He essentially never went any further here. He needed to be guided by this
approach in his own historical science, even though it contained a specific problem of method within it. However, one misunderstands the true scientific vehemence of Weber's thought when one simply carries *this* approach over into psychology and moreover into one's attempts to get at the *whole* of psychology, i.e.,

into one's "observations" about basic *principles* that at bottom have a completely different structure than the type of observations Weber pursued. To emulate Weber truly would rather be to strive just as radically and incessantly as he did to achieve a genuine "systematic" mastery in one's own field of psychology and, more particularly, with reference to the problem of working out the whole of psychology as a science. Objective economic processes and human actions as seen in the context of the development of intellectual history are surely from the start something other than worldviews and "ultimate positions of psychical life," i.e., phenomena of existence. At the very least, one really needs to ask whether the attitude, method, and conceptual structures of sociology can be transferred from this science (taken moreover in the sense of Weber's very specific conception of it) to the problem of the nature of psychology, something that Jaspers broaches, moreover, for the sake of pursuing specifically *philosophical* intentions.

Furthermore, we need to examine that distinction between scientific observation and value, which likewise has a very specific sense in Weber's thought and again derives from his own concrete science. Can one demand it also in the sphere of philosophical knowing without any further discussion? If the meaning of objectivity in philosophical knowledge has not been clarified beforehand, we can decide nothing about the role of this distinction in philosophy.

Concerning Kierkegaard, we should point out that such a heightened consciousness of methodological rigor as his has rarely been achieved in philosophy or theology (the question of where he achieved this rigor is not important here). One loses sight of nothing less than the most important aspect of Kierkegaard's thought when one overlooks this consciousness of method, or when one's treatment of it takes it to be of secondary importance.

Jaspers falls under the spell of a deception when he thinks that it is precisely in mere observation that he would achieve the highest degree of noninterference in the personal decisions of his readers and would thus free these individuals for their own self-reflection. On the contrary, by presenting his investigations as mere observations he indeed appears to avoid imposing on his readers *particular* worldviews, i.e., the ones he has described, but he pushes his readers into believing that his unexamined preconception (life as a whole) and the essential modes of articulation corresponding to it are something obvious and noncommittal, whereas it is rather precisely in the meaning of these concepts and the "how" of their interpreting that everything is really decided. Mere observation does not give us what it wants to, namely, the possibility of radical reexamination, decision and, what is synonymous with these, an intense consciousness of the methodological necessity of questioning. We can set genuine self-reflection free in a meaningful way only when it is there to be set free, and it is there for us only when it has been rigorously awoken. Moreover, it can be genuinely awoken only if the Other is in a certain way relentlessly compelled to engage in reflection and thereby sees that one's appropriation of the objects treated in philosophy is inseparably bound up with a certain rigor in the actualization of method. All sciences fall short of this rigor, since in the sciences it is only the demand for objectivity that is important, whereas in philosophy what belongs together with the matters treated is the philosophizing individual and (his) notorious poverty. One can call something to the attention of another and compel him to engage in reflection only by traveling a stretch of the path oneself.

Jaspers might be able to justify his having allowed the problem of method to recede into the background by pointing out that he did not endeavor to provide a "general psychology" in his investigations. Certainly all problems cannot be dealt with in one fell swoop, but in fundamental investigations dealing with principles, the successive treatment of problems is no mere juxtaposition of them. Any individual problem in philosophy bears within itself directives for us to follow forward and backward into contexts of principles. It is a sign precisely of Jaspers' misunderstanding and undervaluation of the real problem of method that he approaches problems in psychology of worldviews under the assumption that this psychology is a separate science. He fails to see that "general psychology" and "psychology of worldviews" cannot be separated from each other in this way, and that both of these together cannot be separated from fundamental problems in philosophy.

Though Jaspers has only gathered up and depicted what "is there," he has nonetheless gone beyond mere classification by bringing together in a new way what has already been available to us, and this must be evaluated positively as a real advance. However, if it is to be capable of effectively stimulating and challenging contemporary philosophy, his method of mere observation must evolve into an "infinite process" of radical questioning that always includes itself in its questions and preserves itself in them.

APPENDIX

Familiarity with Jaspers' book is assumed. A detailed report has been avoided because this book does not, in a good sense, allow itself to be reported on without simply paraphrasing its different parts. Otherwise the clarity Jaspers has striven for and fully attained in many parts would be missing from the reader's representation and understanding of his book. This also is why certain changes in the various parts of the book that have turned out to be rather sprawling would be welcome in a new edition. These parts could remain as they are, if only Jaspers would show us in his subsequent investigations that a clear, preliminary presentation of the phenomena in question is really already a head start for the philosophical explication that follows.

But one change or another may very well be apropos in the following areas.

1. The Introduction (pp. 1–31) can be left out altogether without this impairing the reader's understanding of the body of the book, or else it must be rewritten and limited to §1, §2, and the section from p. 31 to p. 37. The latter belongs among the best parts of the book, and it makes possible a more funda-

mental understanding and analysis of principles. It is only in a fundamental investigation of principles that §3 (pp. 14–31) could be developed in a way that is appropriate to the sense of the phenomena in question.

2. It would be more germane to the subject matter of the book if chapter 3 (Types of Mental Life) were placed at the beginning, and if chapter 1 (Attitudes) and chapter 2 (Worldviews) also were allowed to emerge as it were from out of the "vital forces" that are presented in chapter 3. Jaspers characterizes these attitudes and worldviews as "emanations" (189) of vital forces. It would be even more effective to organize chapter 3 and "divide it up" into parts in such a way that chapter 1 and chapter 2 were taken up and contained right in the middle of it.

3. It would be more in accordance with the way Jaspers actually proceeds in his book if the methodological expression "psychology of understanding" were specified as a "*constructive* psychology of understanding" ("constructive" is meant here in a positive sense as a formation of types that draws these types out of intuitive understanding and is actualized and developed in a manner always appropriate to such understanding). The problem of understanding has been left undiscussed in our critical observations, because such questions remain unripe for discussion as long as the problem of the historical, roughly indicated in our "comments," has not been laid hold of at its roots and lifted up into the center of philosophical problems. The same goes for the notion of "ideas as driving forces."

Chapter Eight

THE PROBLEM OF SIN IN LUTHER (1924)

JOHN VAN BUREN, TRANSLATOR

Prof. Heidegger proceeded roughly as follows.

The problem of sin will be treated not insofar as it is an object of religious reflection but rather as a theological problem, and it is from the point of view of this question that Luther's theology will then be examined.

The object of theology is God. The theme of theology is man in the how of his being-placed before God. But the being of man is at the same time also a being in the world, and there exists for him also the whole problem of the world. Now Luther followed a particular fundamental direction of theological questioning, one proceeding directly from sin. Thus our question reads like this: What does the word "sin" mean when the relation of man to God is being discussed as a theological problem? This problem is closely connected with the question of man's original state (*iustitia originalis* [original righteousness]). What is asked about here is the being of man at the moment he emerged from the hand of God.

Man must, on the one hand, be regarded as the *summum bonum* [highest good] of creation. On the other hand, he must be so created that the Fall and the being of sin are possible and are not a burden falling on God. And the idea of

---

See pp. 8, 31 for bibliographic and other background information on this transcript of Heidegger's two-part lecture from the start of his Marburg Period, which was presented in Rudolf Bultmann's theology seminar "The Ethics of St. Paul."

redemption is indeed dependent on the way original sin and the Fall are viewed. The sense and essence of any theology are to be read off in light of *iustitia originalis*. The more one fails to recognize the radicalness of sin, the more redemption is made little of, and the more God's becoming man in the Incarnation loses its necessity. The fundamental tendency in Luther is found in this manner: the *corruptio* [corruption] of the being of man can never be grasped radically enough—and he said this precisely in opposition to Scholasticism, which in speaking of *corruptio* always minimized it.

It was now necessary to show:

1. that the tendency toward this problem was already alive in Luther's early period,

2. that the later Luther also displays the same tendency.

I

1. "Quaestio de viribus [et voluntate hominis sine gratia]" [The Question of Man's Capacity and Will without Grace] from the year 1516.[1]

Here Luther does not see sin as the accumulation of errors but rather draws attention to *affectus* [affect], that is, to the mode of man's being-placed in relation to things, to the being-displaced and being-horrified *[Entsetztsein]* by them that arises from his clinging to them. Man is seized by a *horror* [horror] that is based in *quaerere iustitiam suam* [seeking his righteousness]. There thus arises *desperatio spiritualis* [spiritual despair], despair before God not because of a mass of sins but because of the *affectus horrens peccatum* [affect of being horrified at sin]—and sin is something defined by a very particular kind of being-placed in relation to the world. The fundamental requirement for all theology is thus to interpret man's being in the world in such a way that he can get out of this being and come to God. Thus this being may not be presented as something good, for here he does not learn to love God; rather, man must be brought to the point where he grasps his being as a persisting in the world that affords not glories but adversities. God has in His mercy shattered man's *quaerere suam iustitiam* [seeking his righteousness], so that he now knows "I have nothing to expect from the world." Thus Luther puts the emphasis on the *affectus subtilissime carnalis* [simplest affect of the flesh] and arrives at a proposition quite the reverse of Scholasticism: *corruptio amplificanda est* [corruption is something to be amplified].[2]

2. "Disputatio contra scholasticam theologiam" ["Disputation against Scholastic Theology"] of 1517.[3]

a. Thesis 17: Man cannot of himself want God to be God; rather, man wants to be God. And this is precisely the essence of sin: *velle se esse deum et deum non esse deum* [to want himself to be God and God not to be God].[4]

b. Thesis 25: Hope comes not from works but from suffering.[5]

c. Thesis 30: On the part of man nothing precedes grace except rebellion against grace. The possibility of the existence of grace does not lie in him.[6]

d. Thesis 37: All human action is presumptuous and sinful.[7] These assertions distinguish Luther from Aristotle and the whole of Greek ontology, so that he can say in Thesis 50: *Totus Aristoteles ad theologiam est tenebrae ad lucem* [The whole of Aristotle is to theology as darkness is to light].[8]

3. The Heidelberg Disputation of 1518.[9]

Here Luther very clearly characterizes the task of theology by contrasting two theological points of view: The first is *theologia gloriae, quae invisibilia Dei ex operibus intellecta conspicit* (th. 22)[10] *et dicti malum bonum et bonum malum* (th. 21)[11] [the theology of glory, which sees the invisible things of God in works as perceived by man and calls evil good and good evil]. Opposite this stands the *theologia crucis* [theology of the cross], which takes its point of departure only from the actual matter (*dicit id quod res est* [says what the matter actually is]).[12]

The Scholastic takes cognizance of Christ only subsequently, after having defined the being of God and the world. This Greek point of view of the Scholastic makes man proud; he must first go to the cross before he can say *id quod res est* [what the matter actually is].[13]

In the Heidelberg Disputation, we surely find the most pointed formulation of Luther's position in his early period. The demonstration that the same tendency is maintained in Luther's theology even in his later period will come in the next meeting.

(Continuation of Prof. Heidegger's paper [on Feb. 21, 1924]).

II

1. What is useful for assessing the related problems of sin and *iustitia originalis* in Luther is an examination of these problems in Scholasticism. Here the response to the question of *iustitia originalis* is dependent on the basic view that the Church is the authority in matters of faith. But it can be this only insofar as it is a divine institution—something that needs to be demonstrated *rationaliter* [rationally]. What is necessary for this is the proof of (1) the existence of God and (2) the possibility of a historical Revelation that is attested in inspired Scripture and carried forward in the Church that is based on it. In order to be able to carry out these demonstrations, it is presupposed that man of himself, outwardly, possesses the possibility of knowledge of God. This can be assumed only if the *natura hominis* [nature of man] is *integra* [unspoilt], even after the Fall.

If this state is the natural one, then man must have possessed another knowledge of God, a higher one, before the Fall on account of a *donum superadditum* [superadded gift] which, as is well known, consists of the three theological virtues.[14] Man loses this "more" through sin but not—and this is the decisive thing—his natural being-placed before God.

Luther rebels against this and here appeals to *experientia* [experience]. The *natura hominis* is *corrupta* [corrupt]. The being of man as such is itself sin. Sin is nothing other than the antithesis to faith, where faith means: standing (being placed) before God. Thus sin is not an affixing of moral attributes to man but rather his real core. In Luther, sin is a concept of existence, something that his emphasis on *affectus* already points to.

Besides this fundamental definition of man, Luther turns his attention to the movement that sin as a mode of the being of man bears in itself: One sin begets another and drags man down ever deeper. The real sin is *incredulitas*, i.e., unbelief, *aversio dei* [turning away from God]. What is included in it, insofar as man is in this being-turned-away from God placed into the world, is a *pavor* [fear]. And with this in further succession: *fuga* [flight], *odium* [hatred], *desperatio* [despair], *impoenitentia* [impenitence].

2. What was stated above can be elucidated with Luther's lectures on Genesis from 1544 (Erlangen edition app. exeg. lat. tom. I).[15]

a. The difference of opinion comes to expression clearly on p. 208: *Scholastici disputant, quod justitia originalis non fuerit connaturalis, sed ceu ornatus quidam additus homini tanquam donum.* . . . [The Scholastics argue that original righteousness was not a part of man's nature but, like some adornment, was added to man as a gift. . . .] Luther against this: . . . *justitiam . . . fuisse vere naturalem, ita ut natura Adae esset diligere Deum, credere Deo, agnoscere Deum* . . . [righteousness . . . was truly part of his nature, so that it was Adam's nature to love God, to believe God, to know God. . . .][16]

The conclusion coming from this Scholastic definition of *iustitia originalis* would be that if *it* does not belong to the real essence of man, then neither does sin.[17] However: *fugiamus deliria ista . . . et sequamur potius experientiam* [let us shun those ravings . . . and rather follow experience].[18] *Experientia . . . docet nos de his calamitatibus* . . . [experience teaches us about this calamity],[19] i.e., *defectus* [loss] which arose from sin. But we recognize its entire magnitude only when from a correlative point of view we see God as God. For only then do we understand what *aversio Dei*, turning away [from God], means.

b. The Fall through sin: . . . *inveniemus summam et acerrimam omnium tentationum hanc fuisse, quia serpens invadit ipsam voluntatem Dei bonam, et nititur probare, Dei voluntatem erga hominem non esse bonam. Ipsam igitur imaginem Dei . . . petit.* [. . . we shall find that this was the greatest and severest of all temptations; for the serpent directs its attack at God's good will and dares to prove that God's will toward man is not good. Therefore it launches its attack against the very image of God. . . .][20] Thus Adam and Eve are not tempted by a particular, specific sin but are stirred up against God himself and his Word. And their sin consists in the fact that they lend an ear to a Word that is not God's Word, that they let themselves get involved in any way in a *disputatio* [dispute]. Through this, they lose their original being before God.

c. The movement of sin: *Primum enim cadit homo ex fide in incredulitatem et inoboedientiam: incredulitatem autem sequitur pavor, odium et fuga Dei, quae desperationem et impoenitentiam secum adducunt.* [First man falls from faith into unbelief and disobedience. Then fear, hatred, and flight from God, and these bring with them despair and impenitence.][21] God is unbearable to man; man is frightened by Him even in the quiet rustling of leaves, since he is shaken and unsettled in his own proper being.[22] He flees from God and thereby demonstrates his *intellectum depravatum* [depraved intellect]. *An non enim extrema stultitia est . . . Deum fugere, quem non possunt fugere?* [Or is it not the height of folly . . . to flee from God, from whom they are unable to flee?][23] And he flees because he does not see that *sin* itself means the *vera discessio a Deo, nec oportuit majorem fugam addere* [actual withdrawal from God, and it would not have been necessary to add any further flight].[24]

Et tamen haec (*stultitia* and *pavor*) *sunt quasi praeludia.* [And yet these (folly and fear) are, as it were, preludes.][25] The real meaning of sin is this: He who flees once flees in such a way that he constantly wishes to distance himself further, he *fugit in aeternum* [keeps on fleeing forever].[26] And Adam flees *excusando mendaciter peccatum, peccatum peccato addit. . . . Sic peccatum pondere suo semper secum trahit aliud peccatum, et facit aeternam ruinam* [by excusing his sin with lies, heaping sin upon sin. . . . Thus sin by its own gravitation always draws with it another sin and brings on eternal ruin].[27]

Adam has the presumption to make an *excusatio* [excuse], he *perstat in excusatione* [persists in his excuse].[28] He has the presumption to make an *accusatio et culpam a se in Creatorem transfert* [accusation and transfers his guilt from himself to the Creator].[29] *Non enim possunt (peccatores) aliter, quam Deum accusare et se excusare.* [They (sinners) cannot do otherwise than accuse God and excuse themselves.][30] That is the real despair.

And it goes still further: in her excuse, Eve aims her accusation at God as *creator* of the serpent and thereby characterizes him as *auctor peccati* [the originator of sin]. *Ita ex peccato humano ficit peccatum plane diabolicum, et incredulitas vertitur in blasphemiam, inoboedientia in contumeliam Creatoris.* [Thus out of a human sin comes a sin that is clearly demonic; unbelief turns into blasphemy, disobedience into contempt of the Creator.][31] *Hic ultimus gradus peccati est.* [This is the last step of sin.][32]

d. And nonetheless the situation of man in which he distances himself from God is a relation to God that shows itself in a certain looking back on man's part in the sense that God is rejected as *auctor peccati,* in the sense that man says: "God is not God."

And this situation of man is effected by God, insofar as it is the *summa gratia* [highest grace][33] that he did not remain silent after the Fall but *loquitur* [speaks]. What also needs to be taken into account is how the being of God is always conceived of as *verbum* [word], and the fundamental relation of man to him as *audire* [hearing].

e. What is evident from these remarks is how Luther's orientation regarding sin is totally different vis-à-vis Scholasticism, and how he understands Scholasticism as a fundamental antithesis to faith. In theological terms, this means: "One can understand faith only when one understands sin, and one can understand sin only when one has a correct understanding of the being of man itself."

Contemporary Protestant theology does not generally exhibit the above-sketched understanding of sin and of the relation of God and man involved here, and when it is once again explained in the latest theological movement, one underestimates it and fights against it out of a fear of what this understanding amounts to, betraying thereby the principle of Protestantism.

f. A remark about Catholicism and Protestantism in Kierkegaard's journal of 1852 (II, p. 284ff.) can be useful in clarifying what was meant above. Its sense is briefly the following:

Protestantism is only a *corrective* to Catholicism and cannot stand alone as normative, just as Luther is Luther only on the spiritual basis of Catholicism. If Catholicism degenerates, then "surface sanctity" arises—if Protestantism degenerates, then "spiritless worldliness" arises. In the process, what would appear in Protestantism is a refinement that cannot develop in Catholicism. For in the latter, when a representative of its principle degenerates into worldliness, then he brings upon himself the *odium* [disgrace] of worldliness—when a representative of Protestantism degenerates into worldliness, then he is praised for his godliness and frankness. And this is the case, because in Catholicism the universal presupposition exists "that we human beings are really scoundrels"; "the principle of Protestantism has a special presupposition: a human being who sits there in mortal anxiety—in fear and trembling and great spiritual trial."[34]

Chapter Nine

PHENOMENOLOGICAL INTERPRETATIONS IN CONNECTION WITH ARISTOTLE

An Indication of the Hermeneutical Situation (1922)

JOHN VAN BUREN, TRANSLATOR

The following investigations serve the purpose of a history of ontology and logic. As interpretations, they stand under certain conditions of interpreting and understanding. The subject matter making up the content of an interpretation, i.e., the thematic object in the "how" of its being-interpreted, is able to speak for itself in a manner fitting for it only when the particular hermeneutical situation at the time, and every interpretation is relative to such a hermeneutical situation, has been made available by being sketched out in a sufficiently clear manner. All

---

See pp. 8, 29 for bibliographic and other background information on this draft introduction to a planned book on Aristotle from the last years of Heidegger's Early Freiburg Period. Insertions by the translator have been placed in brackets, those by the German editor in the symbols "{ }," and those by Heidegger within quotations in the symbols "< >." References to Aristotle's works have been filled out, missing references added, and mistakes in the German edition regarding the spelling of Greek words corrected. For the convenience of the reader, standard English translations of terms and passages from Aristotle also have been added, though often in modified form, from *The Basic Works of Aristotle*, ed. Richard McKeon (New York: Random House, 1941).

interpretations have, in each case in accord with the particular domain of their subject matter and their knowledge-claims about it: (1) an *initial position of looking* they have more or less explicitly assumed and secured; (2) motivated by this, a *direction of looking* in which is defined the "as-what" (in terms of which the object is to be conceptually grasped in advance) and the "toward-which" *[das "woraufhin"]* (with respect to which *[auf das]* the object is to be interpretively laid out);[1] and (3) demarcated by the position and direction of looking, the *scope of looking* within which their particular claims about the objectivity of their interpretation move at any particular time.

The possible actualization of interpretation and understanding and the appropriation of the object emerging from this actualization will be transparent to the degree that the hermeneutical situation, in which and for the sake of which the interpretation temporalizes and unfolds itself,[2] is elucidated from the above points of view. A hermeneutics of the situation has to work out the transparency of its situation at the particular time and bring this hermeneutical transparency right into the starting point of interpretation.

The situation of interpretation, i.e., of the appropriation and understanding of the past, is always the living situation of the present. As a past that is appropriated in understanding, history itself grows in comprehensibility the more primordial one's resolute choice and working out of the hermeneutical situation is. The past opens itself up only in accord with the degree of resoluteness and power of the capacity to disclose it that the present has available to it. The primordiality of a philosophical interpretation is determined by the particular competence and sureness in which the philosophical research in question maintains itself and its questions. The conception this research has of itself and of the concreteness of its problems also already decides its basic orientation to the history of philosophy. What for these philosophical problems constitutes the proper domain of objects that should be interrogated—this determines the direction of looking into which one inevitably places the past. This reading into the past is not only not contrary to the sense of historical knowing, but it is in fact the basic condition for getting the past to speak to us at all. All of those interpretations in the field of the history of philosophy and likewise in other fields which, in contrasting themselves with "constructions" employed in the history of problems, consider it crucial that one not read anything into the texts will inevitably also themselves be caught in the act of reading something into these texts, only they will be doing so without being informed about it and by using conceptual resources taken from utterly disparate sources over which they have no control. One mistakes this absence of worry[3] about what one is "actually doing" and this ignorance about the conceptual resources one employs for a suspension of all subjectivity.

The elucidation of the hermeneutical situation of the following interpretations, and through this the demarcation of their thematic domain, is developed from the following fundamental conviction. In accord with the basic character of its being, philosophical research is something a "time," as long as it is not merely concerned with it as a matter of education, can never borrow from another time. Such research also is something that—and this is how it needs to understand itself and the nature of what it can possibly achieve in human Dasein—will never want to step forward with the claim that it be allowed to and is able to relieve future times of the burden of having to worry about radical questioning. The possibility that now past philosophical research will have an effect on the future of research can never consist in its results as such, but rather is rooted in the primordiality of questioning which is attained and concretely worked out in each particular case, through which past research can become a present in ever-new ways as a model that evokes problems.

[THE INITIAL POSITION OF LOOKING]

The object of philosophical research is human Dasein insofar as it is interrogated with respect to the character of its being. This basic direction of philosophical questioning is not externally added and attached to the interrogated object, factical life. Rather, it needs to be understood as an explicit taking up of a basic movement of factical life. In this movement, life is in such a way that in the concrete temporalizing of its being, it is anxiously concerned about its being, even when it goes out of its way to avoid itself. A characteristic of the being of factical life is that it finds itself hard to bear. The most unmistakable manifestation of this is the fact that factical life has the tendency to make itself easy for itself. In finding itself hard to bear, life *is* difficult in accord with the basic sense of its being, not in the sense of a contingent feature. If it is the case that factical life authentically is what it is in this being-hard and being-difficult, then the genuinely fitting way of gaining access to it and truly safekeeping it can only consist in making itself hard for itself. This is the only duty philosophical research can be required to fulfill, unless of course it wants to miss its object completely. All making it easy, all the seductive compromising of needs, all the metaphysical tranquilizers prescribed for problems having been for the most part derived from mere book learning—the basic intention of all of this is from the start to give up with regard to the task that must in each case be carried out, namely, bringing the object of philosophy into view, grasping it, and indeed preserving it. Accordingly, the history of philosophical research will be there as object in a relevant sense for present research on it when and only when the latter aims to provide not diverse historical curiosities but rather radically simple *monuments that evoke thinking,* i.e., only when it does not divert understanding within the present into the goal of merely enlarging knowledge about the past but rather forces the present back upon itself in order to intensify its questionability. However, and especially for a present in whose character of being historical consciousness has become constitutive, worrying about history and appropriating it in the above manner means: understanding radically what a particular kind of past philosophical research put forward at a particular time in and for *its* situation in worrying itself with the basic things it did. *Understanding* consists not merely in taking up the past for the sake of a knowledge that merely takes note of it but rather in repeating in an original manner what is understood in the past in terms of and for the sake of one's very own situation. This understanding happens least when one takes over from the past certain theorems, propositions, basic concepts, and principles and updates them in one way or another. When it uses models from the past, and what is at issue here is itself, it subjects these models from the ground up to the sharpest critique and develops them for the sake of a potentially fruitful opposition. Factical Dasein always is what it is only as one's own Dasein and never as the Dasein in general of some universal humanity. Expending care on the latter could only ever be an illusory task. *Critique* of history is always only critique of the present. Such critique should not naively be of the opinion that it is able to calculate for history how it would have happened, if only. . . . Rather, it needs to keep its eye on the present and see to it that it raises questions in accord with the kind of originality it is able to attain. History gets negated not because it is "false," but because it still remains effective in the present without, however, being able to be an authentically appropriated present.

Establishing the basic historical orientation of interpretation develops from an explication of the sense of philosophical research. We already have defined the object of this research in an indicative manner as *factical human Dasein as such*. It is from this its object that a concrete sketch of the philosophical problematic needs to be drawn. Thus what becomes necessary here is that we bring into relief in a preliminary fashion the specific characteristics of the object, factical life. And we need to do this not only because factical life is the *object* of philosophical research, but also because this research itself constitutes a particular *how* of factical life. As such, it co-temporalizes and helps unfold the concrete and historically particular being of life itself, and it does this in its very actualization and not first through some subsequent "application" to life. The possibility of this co-temporalizing is based on the fact that philosophical research is the explicit actualizing of a basic movement of factical life and constantly maintains itself within it.

In our indication of the hermeneutical situation, the structures of the object "factical life" will not be sketched out concretely and presented in their constitutive interrelation. Rather, by enumerating only the most constitutive elements of facticity, what we mean by this term will be brought into view and made available as a *forehaving* for such concrete investigation.

The confusing plurivocity of the word "life" and its usages should not be a reason for simply casting it aside. One would thereby forfeit the possibility of pursuing the various directions in the meaning of this word that are proper to it and alone make it possible to reach the respective object meant in each. In this regard, we must basically keep in view the fact that the term ζωή, *vita* [life], points to a basic phenomenon that the interpretations of human Dasein in Greek thought, the Old Testament, New Testament Christianity, and Graeco-Christian thought made central. The plurivocity of this term's meaning is rooted in the meant object itself. In philosophy, the uncertainty of a term's meaning can only be either an occasion for eliminating it or, if it turns out to be based in the object as necessary, an occasion for making it into an explicitly appropriated and transparent uncertainty. Such a focus on plurivocity (πολλαχῶς λεγόμενον) [that which is said in many ways (cf. Met. 1003a33ff.)] is not a mere poking around in the meanings of isolated words but rather an expression of a radical tendency to gain access to the meant objects themselves and to make available the motivational source of the different ways they are meant.

The basic sense of the movement of factical life is *caring (curare)*. Life's "being out for something" in which it is directed toward and cares about it is such that the toward-which of this care, namely, its historically particular world, also is there. The movement of caring is characterized by the fact that factical life *goes about its dealings* with the world. The toward-which of care is the with-which of these dealings. The sense of the being-real and being-there *[Dasein]* of the world is based in and defined by its character of being the with-which of dealings marked by caring. The world is there as always already having been taken up in care in one way or another. In accord with the possible directions of care, the world is articulated into the *environing world,* the *with-world,* and the *self-world.* Accordingly, caring is the care for one's livelihood, occupation, pleasures, remaining undisturbed, not dying, being familiar with . . . , knowing about . . . , and arranging one's life with respect to its ultimate goals.

The movement of concern displays many different modes of actualizing itself and of being-related to the with-which of its dealings: for example, tinkering with . . . , preparing for . . . , production of . . . , guaranteeing by . . . , making use of . . . , utilizing for . . . , taking possession of . . . , safekeeping of . . . , and loss of. . . . The with-which corresponding to each of these modes, that is, the with-which of dealings directed to a routine task and performing it, stands at any particular time within a definite kind of acquaintance and familiarity. These dealings characterized by caring always have their with-which within a definite kind of seeing of it. *Circumspection* is at work in these dealings, guiding them, cotemporalizing them, and playing its part in unfolding them. Caring takes the form of a looking around and seeing, and as this circumspective caring it is at the same time anxiously concerned about developing its circumspection, that is, about securing and expanding its familiarity with the objects of its dealings. In circumspection, the with-which of dealings is in advance grasped as . . . , oriented to . . . , interpreted and laid out as. . . . Objects are there as objects having been signified in this or that way and as such pointed in this or that direction. Here the world is being encountered[4] in this character of significance. Dealings characterized by caring not only have the possibility of giving up this care for gearing objects in the world in certain directions but rather, on account of a primordial tendency in the movement of factical life, they have an inclination to do so. In this blockage of the tendency to pursue dealings characterized by concern, these

dealings are transformed into a mere looking around without any view to directing oneself to routine tasks and gearing things in certain directions. Such looking around takes on the character of merely *looking at*. . . . In the care of this looking, i.e., in curiosity (*cura* [care], *curiositas* [curiosity]), the world is there for one
not as the with-which of dealings directed to routine tasks but solely from the
point of view of its *look*, its *appearance*. The looking becomes more fully actualized when one proceeds to define the world looked at and as such can organize
itself into the form of *science*. Thus science is a mode of dealings with the world
temporalized and unfolded by factical life itself and concerned with looking at
the world. As the movement of going about these dealings, science is a mode of
the being of factical life and plays a part in shaping its Dasein. The inventory of
ways of looking at the world, i.e., points of view, obtained at any particular time
(i.e., the definition of contexts of objects in the world with regard to how they
look) is something that has accrued to the circumspection out of which it has
grown. Here looking around actualizes itself in the mode of *addressing* and *discussing* the objects it deals with. The world is always being encountered in a particular manner of having-been-addressed, i.e., of an address that has made certain claims about it (λόγος).

In releasing itself from its tendencies to direct itself to its routine tasks and
perform them, going about dealings *takes a break* and *makes a sojourn*. Looking at
the world becomes an autonomous form of dealings with it. As such, this looking
becomes, in holding itself back from its work, a sojourning among objects for the
sake of defining them. Objects are originally there for one as objects having significance, whereas objects in the sense of mere things and facts first emerge from
the world as it is factically encountered (i.e., out of what has significance) within
a multistage process of theorizing directed to the world in a particular manner.

Factical life moves at any time within a certain state of *having-been-interpreted* that has been handed down to it, and it has reworked or worked out anew.
Circumspection makes the world available to life as having been interpreted on
the basis of those points of view within which it is encountered and awaited as
an object of anxious concern, arranged in the forms of tasks, and sought as a
refuge to which one can flee. These points of view, which are for the most part
available in an inexplicit manner and which factical life has more often than not
simply slipped into through habit as opposed to having explicitly appropriated
them, sketch out in advance the paths on which the movement of caring can
actualize itself. The interpretation of the world is factically also the interpretation
that life itself stands in. In it is also laid down the directions in which life takes
itself up into its care. In other words, what is also established in it is the particular sense the Dasein of life has, i.e., the "as-what" and the "how" in which human
beings maintain themselves within their own forehaving.

The movement of care is not a *process* running its course on its own over
and against the world that is there for it. The world is there in life and for life.
However, it is not there in the sense of a mere being-thought-about and being-

observed. This mode of the being-there of the world is temporalized and unfolded only when, in the movement of its going about those dealings characterized by concern, factical life takes a break and sojourns. This being-there of the world—which as actuality and reality, or indeed conceived of in terms of the objectivity of nature that has been stripped of all significance, usually is thought to provide the necessary point of departure for epistemological and *ontological* problems—is what it is only as having developed from a certain taking a break and sojourning. This sojourning is *as such* a sojourning in and for the basic movement of those dealings characterized by *concern.*

And as for this concern, there is more to it than that it is related to its world generally and in an original intentionality. The movement of concern is not an indifferent actualizing, one that is of such a kind that by means of it things simply happen in life and as if life itself were a process. What lives within the movement of caring is its *inclination* toward the world, and it takes the form of a *propensity* toward becoming absorbed in the world and letting itself be taken along by the world. This propensity of the anxious concern of life is the expression of a basic factical tendency in life toward *falling away* from itself and, as included in this, *falling into* the world and itself *falling into ruin.* Terminologically, we can describe this basic characteristic of the movement of caring as "the *inclination* of factical life toward *falling*" (or in abbreviated form, simply as *"falling into . . ."*), and we have thereby at the same time provided an indication of the directional sense and the intentional toward-which of the tendency of caring. Falling should not be understood as an objective happening or as simply "occurring" in life but rather as an intentional how. This propensity *[Hang]* is the most profound *fate [Verhängnis]* that life factically has to endure within itself. The how of having to endure itself in this manner, i.e., the way this fate "is," must be approached along with this fate itself as a constitutive factor of facticity.

This characteristic of movement is not an evil feature of life appearing from time to time and able to be eradicated in more progressive, happier times of human culture. This is so little the case that such approaches to human Dasein in terms of an attainable perfection and a paradisiacal naturality are themselves only extensions of this very inclination toward falling into the world. Here one closes one's eyes to the ownmost character of movement belonging to life and views life in a worldly manner as an object of dealings able to be produced in some ideal form. That is, one views it as the toward-which of simple concern.

That factical life in its inclination toward falling arrives at this worldly interpretation of itself gives expression to a basic characteristic of such movement: namely, it *tempts* life insofar as it spreads out before it and puts in its way possibilities (drawn from the world) of making things easy for itself in an idealistic manner and thereby missing itself. As tempting, the inclination toward falling is at the same time *tranquilizing,* i.e., it holds factical life fast in the circumstances of its fallenness, so that life speaks of these circumstances and concernfully refines them as though they were situations of unworried security and the most ideal possibilities of human activity. (In contrast to *circumstances,* the *situation* of factical life means the stand taken by life in which it has made itself transparent to itself in its falling and has, in worrying about itself in a concrete manner at the particular time, *seized upon itself and stirred itself* in its possibility of a motion running counter to the falling of its care.) As tranquilizing, the tendency toward falling that manifests itself in the manner of temptation is *alienating.* That is, in being absorbed in the world it concerns itself with, factical life becomes more and more alienated from itself, and the movement of caring that has been left to its own devices and comes before itself as the occurrence of life increasingly takes away the factical possibility that life can, in worrying about itself,[5] bring itself into view and take itself up as the goal to return to and appropriate. In the three characteristics of its motion, namely, being tempting, tranquilizing, and alienating, the tendency toward falling is the basic movement not only of going about those dealings that gear things in certain directions and produce but also of circumspection itself and its possible autonomy, i.e., of looking at and the addressing and interpreting that define and provide knowledge. Factical life not only takes itself up and cares for itself as a significant occurrence standing before it and as worldly importance but also speaks the *language* of the world whenever speaking about itself.

What lies in the inclination toward falling is the fact that factical life, which is in each case properly the factical life of the individual, is for the most part not lived as such. Rather, it moves within a certain *averageness* that belongs to its caring, its going about its dealings, its circumspection, and its understanding of the world. This averageness is that of the reigning *publicness*[6] at any particular time, of the social environs, the dominant trends, the "just like the others." It is this "everyone"[7] that factically lives the life of the individual: everyone is concerned about such and such, everyone sees it, judges it to be so, everyone enjoys it, everyone does it, asks about it. Factical life is lived by the *"no one,"* to which all life devotes its concern and apprehensions. Life is always mired in inauthentic traditions and customs of one sort or another. Out of them develop certain yearnings, and in them the paths along which such yearnings are to be satisfied have been mapped out for one's concern. Life conceals itself from itself in the world in which it is absorbed and in the averageness in which it goes about its dealings. In the tendency toward falling, life goes out of its way to avoid itself. Factical life itself gives the clearest attestation to this basic movement in the way it approaches *death.*

If in accord with the basic character of its being factical life is not a process, so death is not a cessation in the sense of the termination of this process that will turn up at one time or another. Death is imminent *for* factical life, standing *before* it as an inevitability. Life is in such a way that its death is always in one way or another there for it, i.e., there as seen in one way or another, even if this takes the form of pushing away and suppressing "the thought of death." Death is given as an object of care precisely in the fact that in the obstinacy of its imminence, it is

encountered as a how of life. The forced absence of worry about death in the caring of life actualizes itself in a flight into worldly concerns and apprehensions.
However, this looking away from death is so little a seizing upon life that it rather
turns out to be an evasion of the life standing before it and of the authentic character of its being. Whether in the form of one's worldly concerns and apprehensions fleeing death, or in that of worrying oneself about it and laying hold of it,
having death imminently before one is a basic constitutive characteristic of facticity. When one *has* death before one as *certain* and *lays hold of it* as such, one's
life becomes visible in itself. When death is in this manner, it gives to life a certain way of seeing itself and constantly leads it before its ownmost present and
past, a past that, burgeoning within life itself, comes toward it from behind it.

When time and again the attempt is made to define the basic characteristics of the object, factical life, and of its being without having also taken death
and "having death imminently before one" as a fundamental starting point to
guide one's approach to this problem, such an omission cannot be rectified merely
by a subsequent addition of these themes. The above-sketched problem of the
basic characteristics of the being of death, a problem absolutely constitutive for
ontology, has nothing to do with a metaphysics of immortality and its treatment
of the question of "what comes after death." Since death as imminently *before* one
characteristically makes the present and past of one's life visible, it is as such a
constituent moment of facticity at the same time the key phenomenon in which
the specific kind of *"temporality"* belonging to human Dasein is to be brought
into relief and explicated. It is on the basis of the sense of this *temporality* and not
at all through a formal analysis of concept-formation in historio*graphy* that the
basic sense of the *historical* needs to be defined.

The constitutive characteristics of facticity indicated above, namely, caring,
the tendency toward falling, and the how of having death imminently before one,
seem to contradict what we previously brought into relief as a basic characteristic of factical life, namely, that it is a being for which what is at issue, what it
comes to, in its manner of temporalizing is its own being. But this only seems to
be the case. Whenever it goes out of its way to avoid itself, life is factically there
for itself. It is precisely in this "away from itself" that life presents itself and pursues its absorption in its worldly concerns and apprehensions. Like all other kinds
of movement of factical temporality, this "absorption in" has in itself a more or
less explicit, though unacknowledged view *back* to that *before which* it is in flight.
The before-which of its fleeing is life itself as the factical possibility of being
explicitly seized upon and stirred as an object one worries oneself about. All going
about dealings has its circumspection, and what such circumspection provides for
these dealings is a certain guiding foresight into their with-which and the kind of
authenticity it is possible to achieve at the particular time regarding it. The being
of life accessible in facticity is in itself such that it can be made visible and reached
only on the path of a *detour* through a motion running counter to the falling of
care. As the worry of life about not becoming lost, this countermotion is the way

the possibility of seizing upon the being of life, stirring it, and authenticating it is temporalized and unfolded. This be-ing itself, which is possible in and for factical life, can be described as its *"existence."* Whenever factical life worries about its existence, it finds itself *on the path of a detour.* The possibility of seizing upon and stirring the being of life in its worry about itself is simultaneously the possibility of failing to exist. Insofar as existence is possible for factical life at any particular time, but also in itself something life can fail at, it is in principle something that warrants questioning. The possibility of existence is always the possibility of concrete facticity as a how of the temporalizing and unfolding of this facticity in its temporality. The question of what will show up in such existence cannot in any sense be asked in direct and universal terms. Insight into existence itself can be gained only through that kind of actualizing in which facticity is rendered questionable, i.e., through a concrete *destruction* of facticity at some particular time with respect to the motives of its movement, its directions, and what is available to it on a volitional level.

The motion running counter to the tendency toward falling should not be interpreted as an escapist flight from the world. What is typical of all such flight from the world is that it does not intend life in terms of its existential[8] character. That is, it does not seize upon and stir it up in its fundamental questionability but rather imaginatively inserts it into a new *world* of tranquility. Worrying oneself about existence changes nothing in the factical circumstances of one's life at the particular time. What is changed is the how of the movement of one's life, and this how can as such never become a matter of publicness and the "everyone." Here the concern and apprehension involved in going about one's dealings are such that in them one is worried about one's self. And when in factical life one worries about existence in this way, this is not a matter of brooding over oneself in egocentric reflection. Rather, such worry is what it is only as a motion running counter to the tendency of life toward falling, i.e., it is what it is precisely in the concrete movement of going about one's dealings and of the concern involved. Here the *"counter to"* as a *"not"* attests to a primordial achievement that is constitutive on the level of being. In view of its constitutive sense, negation has an original primacy over any position-taking. And this is because the character of the being of human beings is factically defined by its falling, i.e., by its worldly propensities. The sense of this primal fact itself and the sense of this factuality as such can, if at all, only be interpreted within and relative to facticity *insofar as it has been seized upon and stirred.* The actualization of having insight into life and addressing it with respect to its existential possibility has the character of a worry about life in which life is interpreted with respect to the sense of its being. "Facticity" and "existence" do not mean the same thing, and the factical character of the being of life is not determined by existence. The latter is only one possibility that temporalizes itself and unfolds itself in the being of life we have described as "factical," and this means that it is in facticity that the possibility of radically formulating the problem of the being of life is centered.

If in the first place philosophy is not an artificial occupation that merely accompanies life and deals with "universals" of one sort or another and arbitrarily posited principles but rather is as a knowing that *questions,* that is, as *research,* simply the explicit and genuine actualizing of the tendency toward interpretation that belongs to the basic movements of life in which what is at issue is this life itself and its being; and if secondly philosophy is set on bringing into view and conceptually grasping factical life in terms of the decisive possibilities of its being, i.e., if relying upon its own resources and not looking to the hustle and bustle of worldviews, it has radically and clearly resolved to throw factical life back on itself as this is possible in this factical life itself and to let it fend for itself in terms of its own factical possibilities, i.e., if philosophy is *in principle atheistic*[9] and understands such about itself—then it has resolutely chosen factical life with a view to its facticity and, in acquiring it as an object for itself, it has preserved it in its facticity. The how of its research is the interpretation of the sense of this being *[Seinssinn]* with respect to its basic categorial structures, i.e., the modes in which factical life temporalizes itself, unfolds itself, and *speaks* with itself (κατηγορεῖν [predicating in terms of categories]) in such temporalizing. As long as philosophical research has understood, simply on the basis of the object it has seized upon, that what this object entrusts it with as its topic of inquiry consists of those primordial ontological conditions of the possibility of any worldview that can be made visible only in the rigor of its research, it will have no need for the finery of worldviews and the zealous care about not arriving too late for the turmoil of some present times in which one wants to go along for the ride. These conditions are not "logical forms." Rather, understood as categories, they are possibilities of the factical temporalizing and unfolding of existence that have been grasped in their genuine availability.

The basic problem of philosophy concerns the *being* of factical life. In this respect, philosophy is a *fundamental ontology that deals with principles,* so that this ontology of facticity provides the particular specialized regional ontologies of the world with a foundation for their problems and a clarification of the sense of these problems. The basic problem of philosophy has to do with the being of factical life in the how of its being-addressed and being-interpreted at particular times. In other words, as the ontology of facticity, philosophy is at the same time the interpretation *[Interpretation]* of the categories of this addressing and interpreting *[Auslegen],* i.e., it is *logic.*

Ontology and logic need to be brought back to their original unity in the problem of facticity and understood as offshoots of fundamental research into principles that can be described as "the *phenomenological hermeneutics* of facticity."

The interpretations of factical life found in the circumspection of caring and the insight of worry are in each case concrete, and it is with a view to their *forehaving* (the basic sense of being into which life places itself) and with reference to their *foreconception* (the modes of addressing and discussing in which factical life converses with itself and speaks about itself) that philosophical research needs to render these interpretations categorially transparent in the factical unity of their temporalizing and unfolding of life. This hermeneutics is a phenomeno-logical hermeneutics, i.e., the object making up its domain of research, namely, factical life with respect to the how of its being and speaking, is thematically and methodologically brought into view as a *phenomenon*. The structure of an object that characterizes it as a phenomenon, i.e., *intentionality in toto* (being related to . . . , the toward-which as such of the relation, the actualization of the relating itself to . . . , the temporalizing and unfolding of the actualization, and the true safekeeping of this temporalizing and unfolding), is none other than the struc-ture of that object which has the character of being of factical life. Taken simply as being related to . . . , intentionality is the first phenomenal characteristic of the basic movement of life, i.e., of caring, that one can directly bring into relief. Phe-nomenology itself is radical philosophical research, as it was when it first burst onto the scene with Husserl's *Logical Investigations*. Phenomenology has not been seized upon and understood in its most central motives if, as happens in some areas of phenomenological research itself, one sees in it only a philosophical propaedeutic whose purpose is supplying clear concepts and with whose assis-tance one is then supposed to set to work for the first time in *actual* philosophy— as if one could clarify basic philosophical concepts on a descriptive level without that fundamental orientation to objects that is central in philosophical problems and needs to be constantly appropriated anew.

[THE DIRECTION OF LOOKING]

We have now given an indication of the initial *position of looking* to be adopted by the following interpretations, insofar as they are phenomenological interpre-tations and are for the sake of a history of ontology and logic. The idea of a phe-nomenological hermeneutics of facticity includes within it the tasks of a formal and material theory of objects and logic, a theory of science, a "logic of philoso-phy," a "logic of the heart," and a logic of "pretheoretical and practical" thought. And such is the case not because this "hermeneutics" is a collective term that combines the above tasks but rather in consequence of its effective force as the fundamental approach to all philosophical problems.

But we still have not yet gained an understanding of what historical inves-tigations are supposed to accomplish for such a hermeneutics, why we are focus-ing especially on *Aristotle* as a theme of investigation, and furthermore how this investigation is to be carried out. The motivations for the particular *directions of looking* we will be taking result from the *concrete* understanding gained in our above-sketched initial position. What lies in the idea of facticity is that the gen-uine object of research is *in each case always authentic facticity* ("authentic" is being understood literally here as *"one's own"*), i.e., the facticity of one's own times and generation. Due to its tendency toward falling, factical life lives for the most part in what is inauthentic, in what has been handed down to it, in what has been transmitted and reported to it from the past, in what it has appropriated and learned in an average way. Even what has been worked out in an original manner as an authentic possession falls into averageness and publicness. It loses the specific sense of its provenance out of its original situation and in this free-floating manner enters into the common practices of the "everyone." This falling touches all of the dealings of factical life, all of its circumspection, and not least of all its own actualization of its interpretation with respect to the forehaving and foreconception of this interpretation. In the ways it formulates questions and finds answers to them, philosophy too is situated in this movement of facticity, since it is only the explicit interpretation of factical life.

Accordingly, it is necessary for the philosophical hermeneutics of facticity to begin within its factical situation by inserting itself into the particular state of the having-been-interpreted of factical life given in advance for hermeneutics. This having-been-interpreted initially supports hermeneutics and can never be completely eradicated. According to what was said above about the tendency toward falling effecting all interpretation, it is precisely *"what is self-evident"* in this pregiven interpretation, i.e., what is not discussed in it, what is thought to require no further explanation, which will turn out to be what *inauthentically*, i.e., without being explicitly appropriated from out of its origins, sustains the reigning effective force of pregiven problems and directions of questioning.

The addressing and interpreting of factical life actualized by factical life itself allow the ways of seeing and speaking here to be given to them in advance from objects in the world. Whenever human life, Dasein, the human being becomes an object of inquiry and is defined in interpretation, this objectivity stands within forehaving as a worldly occurrence, as "nature" (the psychical is understood as nature, as are spirit and life in the analogous categorial articulation involved here). That today we still speak of the "nature" of man, the "nature" of the soul, and more generally the "nature of things," and that we also discuss the categories of this kind of objectivity in the same way, i.e., employing categories developed from a particular kind of explication, namely, a particular way of looking at "nature"—this has its motives in intellectual history. Even when the objects in question are in principle no longer crudely spoken of as "substances" (a way of speaking Aristotle was, one should add, far more removed from than is generally taught) and interrogated in terms of their occult qualities, the interpretations of life move nonetheless within basic concepts, starting points for questions, and tendencies of explication that have sprung from experiences of objects we today have for a long time no longer had available to us.

In its contemporary situation, philosophy moves inauthentically within *Greek* conceptuality and, indeed, this conceptuality has been permeated by a chain of diverse interpretations of it. The basic concepts of Greek philosophy have lost their original expressive functions that were tailored to particular regions of objects that were experienced in a particular manner. But in spite of all of the analogizing and formalizing these basic concepts have undergone, a certain

aspect of their provenance still survives. They still bear within themselves something of the genuine tradition of their original sense, insofar as one can point out
in them the way their sense is directed back to their source in certain objects.
When in its contemporary situation philosophy takes as its starting point the idea
of man, ideals of life, and notions of the being of human life, it moves within
points of departure in certain founding experiences temporalized and unfolded
in Greek ethics and, above all, in the Christian idea of man and human Dasein.
Even the views found in contemporary anti-Greek and anti-Christian trends
maintain themselves at bottom within these same directions and modes of interpretation. Accordingly, insofar as the phenomenological hermeneutics of facticity endeavors, in its interpretation, to play its part in helping the contemporary
situation with the possibility of its being appropriated in a radical manner, doing
this by calling attention to concrete categories and allowing them to be given in
advance, it sees itself directed to the task of loosening up the reigning state of traditional interpretation today with respect to its hidden motives and its unex-
pressed tendencies and modes of interpreting so that it can, by way of a *decon-
structive regress,* penetrate into the original motivational sources of these
explications. *Hermeneutics carries out its tasks only on the path of destruction.* If
philosophical research has really understood the kind of objectivity and being
belonging to its thematic toward-which (namely, the facticity of life), it takes the
form of *"historical"* knowing in the radical sense of the term. In philosophical
research, this destructive confrontation with its own history is not merely a supplement for illustrating how things stood in earlier times, an occasional overview
of what others before us "came up with," or an opportunity for depicting enter-
taining perspectives in world-history. Rather, destruction is the authentic path
upon which the present needs to encounter itself in its own basic movements,
doing this in such a way that what springs forth for it from its history is the per-
manent question of the extent to which it itself is worried about appropriating
radical possibilities of founding experiences and of their interpretation. It is by
means of this question that contemporary tendencies toward a radical logic of
origins and toward formulating the starting points of ontologies can gain a fundamental, critical clarification. Here the sort of critique already arising precisely
through the concrete actualization of destruction is thereby centered not on the
fact *that* we always stand within a tradition but rather on the *how* of our standing within a tradition. What we have not interpreted and brought to expression
in an original manner amounts to something we do not truly have in an authentic safekeeping[10] of it. And it is factical life itself (i.e., also the possibility of existence found in it) that needs to be taken up into, temporalized by, and unfolded
in this true safekeeping. Thus if this life relinquishes the originality of interpretation, it relinquishes the possibility of ever coming into possession of itself in a
radical sense, i.e., the possibility of radically *be-ing* [zu sein] itself.

The tangled complexity of central, constitutive effective forces at play in the
being of our contemporary situation will, with respect to the problem of facticity,

be referred to in brief as the *Graeco-Christian interpretation of life*. This also will include those contemporary anti-Greek and anti-Christian trends of interpretation that are determined by and relative to the Graeco-Christian interpretation of life. The idea of man and of human Dasein taken as the starting point in this Graeco-Christian interpretation determined the philosophical anthropology of Kant and that of German Idealism. Fichte, Schelling, and Hegel came out of *theology* and received from it the basic impulses of their speculative thought. This theology is rooted in the theology of the Reformation, which succeeded, only in very small measure, in providing a genuine explication of Luther's new fundamental religious position and its immanent possibilities. As for this new position, it itself grew out of those interpretations of Paul and Augustine that Luther had taken up in an original manner, as well as out of his confrontation at the same time with the theology of late Scholasticism (Duns Scotus, Ockham, Gabriel Biel, Gregory of Rimini).

The doctrines of late Scholasticism concerning God, the Trinity, the original state of man, sin, and grace worked with the conceptual resources that Thomas Aquinas and Bonaventure provided for theology. But this means that the idea of man and of the Dasein of life initially taken as the starting point in all of the above domains of theological problems was based on an Aristotelian "physics," "psychology," "ethics," and "ontology," in which Aristotle's basic teachings were treated in a particularly selective manner and worked with on the basis of a particular interpretation of them. Augustine also was decisively influential and through him Neoplatonism and, through it and to a greater degree than is commonly supposed, again Aristotle. These connections are more or less well known to us on the crude level of the historical textual filiations involved, but what is still completely lacking is an authentic interpretation of these connections that has its central basis in the fundamental philosophical problem of facticity outlined above. The prospect of pursuing comprehensive research on the Middle Ages is in its guiding points of view entangled at present in the schematism of a neo-Scholastic theology and in the framework of an Aristotelianism having taken shape in this neo-Scholasticism. What is first necessary is that we understand the exegeses and commentaries of medieval theology (i.e., its scientific structure) as interpretations of life conveyed in a particular form. Theological anthropology needs to be traced back to its founding philosophical experiences and motives, so that with reference to them we can make sense of the force of influence and kind of transformation that issued from the particular basic religious and dogmatic position at the time.[11] Not only has the hermeneutical structure of commentary on the *Sentences* of Peter Lombard (something supporting the actual development of theology up to Luther) not as such been uncovered, but *the very possibility of questioning and approaching it* is utterly wanting. What was taken up in the *Sentences* in the spirit of and through selections from Augustine, Jerome, and John Damascene is by itself already of importance for the development of medieval anthropology. If one is to have any sort of standard for assessing these transformations, an adequate interpretation of Augustinian anthropology needs to be available for this purpose, one that does not, for example, simply attempt to extract propositions on psychology from his works on the model of a textbook in psychology or moral theology. An adequate interpretation of Augustine with respect to the fundamental ontological and logical constructions in his teachings about life needs to take its central focus from his writings on the Pelagian controversy and his teachings on the Church. The idea of man and of Dasein at work here points back to Greek philosophy, to the patristic theology based on Greek philosophy, to Pauline anthropology, and to the anthropology of the Gospel of John.

In connection with the task of the above phenomenological destruction, the important thing is not merely to paint a picture of various intellectual currents and their relations of dependency but rather to bring into relief the central ontological and logical structures at each of the decisive turning points in the history of Western anthropology by making a primordial regress to the relevant sources. One can bring off this task only if a concrete interpretation of Aristotle's philosophy taking its orientation from the problem of facticity, i.e, from a *radical phenomenological anthropology,* has been made available.

Looking at Aristotle in light of the problem of facticity we have taken as our starting point, we can see that he was simply the completion and concrete refinement of the philosophy preceding him. But it also is true that his "physics" succeeded in working out a new fundamental approach to principles, and what grew out of this was his ontology and logic, which in turn permeated the history of philosophical anthropology that we schematically and retrospectively sketched out above. Beings in the how of their being-moved became the central phenomenon for Aristotle, and the explication of this phenomenon was the main topic of his physics.

The only appropriate basis for the particular methodological aims of the following investigations is the actual textual corpus in which Aristotle's research has been handed down to us (namely, discussions in the style of thematic outlines and investigations). It is only by working back from Aristotle that we can properly define Parmenides' doctrine of being and understand it as the crucial step that decided the sense and fate of Western ontology and logic.

These investigations seeking to carry out the task of a phenomenological destruction set their sights ultimately on late Scholasticism and Luther's early theological period. Accordingly, their range encompasses tasks whose difficulty should not be underestimated. Moreover, it is our initial position (i.e., our having taken the problem of facticity as our starting point and our exposition of it) that determines our basic approach to history and the way in which the particular direction of looking at it focuses on Aristotle.

[THE SCOPE]

In accord with its initial position and direction of looking, each and every interpretation necessarily elucidates its thematic object in overprecise terms. One is able to define the object in a fitting manner only when one first sees it in over-precise terms (not arbitrarily but on the basis of access to the content in it one defines) and then manages, by a retraction of this overprecise elucidation, to arrive at a demarcation of the object that is as fitting as possible to it. An object that is always seen only in semi-darkness can be correctly understood in *its* semi-dark givenness only by a detour passing through an overly clear elucidation of it. However, insofar as it does elucidate in overprecise terms, interpretation should not question too broadly and claim for itself an utterly fantastic kind of objectivity in historical knowledge, as if it could eventually meet up with an "in-itself." Merely inquiring into such a thing in any sense whatsoever means that one has misunderstood the basic character of the object of *history*. Inferring relativism and skeptical historicism from the fact that an "in-itself" cannot be found is only the flip side of the *same* misunderstanding. The translation of interpreted texts and above all the translation of their decisive basic concepts is something that has grown out of the concrete interpretation of them and contains it, so to speak, *in nuce* [in a nutshell]. Coinages employed in translations do not spring from an obsession with innovation but rather from the content of the translated texts.

We now need to clarify the basic approach we will be taking in our interpretation of Aristotle, an approach determined by our above-sketched initial position. We will at the same time provide a summary sketch of the first part of our investigations.

The question that must guide our interpretation of Aristotle is: *As what kind of object, with what kind of characteristics of being, was human being, i.e., "being in life," experienced and interpreted?* What is the sense of Dasein in terms of which Aristotle's interpretation of life initially approached human being as an object? In short, in what kind of *forehaving of being* did this object stand? Further, how was this being of the human being explicated in concepts, out of what soil did this explication arise as a phenomenon, and which categories of being grew out of what was viewed in this manner as its explicata?

Was the sense of being Aristotle employed to define the being of human life drawn in a genuine manner from a simple, founding experience of this object only and its being, or was human life understood as only one being within a more comprehensive domain of being, i.e., did Aristotle apply to it a sense of being that he took to be archontic for investigating it? What did being in any sense whatsoever really mean for Aristotle? How was it able to be accessed, grasped, and defined? The domain of objects supplying the primordial sense of being was the domain of those objects *produced* and put into use in dealings. Thus the toward-which this primordial experience of being aimed at was not the domain of being consisting of *things* in the sense of objects understood in a *theoretical* manner as facts but rather the world encountered in going about dealings that produce, direct themselves to routine tasks, and use. What *is* amounts to what has been finished and made ready in the movement of going about the dealings of production (ποίησις), i.e., what has come into a being-on-hand and is now available for certain tendencies to use it.

Being means *being-produced* and, as having been produced, being of significance relative to certain tendencies to have dealings with it, i.e., being-available for them. Insofar as they are objects of circumspection or indeed of that kind of understanding that in its autonomy simply looks at them, beings are addressed with respect to *the way they look* (εἶδος [idea, form]). The understanding that simply looks at beings explicates itself by addressing and discussing (λέγειν) these beings. The "what" of these objects that is addressed (λόγος [discourse]) and their look (εἶδος) are in a sense the same. And this means that what is addressed in λόγος makes up as such these beings in the authentic sense. With the objects it addresses, λέγειν takes beings in the beingness (οὐσία [substance]) of their look into true safekeeping. But in Aristotle and also after him, οὐσία still retains its original meaning of the household, property, what is at one's disposal for use in one's environing world. Οὐσία means *possessions, what one has* [die Habe]. What it is in beings which, as their being, comes into the true safekeeping that deals with them, i.e., what allows them to be characterized as *possessions,* is their *being-produced.* It is in production that the objects of dealings first appear and come to look the way they do.

The domain of being consisting of objects of dealings (ποιούμενον [what has been produced], πρᾶγμα [a thing done], ἔρλον [a work], κινήσεως [what has been set in motion]) and the mode of addressing these objects in such dealings, namely, a particular "logos" or more precisely the objects of such dealings in the how of their being-addressed, mark out the forehaving from which Aristotle drew the basic ontological structures and also the modes of addressing and defining for approaching the object "human life."

How did these ontological structures arise? As the explicata of a defining that looks at *[hinsehend]* . . . and addresses . . . , that is, insofar as they grew out of Aristotle's having moved along a certain path of research in which, adopting particular points of view *[Hinsichten],* he took up and articulated the domain of being that had been brought into forehaving through a founding experience of it. In other words, those researches in which objects were experienced and thought in their basic character of being-moved and something like motion also was initially seen to be given in these objects must provide the possibility of gaining access to the authentic motivational source of Aristotle's ontology. It is in Aristotle's *Physics* that we find this sort of research. In the method of interpreting it, this research needs to be treated as *a phenomenon in toto* and interpreted with respect to its object in the *how* of the investigative dealings with it, the founding experience in which this object was initially given as the starting point of research, the constitutive movements that actualize this research, and the concrete modes of thinking the object and conceptually articulating it. What becomes visible in this way are beings in motion with regard to the basic character of their being, movement with regard to its categorial structure, and thereby the ontological constitution of the archontic sense of being. For a phenomenological interpretation of this research, we also need to gain an understanding of the sense in which Aristotle generally understood research and the way it is pursued and actualized. Research is a mode of dealings in which one looks at something (ἐπιστήμη [scientific understanding]). It has its particular genesis out of dealings characterized by concern and directed to routine tasks. And it is only with reference to this genesis that we can understand its mode of circumspection, i.e., of interrogating something from the point of view of its "in what way" (αἴτιον [cause]) and its "from-out-of-which" (ἀρχή [origin, first principle]).[12] Insights into the genesis of research will be provided in our preliminary interpretation of {*Met.* A 1–2}. But the kind of understanding in which one looks at and defines (ἐπιστήμη) is only one way that beings are brought into true safekeeping. It has to do with those beings that necessarily and for the most part are what they are. Another kind of dealings in the sense of those that gear beings in certain directions and deliberate about them in a concerned manner exists for those beings that also can be other than they are at present and first need to be brought about in the dealings themselves, either by handling them or producing them. This mode of the true safekeeping of being is {τέχνη [art]}. Within a primordial context of problems, Aristotle interprets the modes of the illumination of dealings, namely, circumspection, insight, and looking at . . . (each of which is different in accord with the particular region of being it corresponds to), as modes of the actualization of that pure and simple *perceiving* that gives sight in any sense and with respect to the possibility of their basic achievement of appropriating being and truly safekeeping it (*Eth. Nic.* Z). By providing an interpretation of this text, we will at the outset be able to gain access to the phenomenal horizon within which research and theoretical knowing need to be located as modes οἷς ἀληθεύει ἡ ψυχή [in which the soul is true] (Z 3, 1139b15). Accordingly, the first part of our investigation will include interpretations of the following texts:

1. *Eth. Nic.* Z;
2. *Met.* A 1–2; and
3. *Phys.* A, B, and Γ 1–3.

Eth. Nic. VI

Temporarily leaving aside the specific problem of ethics in these discussions, our interpretation of them explains the "dianoetic virtues" as different modes of having available the possibility of actualizing a genuine *true safekeeping of being*. Σοφία [wisdom], i.e., authentic understanding that consists in looking at . . . , and φρόνησις [prudence], i.e., circumspection in the care for human well-being, are interpreted as the authentic modes of actualizing νοῦς [intellect], i.e., of pure and simple *perceiving* as such. What becomes accessible in them and comes to be appropriated and taken into true safekeeping are the kinds of beings corresponding to each of these characteristic ways of perceiving. And this means that what is given, along with this interpretation of these phenomena, is the possibility that the beings taken into true safekeeping in σοφία and φρόνησις can now be defined and demarcated in the how of their being-perceived and thereby also with respect to the genuine characteristics of their being. Thus we can clearly see the way this interpretation of the "virtues" is connected with the problem of ontology broached above. The principle of the phenomenal difference between the structures of the two basic ways of perceiving allows the two corresponding and quite different regions of being to become visible. Ἔστω δὴ οἷς ἀληθεύει ἡ ψυχὴ τῷ καταφάναι καὶ ἀποφάναι πέντε τὸν ἀριθμόν· ταῦτα δ᾽ἐστὶ τέχνη, ἐπιστήμη, φρόνησις, σοφία, νοῦς· ὑπολήψει γὰρ καὶ δόξῃ ἐνδέχεται διαψεύδεσθαι. "Thus let us begin by assuming that the modes in which the soul brings and takes beings into true safekeeping as unveiled—actualizing this by means of explication in speech which either affirms or denies—are five in number: procedures in which one is directed to certain tasks and produces [τέχνη (art)]; defining by way of looking at, discussing, and identifying [ἐπιστήμη (scientific understanding)]; the kind of seeing around one which has to do with care for human well-being (circumspection) [φρόνησις (prudence)]; the kind of understanding which sees in an authentic manner [σοφία (wisdom)]; and pure and simple perceiving [νοῦς (intelligence)]. <Only these ones come into consideration> since it lies in the very sense of supposition and having a viewpoint [δόξα (opinion)] that they do not necessarily give us beings as unveiled, but rather such that what is meant by them only looks as if it were . . . and this puts itself in front of the beings in question and deceives us" (*Eth. Nic.* Z 3, 1139b15–18, cf. ibid., Z 6, 1141a3).[13] These modes καθ᾽ἃς μάλιστα . . . ἀληθεύσει ἡ ψυχή [in accord with which . . . the soul is most of all true] (ibid., Z 2, 1139b12), i.e., in accord with whose pure and simple characteristic actualization the soul "most of all" brings to givenness beings (and these are given in advance for each of the above modes) as *unconcealed* in a primordial true safekeeping of them, constitute the "virtues" under discussion in Aristotle's text. A correct interpretation of the meaning of the terms ἀληθές [true] and ἀλήθεια [truth] is of fundamental importance in understanding Aristotle's analysis of the above-mentioned phenomena, how they differ from each other as phenomena and, as part of this, how they constitutively achieve different things in actualizing the true safekeeping of being, and finally how they are characterized by the fact that they are in each case concrete ways of actualizing the underlying vitality of perceiving as such (νοῦς, νοεῖν). Likewise, it is only by gaining a phenomenological understanding of νοῦς that we can explain the structural context of the phenomena falling under it.

When defining what "truth" means, one usually appeals to Aristotle as the source of its original meaning. We are told that for Aristotle "truth" "occurs in judgment" and is more precisely the "agreement" of thought with its object. Moreover, one then takes this concept of truth as a basis for putting forward the so-called "representationalist theory" of knowledge. No trace of the concept of truth as "agreement," the common conception of λόγος as valid judgment or, above all, a "representationalist theory" can be found in Aristotle. When the misbegotten epistemology of so-called "critical realism"[14] indeed uses Aristotle as the main authority in its apologetics against "idealism," which it misunderstands, it also misunderstands from the ground up the original situation of Aristotle's thought from which the phenomena in question arose and which is still available to us through a study of the relevant sources.

The meaning of ἀληθές, namely, being-there as unconcealed, i.e., being-meant in itself, is in no way drawn from and explicated on the basis of judgment and thus does not originally reside in it or refer to it. Ἀληθεύειν [being-true] does not mean "possessing the truth" but rather taking the *beings* meant in each case and as such into true safekeeping as unveiled.

Αἴσθησις [sense perception], i.e., *perceiving* in the how of the sensory, is not *"also"* called true merely because the "concept of truth" has been *transferred* from λόγος to it. Rather, in accord with its own intentional character, it in itself primordially brings to givenness its intentional toward-which "in the original." It means "bringing an object to givenness as unveiled." Hence, ἡ μὲν γὰρ αἴσθησις τῶν ἰδίων ἀεὶ ἀληθής [sense perception of the proper objects of each of the individual senses is always true] (*De an.* Γ 3, 427b12).[15] We can see that with respect to the phenomenal situation intended here, the expressions "truth" and "true" do not really tell us anything. In contrast, "falsehood" (ψεῦδος, ψευδές) can be found only where there is "synthesis": τὸ γὰρ ψεῦδος ἐν συνθέσει ἀεί [falsehood always involves a synthesis] (ibid., Γ 6, 430b). Falsehood presupposes as the condition of its possibility a *different* intentional structure of meaning something as an object, an approach to beings from the "point of view" of another kind of being-meant. When a being is intended in itself not in a plain and simple manner but rather as this or that, i.e., in its character of being "as" something, perceiving takes place in the how of a *taking-together* and *taking-with*. When, as sense perception, perceiving actualizes itself in the mode of addressing and discussing its object "as" this or that (i.e., in λέγειν), it can happen that in the course of this the object winds up giving itself out as something that it is not. And this tendency toward meaning the object in its "as" is utterly foundational for the possibility of ψεῦδος: ὅτι μὲν γὰρ λευκόν, οὐ ψεύδεται, εἰ δὲ τοῦτο τὸ λευκὸν ἢ ἄλλο τι, ψεύδεται [while the perception that white is there before one cannot be false, the perception that what is white is this or that may be false] (ibid., Γ 3, 428b20); διανοεῖσθαι δ᾽ ἐνδέχεται καὶ ψευδῶς καὶ οὐδενὶ ὑπάρχει ᾧ μὴ καὶ λόγος [it also is possible to think falsely, and thought is found only where there is discourse as well as sense perception] (ibid., 427b13). That is, only what is perceived in the mode of being-addressed with respect to an "as" can give itself to such addressing "as deceptively like." In accord with its meaning, the "being-true" of the λόγος of addressing is constituted only circuitously through a reference to ψεῦδος. Λόγος itself needs to be understood in terms of its own basic *intentional* characteristic, namely, that it is ἀπόφανσις [assertion], i.e., an addressing and discussing which means its object in such a way that what it says is said on the basis of this object and is drawn from (ἀπό) it. Accordingly, ἀποφαίνεσθαι [asserting] is to be understood as: letting the object "appear" for itself (middle voice) from out of itself and as it is in itself. This is of importance for our interpretation of φαντασία [imagination].

What λέγειν brings to givenness is beings themselves, and we now know that this means that it brings them to givenness in their unveiled "as-what" inasmuch as a deceiving "what," which merely passes off the being in question as such and such, does not put itself in front of this being. Insofar as it is a deceptive self-veiling, ψεῦδος has this sense only on the basis of that meaning of ἀληθές that does not originally refer to λόγος: δόξα ψευδής ἐγένετο, ὅτε λάθοι μεταπεσὸν τὸ πρᾶγμα [opinion becomes false when, upon changing, its object becomes concealed and escapes notice] (ibid., 428b8). Here, *remaining-concealed, being-veiled,* is explicitly specified as what determines the meaning of ψεῦδος and thus also that of "truth." Aristotle sees being-concealed as in itself positive, and it is no accident that the sense "truth" had for the Greeks was defined privatively on the level of its meaning and not just on a grammatical level. Beings in the how of their possible "as-what-definitions" are not simply there for one, but rather they are a "task." And beings in the how of their being-unveiled, i.e., ὄν ὡς ἀληθές [being as being true], need to be taken into true safekeeping and protected against possible loss. This is the meaning of ἕξεις, αἷς ἀληθεύει ἡ ψυχή [states of having in which the soul is true]. The highest and authentic of these states of having are σοφία and φρόνησις, since they each within their own domain of being hold the ἀρχαί [first principles] in true safekeeping. Ὄν ὡς ἀληθές is not the authentic being of true judgments and their domain of being or validity but rather beings themselves in the how (ὡς) of their unveiled being-meant. Beings are ἐν διανοίᾳ [in thought] as νοητόν [what is thought], i.e., they are in the "intellect" as the toward-which of its perceiving. The above interpretation of ἀληθές and ἀληθεύειν, which eliminates a series of mere pseudo-problems in interpreting their meaning, will be concretely demonstrated in detailed phenomenological analyses of *Met.* E 4, *De an.* Γ 5ff., *De interp., Met.* Δ 29, and above all *Met.* Θ 10.

Λόγος i.e., λέγειν, is the way νοεῖν [perceiving] actualizes itself, and as such it is διανοεῖσθαι [discursive thought], a perceiving in which what is meant is taken apart. That is, it is διαίρεσις [division]: ἐνδέχεται δὲ καὶ διαίρεσιν φάναι πάντα [it is possible to call all of these cases division as well as synthesis (*De an.* Γ 6, 430b3). Addressing and discussing, when it takes the form of synthetically defining, also can be described as a taking-apart and making ex-plicit.

The basic character of νοεῖν is perceiving. Νοῦς is the perceiving as such, i.e., is what generally makes possible and initially gives a toward-which for dealings to be directed toward and to do something with. It is τῷ πάντα ποιεῖν, ὡς ἕξις τις, οἷον τὸ φῶς [what produces all things, a state of having like light] (ibid., Γ 5, 430a15). That is, perceiving produces *everything* in that it is able to have everything available to it, doing so like light. Νους gives sight, a something, a "there" in any sense whatsoever. As the ἴδιον τοῦ ἀνθρώπου [what is proper to human being], νοῦς is—in its concrete actualization as ἐνέργεια [actuality] (i.e., literally as "being at work," namely, its own work [*Eth. Nic.* Z 2, 1139a18ff.], which is that of giving sight)—always νοῦς in the mode of concrete dealings with beings, i.e., gearing these beings in certain directions, producing them, handling them, and determining something about them. Insofar as νοῦς gives to dealings their sight, it also can be characterized as the illumination of these dealings, and such illumination has the sense of a true safekeeping of being. The genuine objects of νοῦς are what it perceives ἄνευ λόγου [without discourse], i.e., without the mode of addressing something with respect to its "as-what-definitions" (οὐ τὶ κατά τινος [it is not the assertion of something about something]) (*De an.* Γ 6, 430b28). In other words, they are the ἀδιαίρετα [indivisible objects], what in itself cannot be taken apart, what is not able to be explicated any further. As such, νοῦς brings to givenness objects purely as such in their unveiled "what," and as such it "can only be true": ἡ μὲν οὖν τῶν ἀδι-αιρέτων νόησις ἐν τούτοις, περὶ ἃ οὐκ ἔστι τὸ ψεῦδος [the perceiving of indivisible objects is found in those cases where falsehood is impossible] (ibid., 430a26). Here, "only" means "not yet at all" having the possibility of being-false and not "no longer" having this possibility. Νοῦς gives to all concrete discussing its possible about-which, and this about-which is itself not something the discussing as such would in the end be able to gain initial access to on its own. Rather, it is initially accessible only in ἐπαγωγή ("induction"), but this word needs to be understood purely in its literal sense, i.e., not in the sense of empirically gathering things together and understanding them collectively, but rather as a simple and direct leading to . . . , a letting be seen of. . . . Νοῦς is αἴσθησίς τις [perception of something], a perceiving which at any particular time initially gives the look of objects in a simple manner: ὁ νοῦς εἶδος εἰδῶν καὶ ἡ αἴσθησις εἶδος αἰσθητῶν [intellect is the form of forms and sense perception the form of sensible things] (ibid., Γ 8, 432a2). Just as the hand ὄργανόν ἐστιν ὀργάνων [is the tool of tools] (ibid.), i.e., just as it is the case that a tool used in some work first comes to its authentic being, namely, *doing work,* when it is taken in hand, so the *look* [Aussehen] of objects is seen only by means of νοῦς and "in" νοῦς as its toward-which. The look of objects as it were *looks out* [es sieht aus] at one by means of νοῦς. Insofar as a domain of objects itself poses the problem of gaining access to it in an explicit manner, and this not exclusively in the sense of defining it in theory, the "from-out-of-which" and "from-the-point-of-view-of-which" (ἀρχή) of one's λέγειν must be available in advance as having been unveiled. Insofar as its view is directed toward this ἀρχή, one's λέγειν makes it its point of departure, and indeed it keeps this point of departure "before its eyes" as its constant and fundamental orientation. As unveiled, such ἀρχαί are explicitly taken into true safekeeping in ἐπαγωγή (τῶν ἀρχῶν ἐπαγωγή [induction of the first principle]) (*Eth. Nic.* Z 3, 1139b31). Λείπεται νοῦν εἶναι τῶν ἀρχῶν [the remaining alternative is that it is intelligence that grasps the first principle] (ibid., Z 6,1141a7), i.e., the highest and authentic achievement of νοῦς consists in this bringing to givenness and true safekeeping of the ἀρχαί corresponding to each region of being (μάλιστα ἀληθεύει [it is most of all true]). The concrete modes of the actualizing of this authentic true safekeeping of being are σοφία and φρόνησις.

The kind of understanding consisting in a pure and simple looking at . . . brings into true safekeeping those beings whose "from-out-of-which" is, as they themselves are, in such a way that it necessarily always is what it is. In contrast, circumspection with regard to the care for and discussion of human well-being brings into true safekeeping those beings which, along with their "from-out-of-which," *can* in themselves *be otherwise.*

Both modes of true safekeeping temporalize and unfold themselves μετὰ λόγου [within discourse] [ibid., Z 4, 1140a4ff.] , i.e., in the discussing and expli-cating within which they are actualized. This explication is constitutive for them, insofar as they bring the ἀρχαί into view not as isolated things existing on their own but rather *such as they in fact are,* i.e., in their ownmost sense as ἀρχαί *for.* . . . As the for-which of the ἀρχαί and as needing to be defined, the for-which comes into true safekeeping along with the ἀρχαί. Λόγος is here an ὀρθὸς λόγος [correct discourse that hits its mark].[16] The discussing is a kind of discussing that moves in a certain direction and keeps to this direction in a pri-mordial manner, i.e., it has in each case an "end" it has fixed upon, and it is this end that is, in accord with the sense of the particular mode of true safekeeping in question, what is at issue for the illuminative explication of this true safekeeping and what it endeavors to arrive at. What φρόνησις brings into true safekeeping is the toward-which of going about those dealings that human life has with itself and the how of these dealings in their own being. These dealings are πρᾶξις [action]: i.e., how one handles oneself in dealings that are not productive but rather in each case simply perform *actions* in the precise sense of this term. Φρόνησις is the illumination of dealings that co-temporalizes and unfolds life in its *being.*

Our concrete interpretation of φρόνησις shows how these kinds of beings (actions) are constituted in it, namely, in terms of the καιρός [timeliness, the moment]. Handling oneself, i.e., performing actions in which one's care is directed toward human well-being, is always a handling oneself in the concrete how of concerned dealings with the world. Φρόνησις makes the circumstances of the actor accessible by keeping a firm hold on the οὗ ἕνεκα ("for the sake of which") [ibid., Z 2, 1139a32ff.] of an action, by making available its more pre-cisely defined "what-for," by grasping the "now" it is to be performed at, and by mapping out its how. Φρόνησις moves toward the ἔσχατον, "the ultimate par-ticular fact" [ibid., Z 8, 1142a25ff.], in which the concrete situation seen in these definite terms culminates at the particular time in question. What makes it possi-ble for φρόνησις to discuss and deliberate about what it does in its care for human well-being is the fact that it is primarily an αἴσθησις [ibid., 1142a28ff.], i.e., ulti-mately an immediate, overall view of the moment from the point of view of the end of action in question. As beings becoming unveiled and available through the ἀληθεύειν of φρόνησις, πρακτά [actions] are as a "*not yet* being such and such." As "not yet such and such" and, indeed, as the toward-which of concern, they are at the same time *already* such and such, i.e., insofar as they are a toward-which that belongs to a concrete readiness for dealings, the constitutive illumination of which is provided by φρόνησις. This "not-yet" and this "already" need to be understood in their "unity," i.e., on the basis of an original givenness, with reference to which they are particular explicata. We say "particular" because here the objects in question are placed under determinate aspects of movement. The concept of στέρησις [privation] is the category of the above-mentioned explicata. It is in this category that Hegelian dialectic is rooted within intellectual history.

᾽Αλήθεια πρακτική [practical truth] is nothing other than the whole unveiled moment (at the particular time) of factical life in the how of its decisive readiness for dealings with itself, and this how is within life's factical relation of concern to the world it is presently encountering. Φρόνησις is *epitactical* [ibid., Z 10, 1143a8]: it brings beings to givenness in their basic character that they are something one should be concerned with in this or that way, and within this point of view it provides and maintains each definite aspect of the moment (the particular how, what-for, to-what-extent, and why at the particular time). As epitactical illumination, it brings one's dealings into their basic orientation of a readiness for . . . , breaking out toward. . . . The kinds of toward-which one intends here, i.e., the beings within the moment, stand within the point of view of their significance for . . . , their being a concern one is able to attend to, their being something one needs to do right now. Φρόνησις is a looking κατὰ τὸ συμφέρον πρὸς τὸ τέλος [from the point of view of what is conducive to the end] (ibid., Z 9, 1142b32). Because it is the true safekeeping of the moment as a whole, circumspection in the authentic sense is what genuinely maintains the "for the sake of which" of action (i.e., its ἀρχαί) in true safekeeping. The ἀρχή always is what it is only in its concrete reference to the moment. In being seen and being seized upon, it is there for one in the moment and for it.

Our interpretation of φρόνησις also provides a concrete description of the method Aristotle uses to explicate this phenomenon, namely, descriptive comparison and elimination, which is done in accord with the different phenomenal points of view of being-related to . . . , the toward-which of the relation, and the how of the actualization of the relation. His description is always actualized by simultaneously holding the different ἕξεις [states of having] up against one another. Especially instructive in this regard is his analysis of εὐβουλία [deliberating well] (ibid., Z 9), which is the concrete way of actualizing the λέγειν immanent in φρόνησις. From out of the moment itself it brings into view for circumspection the how of the fitting way to set to work and authentically achieve the end in question.

However, not only does Aristotle's interpretation bring into relief the kinds of beings and the basic characteristics of their being that φρόνησις takes into

true safekeeping, but it also provides an initial understanding of the basic characteristics of being that φρόνησις *itself* has. Φρόνησις is a ἕξις, i.e., a how of
having available the true safekeeping of being. And as a ἕξις, it is a γινόμενον
[a having-become of the soul], which temporalizes and unfolds itself in life itself
as its own possibility, brings life into a particular state, and in a certain sense actually brings it about. Thus what shows itself in φρόνησις is a doubling of the
point of view into which Aristotle placed the human being and the being of life
and which became decisive within intellectual history for the fate of the categorial explication of the sense of the being of facticity. In circumspection, life is
there for itself in the concrete how of the with-which of going about its dealings.
However, and this is decisive, in Aristotle it is not on the basis of this phenomenon and not in a positive manner that the being of the with-which of dealings is
ontologically defined. Rather, it is defined simply in a formal manner as capable
of being otherwise than it is and thus not necessarily and always what it is. This
ontological definition gets actualized through a *negative* comparison with
another kind of being that is considered to be being in the *authentic* sense. In
accord with its basic characteristics, this kind of being is for its part not arrived
at through an explication of the being of human life as such. Rather, in its categorial structure, it springs from an *ontological radicalization of the idea of beings
that are moved,* and this is *carried out and actualized in a particular manner.* It is
the motion of *production* that is taken into forehaving as exemplary for these
kinds of beings and for the possibility of bringing into relief their structural sense.
Being is *being-finished-and-ready,* i.e., a kind of being in which motion has
arrived at *its end.* The being of life is seen as movement running its course in this
life, and indeed human life is in this movement when it has arrived at its end with
regard to its ownmost possibility of motion, namely, that of pure and simple perceiving. This movement is in the ἕξις of σοφία. In accord with *its* intentional
characteristics, pure understanding does not take into true safekeeping human
life in the how of its factical being. Rather, σοφία does not in any sense have
human life as its intentional toward-which. Human life is actually a being that is
precisely insofar as it can in each case be otherwise. For Aristotle, the being of life
must be looked at simply in terms of the pure temporalizing and unfolding of
σοφία as such, and this is due to the authentic kind of movement available in
σοφία. First, as pure and simple perceiving, νοῦς is in its genuine movement
when it has given up all concern for *gearing beings in certain directions and only*
perceives. Second, as this perceiving, it is a movement that, in having arrived at
its end insofar as what it is able to perceive in a pure and simple manner now
stands before its gaze, not only does not cease, but rather now—precisely as having arrived at its end—really *is motion* for the first time.

As a βάδισις εἰς [going toward], i.e., a being on the way to . . . *[Unter-
wegssein zu],* motion *[Bewegung]* is in accord with its sense motion that has not
reached its toward-which. As a presently going toward . . . , it is, for example,
learning, walking, or building a house. In accord with the basic character of hav-

ing-gone, the going is fundamentally different from this having-gone: ἕτερον καὶ κινεῖ καὶ κεκίνηκεν [what is moving is different from what has moved] (*Met.* Θ 6, 1048b32). In contrast, having-seen is at the same time as and along with the seeing. He has seen—in sight—only insofar as he is seeing just now. He has perceived just now precisely in his act of perceiving (νοεῖ καὶ νενόηκεν [is perceiving and has perceived]) (ibid.). Such movement is a kind of being that consists in both a temporalizing and unfolding of itself that takes itself in true safekeeping *and* a taking itself into true safekeeping that temporalizes and unfolds itself (ἅμα τὸ αὐτό [the same thing at the same time] (ibid., 1048b33). It is only νόησις as pure θεωρεῖν [contemplation] that satisfies the highest idea of pure movement. The authentic being of human beings temporalizes and unfolds itself in the pure actualization of σοφία as a tarrying alongside and pure perceiving of the ἀρχαί of those beings that always are, a tarrying that is *unworried* and always has time to spare (σχολή [leisure]). The basic character of the being of ἕξις and thus also of ἀρετή, i.e., the ontological structure of human being, is understood on the basis of an ontology of beings in the how of a particular kind of movement and on the basis of an ontological radicalization of the idea of *this* kind of movement.

Met. A 1–2

Our interpretation of these two chapters brings to light *three things* regarding our guiding problem of facticity:

1. The phenomenal structure of the intentional toward-which and relation found in going about those dealings (ἐπιστήμη) that simply look at . . . and define contexts having to do with the question of "why," as well as the phenomenal structure of the highest possible kind of temporalizing and unfolding of these dealings, namely, authentic understanding (σοφία), which looks at the ἀρχαί and brings them into true safekeeping. It is on the basis of this that concrete ἀρχή-research, which "physics" is understood to be, will be clarified in advance with regard to the *demarcation of its objects* that is drawn from the idea of pure understanding *in its starting point* (its specifically critical basis) and with regard to its method of categorial explication.

2. The *path* on which Aristotle gains all access to the phenomenon of pure understanding and the kind of interpretation he employs for this phenomenon. Both of these are characteristics of the fundamental meaning of "philosophy."

3. The basic character of the being of σοφία as such and its constitutive achievement for the being of human life.

These three points of view of our examination are intrinsically related, so that the structure of pure understanding will become intelligible simply on the basis of the fact that with regard to its being it is rooted in factical life and has a particular mode of *genesis in it.* This is why the real emphasis of our interpretation consists in bringing to light what was mentioned in point two above.

The question we ask is: How is that which Aristotle defines as research there for him *in its point of departure?* Where is it found and as what? How does Aristotle approach it, and how does he deal with it? From factical life and its own way of speaking in its dealings, Aristotle takes up a certain talk about σοφώτερον [being wiser], i.e., having more understanding than. . . . In other words, he focuses on the factical ways of *supposing-something-to-be-something* in which life interprets its own modes of dealings (i.e., ἐμπειρία [experience], τέχνη [art]): οἰόμεϑα [we consider], ὑπολαμβάνομεν [we assume], νομίζομεν [we usually think], ἡγούμεϑα [we hold] [*Met.* A 1, 981a13ff.]. He begins with a *comparative* expression. What becomes visible in it is what is at issue in life when it addresses something as σοφώτερον, namely, a μᾶλλον εἰδέναι [knowing more] [ibid., 981a31], i.e., a looking and seeing more. Factical life is anxiously concerned about developing its dealings, indeed, those original ones directed to routine tasks and producing, into a kind of dealings that always has available to it a looking and seeing more in the sense of that which has been proposed at any particular time in its dealings. It is in this looking and seeing more that the "look" of the with-which of dealings becomes visible and indeed not as an object to be defined in theory but rather as the toward-which of that concern which gears beings in certain directions. The "look" (of an illness, for example) is characterized by a "why" (αἴτιον) for the concern of those dealings directed to certain routine tasks (ἰατρεύειν, "doctoring" [ibid., 981a18ff.]). The why originally has a "practical" sense.

In its tendency toward this looking and seeing more, factical life eventually gives up the care of directing itself to routine tasks. The with-which of those dealings directed to routine tasks changes into the toward-which of a *mere* looking at. . . . The look of an object comes to be viewed and explicated with respect to those relations in its why that characterize the what of this object itself. Here the tendency of caring has displaced itself into a looking at . . . for its own sake. This looking at . . . becomes an autonomous kind of dealings and as such the toward-which of a unique kind of concern.

In Aristotle's interpretation of the meaning of looking and seeing *[Hinsehen]* more, a meaning *first put forward* by life *itself,* is also found the ultimate direction he takes toward what is μάλιστα εἰδέναι [the knowledge that sees most] [ibid., A 2, 982a30ff.]. He accompanies factical life in its own direction of interpretation and adopts from it the ways of supposing-something-to-be-something in which it addresses a human being as σοφόν [wise], i.e., as someone who has authentic understanding. His interpretation of these modes of addressing yields that meaning of σοφία all can agree with: someone who has authentic understanding is concerned with the *ultimate viewpoints* [Hinsichten] in which beings can in themselves be defined. These viewpoints have as their toward-which the first "from-out-of-whiches" and "from-the-points-of-view-of-which" with respect to which beings need to be initially unveiled, if they are indeed to be taken into true safekeeping in a fitting manner in the concrete addressing, discussing, and defining undertaken in research. Thus Aristotle arrives at an understanding of the meaning of philosophy *through an interpretation of a factical movement of care with respect to its ultimate tendency*. However, these dealings consisting in a pure and simple looking at . . . prove to be such that they cannot any longer really see in their toward-which that very life in which they are. Insofar as these dealings, as pure understanding, still temporalize and unfold life, they do this only through *their* kind of movement.

The concrete possibility of actualizing this pure understanding lies in freeing oneself from the concerns and apprehensions of going about those dealings directed to routine tasks. This is the how in which life, with a view to one of its basic tendencies, makes a sojourn. Θεωρεῖν is the purest kind of movement life has available to it. It is due to it that life is something "divine." But in Aristotle the idea of the divine did not grow out of an explication of an object to which access was first gained in a founding religious experience. Rather, ϑεῖον [divine] is a term for the *highest* character of being coming to light in an ontological radicalization of the idea of beings that are moved. The ϑεῖον is νόησις νοήσεως [thinking of thinking] [ibid., Λ 9, 1074b35] only because of the fact that with regard to the basic character of its being, i.e., of its movement, such perception *satisfies most purely the idea of being-moved as such*. This divine being *must* be pure perceiving, i.e., it must be free of *any emotional relation* to its toward-which. The "divine" is incapable of jealousy, not because it is absolute goodness and love but rather because in its being as pure movement it can neither hate nor love at all.

But this means that the *forehaving* of being that is decisive here, namely, beings in their motion, and the particular ontological explication of *these* beings are the motivational sources of the basic ontological structures that later decisively influenced the notion of divine being in the specifically Christian sense (*actus purus* [pure act]), the inner life of the divine (the Trinity), and thereby also the being of God's relation to man, as well as consequently the sense of man's own being itself. Christian theology, the philosophical "speculation" standing under its influence, and the anthropology always also growing out of these contexts all *speak in borrowed categories that are foreign to their own domains of being*.

That nonetheless precisely Aristotle's ontology of the soul provided support for the temporalizing and unfolding of a rich, far-reaching interpretation of the being of life within the Christian life-world is due to the fact that it was within his concept of motion and precisely by means of it that the decisive phenomenal character of intentionality came into view and consolidated a particular direction of looking.

Phys. A, B, Γ 1–3

The phenomenon of motion is ontologically explicated according to its categories in that kind of research having been handed down to us under the title of

Aristotle's *Physics*. Our interpretation needs to bring to light the following things right within the phenomenal movement of this research: the founding experience at work in it, i.e., the way its object has initially been given (κινούμενον [what is moving]); the points of view into which the object has been placed; and the explicata having grown out of the analysis that looks at the object from these points of view.

The above research is characterized as ἀρχή-research, i.e., it has to bring into true safekeeping the "from-out-of-whiches" and "from-the-points-of-view-of-which" (ἀρχαί) on the basis of which the κινούμενον comes to be seen. But if these ἀρχαί are to be capable of achieving what they are supposed to in accord with their sense, they themselves must be drawn from the phenomenal content of the objects in question. The ἀρχαί of beings are *not there* for those concerned dealings and their circumspection in which one goes about gearing beings in certain directions. This concern and apprehension lives within other points of view, namely, within those directed to the immediately encountered world of its dealings. Within the scope of going about dealings in the concern of factical life, the "from-out-of-whiches" of beings are as such concealed. The primordial sense of the "concept of truth" proves to be at work in *Phys.* A 1 and indeed in Aristotle's initial approach to the problem of research in physics.

'Αρχή-research is *research into the question of access.* As such, (1) it has to secure its *forehaving,* i.e., its thematic domain of objects in the how of the basic phenomenal character of their content, and (2) it has to work out its *foreconception,* i.e., supply the points of view in which the actualization of its explication of its domain of being is supposed to maintain itself. The *initial approach* of this research is *critique* and more precisely fundamental critique concerned with principles. Aristotle's interpretation makes clear why such research into the question of access must necessarily take a critical approach: namely, because all research moves within a particular level of some pregiven interpretation of life and within certain pregiven ways of discussing the world. What is still there and at work in the facticity of Aristotle's own research is the how in which the "ancient physicists" had already seen, addressed, and discussed "nature."

Accordingly, the critical question Aristotle's ἀρχή-research poses to former times runs as follows: Were those beings that were thought of as φύσις [nature] brought into the forehaving of research in such a way that their decisive phenomenal character, namely, motion (a character previous research always also had in mind in one way or another when it addressed beings in the ways it did), was taken into true safekeeping and explicated in a primordial manner? Or was the way traditional research sought to gain access to the domain of being in question such that this research moved from the outset within "theories" and thematic principles that not only were not drawn this domain of being itself but blocked almost all access to it?

The sense of Aristotle's critical stance consists in posing this question. His critique is positive in a distinctive sense, and it is based explicitly on a decisive founding experience: namely, "we assume from the outset <ἡμῖν ὑποκείσθω> that there are beings in motion" [*Phys.* A 2, 185a13]. These beings in this how are accessible in a plain and simple manner in ἐπαγωγή. The first book of the *Physics* exhibits a very tight structure, and the first stage of its critique, namely, that of the Eleatics, makes sense only on the basis of its concrete task of research into the question of access and the necessity of a critical approach here.

According to Aristotle's explicit comments, the Eleatics in fact do not "really" belong in any sense within the thematic compass of his critique [ibid., 184b27]. Their foreconception, i.e., their theory of being, was such that it, in principle, blocked access to beings as beings which are moved, and thus access to φύσις. The Eleatics were thereby not in a position to catch sight of the basic phenomenon in the subject matter taken up as the theme of research in physics (namely, motion) and to allow this motion itself to provide the decisive points of view for concrete inquiry into it and for concretely defining it.

Aristotle draws the Eleatics into the discussion in spite of their "not belonging there" not, as Bonitz thinks, to have an easy target for refutation but rather so that *in this critique of them he can secure the horizon that is decisive for looking at all subsequent problems in physics:* namely, that of λόγος, i.e., the κινούμενον as λεγόμενον. Here Aristotle points out the following things. What has been taken up as a theme of research, i.e., the κινούμενον, is as an object of ἐπιστήμη one that is addressed and discussed: ἐπιστήμη and σοφία (as νοῦς καὶ ἐπιστήμη [intelligence and scientific understanding] (*Eth. Nic.* Z 6, 1141a5) are μετὰ λόγου. These beings must be approached initially within their ontological structure that is constituted in advance in such a way that they are in principle always the "toward-which" of an addressing and discussing, i.e., they are meant in the how of their "as-characteristics." Beings are always categorially something *as* such and such, and this means that their sense of being is in principle *manifold* (having more than one sense). What is prescribed in an a priori manner in the sense of λέγειν is that everything addressed is addressed *as* something. The idea of the ἀρχή, of the from-"out-of-which" *for* something, i.e., the "point-of-view as in regard to and *for* . . . ," becomes categorially impossible if being is not articulated as having more than one sense, i.e., if the science of physics approaches its domain of objects with the Eleatic thesis, ἕν τὰ πάντα [all things are one] [*Phys.* A 2, 185a23].

In an intermediary set of reflections in which we provide an interpretation of the decisive ontological contexts in the doctrinal poem of Parmenides, it is shown that Parmenides was the first to have brought the being of beings into view, though in ontological terms things remained at this first "impression of being." With this first, though decisive view, ontological seeing was already at its end. The idea that everything experienced is in the how of being-an-object became of such importance for the domain of objects in question that this being-an-object was itself in fact thought of as being that "really" is, and from this point of view its sense was decided in a negative manner by exciding all other possible definitions of being. Νοεῖν as a pure and simple meaning something and φάναι [speaking], i.e., addressing, were at first viewed in the same way and indeed in their unity with being. The ἀλήθεια operative here was not, however, brought into relief with regard to the basic phenomenal structures that are primary and decisive for it.

The first stage of Aristotle's critique endeavors to show that if ἀρχή-research wants to gain access to the domain of objects that initially should be given for it and to the proper points of view for this domain, it must work out the ontological constitution of this domain by taking a look at the basic phenomenon of motion. It is simply an internal consequence of the formulation of this problem that in the context of his critique of the Eleatics, Aristotle comes across the problem of ὁρισμός [definition], i.e., the simple explicative definition of an object in the what of its beingness. The object in question here is that phenomenon of motion which Aristotle wishes to explicate.

Proceeding from this first stage of Aristotle's critique, which secures the general horizon of research, our interpretation shows how he interrogates the opinions and explications found in the "ancient natural philosophers" with respect to how far they got in allowing the phenomenon of motion to speak for itself, and how they were always in principle impeded in their explication of this phenomenon because of their preconceived theories about the sense of being. Through this interpretation, it will become clear that behind the seemingly formalistic question, how many ἀρχαί should be posited with respect to φύσει ὄντα [natural beings], and what are they, there is concealed a question that Aristotle always considers, namely, to what extent is motion itself being seen and genuinely explicated on the basis of itself? If it is seen and explicated on the basis of itself, then there is necessarily *more than one* "from-out-of-which" and "from-the-point-of-view-of-which" in its categorial structure and just as necessarily *not more than three*. It is in Chapter [7][17] that Aristotle offers a positive explication of the phenomenon of motion, doing this at first solely in the context of the problem of λόγος that has been introduced, and in fact we need to *look back* from this chapter to the preceding ones. The "fundamental category" of στέρησις pervading Aristotle's ontology grows out of the explications that he pursues in Chapter 7, i.e., out of his explication of a particular kind of addressing of movement which is viewed in a definite manner. Characteristically, the "coming to be of a statue from bronze" [ibid., A 7, 190a25] (i.e., in the movement of going about the dealings of *production*) plays the role of an example in problems directed to the κίνησις [movement] of φύσει ὄντα.

The problem of the ἀρχή is approached from another direction of looking when we come to Book Two of the *Physics*. The question raised here is, what are the possibilities of *being-interrogated* (αἴτιον, "why") in theory that are motivated by the content of φύσει ὄντα and their fundamental categorial structure? Our interpretation shows how the notion of the "four causes" springs from the problem of ontology that has already been sketched out. But at the same time this book (Chapters 4–6) is of decisive importance with respect to the problem of facticity as such. It is shown that under the headings of τύχη [chance], αὐτόματον [spontaneity] (terms utterly untranslatable when it comes to their authentic meaning), Aristotle ontologically explicates the "historical" movement of factical life, i.e., the movement of "what happens and can happen in such and such a way to someone everyday" [ibid., B 8, 198b36]. These ontological analyses have to this day not only remained unsurpassed but have not even been understood and utilized for what they are. They have been treated as an awkward and no longer usable supplement to the definition of the "real causes," though these causes themselves clearly bear witness to the fact that they are *conditioned* by a particular approach to the problems in question.

In Book Three, Aristotle initiates his properly thematic analysis of the phenomenon of motion. Our interpretation (of Chapters 1–3 above all), which must contend with almost insurmountable textual difficulties (Simplicius [395, 20][18] complained about this early on), can really only be laid out when we work through the concrete contexts of this book. What is decisive for Aristotle is to show that the phenomenon of motion cannot be understood in a fundamental, categorial manner by using the traditional categories of "being" and "non-being" ("being-different," "being-unequal") [ibid., Γ 2, 201b21] that had until that time been made available in ontology. The phenomenon of motion provides of itself the structures that are primordial and ultimate in it: namely, δύναμις [potentiality], i.e., the in each case particular availability of . . . ; ἐνέργεια [actuality], i.e., the putting to work of this availability; and ἐντελέχεια [the fulfillment in which something has reached its end], i.e., the maintaining (in true safekeeping) of this availability that has been put to work.

The second part of our investigations is focused on an interpretation of *Met.* Z, H and Θ. What is shown here is how Aristotle develops the fundamental problem of beingness through a specifically executed explication of what is addressed in a particular manner in λόγος as such (and in terms of the forehaving at work here, this λόγος is at the same time the look of something being moved in some way, i.e., of something having arisen from motion [κίνησις—ποίησις—πρᾶξις]), as well as how, on the basis of this, he arrives at an ontological formulation of the "categories" of δύναμις and ἐνέργεια, which are, along with his categories in the narrower sense, constitutive for the being "of beings."

Aristotle's "ethics" is then to be placed into this ontological horizon, so that this "ethics" is seen as the explication of beings in the sense of human beings, i.e., human life and its movement. This is done in such a way that we first provide an interpretation of *De anima* with respect to its ontological and logical structure, and indeed this itself is carried out on the broader basis of an explication of the domain of the being of *life* as a particular kind of movement (i.e., on the basis of an interpretation of *De motu animalium*). What is shown here is how "intentionality" comes into view for Aristotle and indeed as "objective," i.e., as a how of the movement of life that is somehow "noetically" illuminated when it goes about its dealings. Beings in their basic aspect of being-moved, i.e., their "being out for" and "going toward," constitute the forehaving and condition that makes it possible for us to bring intentionality into relief in accord with how it becomes explicit in Aristotle and for its part makes visible the basic characteristic of λόγος. We will then for the first time have at our disposal the concrete motivational basis allowing us to understand the final stage that Aristotle reached in the problems of ontology and logic. What this final stage is rooted in will be exhibited in an interpretation of *Met. Γ, E, B,* and *I* and in an interpretation of *De interp.,* the *Prior Analytics,* and the *Posterior Analytics.* What becomes clear on the basis of these interpretations is the extent to which a particular ontology of a particular domain of being and the logic of a particular kind of addressing came to be regarded, in consequence of the inclination toward falling found in interpreting, as *the one and true ontology* and *the one and true* logic, and as such came to dominate in a decisive manner not only the history of ontology and logic but also that of spirit itself, i.e., the history of human existence.

The origin of the "categories" does not lie in λόγος as such. Nor are these "categories" read off from "things." Rather, they are the basic modes of a particular kind of addressing of a particular domain of objects that are maintained in forehaving *in terms of their "look"* and consist of those objects of dealings one can be concerned with and directed to in terms of routine tasks. As such, they are the "phyla" of the sense of the as-what-characteristics in terms of which these objects are able to be addressed [for this and the following, see *Met.* Θ 10, E 2–4, Δ 7]. They are found together with δυνάμει and ἐνεργείᾳ ὄν [being possible and being actual], since, in growing out of the what of objects and being for it, they are constitutive for the being of objects in the sense of states of "affairs" *["Tuns"-Gegenstände]* (ὄν ὡς πρᾶγμα [being in the sense of things]). In contrast, ὄν ὡς ἀληθές [being in the sense of being true], i.e., truth as a characteristic of beings, as the how of their unveiled being-there as they are in themselves, is not constitutive for the πρᾶγμα [thing], and yet it is the κυριώτατον [being in the strictest sense] (*Met.* Θ 10, 1051b1), i.e., what is decisive, what leads the way, with respect to gaining access to beings in the mode of a simple perceiving of them and an explicative defining of them. Ὄν κατὰ συμβεβηκός [being in the sense of accidental attributes], i.e., being in the how of being-found-along-with, is as little constitutive for beings as ὄν ὡς ἀληθές. For the primordial sense of being is *being-produced* [Hergestelltsein]. Such beings are originally there, as what they are, only for a productive kind of dealings, only that these dealings now no longer make use of them, in that they are able to take up the now finished and ready objects within different and no longer original points of view for caring about them.

The being of a house is being as being-built *[Erstelltsein]* (οὐσία γινομένη, ποιηθεῖσα [being that is coming into being, is being produced].[19] Thus the sense of being is for Aristotle a *very particular sense of being,* not the vague, indifferent sense of reality in general. Here being is relative to production, i.e., to the circumspection (procedures) illuminating these dealings. As a consequence of this sense of authentic being having been taken as the fundamental starting point, the modes of the look and the encountering of the objects of dealings in which these objects are given in terms of their full significance in the environing world (e.g., the being-comfortable of the house, its being-pleasant, being-conveniently-located, and being-well-lit [ibid., E 2, 1026b8–9]) must appear as *a mere being-found-along-with* and as ἐγγύς τι μὴ ὄν—ὥσπερ ὀνόματι μόνον [something closely akin to non-being—as if it were a mere name] (ibid., 1026b22, 1026b14). But the fact that Aristotle was able to bring this being-found-along with into relief as a separate sense of being is at the same time the strongest expression of the fact that he did take up the environing world as it is fully experienced, that he did see the sorts of things here that are found along with . . . , only that—and this happened already with the term he used for it—all of this was ontologically interpreted on the basis of the guiding theme of a particular sense of being that had been worked out and refined as the decisive one. For its part, this sense of being had its provenance in the environing world as it is originally given in experience, but then, and this is found even in Aristotle himself, it lost the sense of this provenance due to the pressure exerted by the kind of ontology worked out and refined. In the course of the subsequent development of ontological research, it fell into the averageness of having its vague traditional meaning of "reality" or "actuality" and as such then provided the starting point for the problems of epistemology. The "objectivity" of the theoretical definition of objects in the sense of "nature," an "objectivity" that in turn first grew out of this starting point for epistemology, then took the lead regarding the problem of the sense of being.

Chapter Ten

WILHELM DILTHEY'S RESEARCH AND THE STRUGGLE FOR A HISTORICAL WORLDVIEW (1925)

CHARLES BAMBACH, TRANSLATOR

CONTENTS

See pp. 8–9, 32 for bibliographic and other background information on this ten-part series of lectures from Heidegger's Marburg Period, delivered in Kassel the year before the composition of *Being and Time*.

I

The theme of these lectures will appear somewhat remote and unfamiliar perhaps, but it involves a fundamental problem pervading the whole of Western philosophy: the problem of the sense of human life. What kind of reality is life? In terms of the question of what reality is, immediate reality is taken to be the world or nature. Yet always already included in such a question is the question of the being of human being itself. The discovery of the authentic sense of the being and reality of human life has a muddled history. Only in recent times has it arrived at a basis so that it can be investigated in a scientific, philosophical manner. In the history of this question, the work of Dilthey has a central place. At the same time, in conjunction with this question, there has been an upheaval in the way philosophical questions have been formulated, a crisis of philosophy as science. And philosophy is not the only science in crisis. All sciences and groups of sciences are undergoing a great revolution of a productive kind that has opened up new modes of questioning, new possibilities, and new horizons. In physics, there is the appearance of the theory of relativity; in mathematics, where the foundations have become questionable, one speaks of a crisis of foundations. In biology, attempts are being made to overcome mechanism; in the historical *[historischen]* sciences, questions are raised concerning our understanding of historical *[geschichtlichen]* reality and the possibilities of interpreting the past.[1] Even in theology (i.e., Protestant theology) a rejection of mere history of religion is taking place, and theologians are beginning to reflect on their theme and method in a new way. Philosophy also stands within this general crisis, a crisis whose roots go back before the war. It develops out of the continuity of science itself, and this is the guarantee for the earnestness and reliability of its upheavals.

First we have to make clear what kind of question is being raised in the theme of these lectures. What does "historical *[historische]* worldview" mean? What is a "struggle for" a historical worldview? Who is Dilthey, and what does he have to do with all of this?

To begin, we address the theme, method of treatment, and structure of the following discussions.

HISTORICAL WORLDVIEW:

What is the meaning of this expression, and how did it arise as a problem? Worldview: the expression is first used in the eighteenth century. In itself, the term is ambiguous, not really reflecting what it literally means: having a view of the world, of nature. At the same time, it also means knowledge about life and one's own being in the world. From this knowledge are formed certain posited goals that regulate one's actions. In a worldview, a certain attitude thus manifests itself. A worldview is not merely a theoretical form of knowledge but a practical attitude about the world and one's own existence that is not momentary but enduring. It is formed and appropriated by human beings themselves. This possibility has only come to light since the Renaissance, with the freedom from religious ties. In another sense, one also can speak of a natural worldview that all human beings as such already also bring with them through milieu, aptitude, education, etc. This is a prescientific worldview in contrast to a scientific one, i.e., a position formed on the basis of theoretical-scientific knowledge.

A *historical* worldview is one in which knowledge of history determines one's understanding of the world and Dasein. It is grounded in the historical character of the development of the world and of human Dasein. Here *struggle* means a struggle for the attainment of such a position from out of one's knowledge of the historical character of the world and Dasein. Its concern is to make these decisive historical forces primary for the shaping of beliefs and the consciousness of Dasein. That is only possible where history as our own reality has entered human consciousness. This is not something self-evident. Primitive peoples have lived a long time without history *[Geschichte]*, as we ourselves have. The Greeks no doubt already had a certain experience of the historical. However, knowledge of change is hardly the same thing as historical *[historisches]* consciousness. The latter is tied to certain presuppositions. In humanism and the Reformation, there arose a certain historical critique and debate with Catholicism. One sought to return to the pure forms of Christian life, something that led one back into history. On the other hand, there developed a national consciousness among individual peoples that led to a push for knowing one's own origins. But all of this still cannot be called "historical consciousness." Only when history is so viewed that one's own reality also is seen within a historical context can it be said that life knows about the history in which it stands, that a historical consciousness is found there. One's own epoch is experienced as a situation in which the present itself stands, and this not merely in the sense of standing over against the past but rather simultaneously in the sense of a situation in which the future will be decided or has been decided. Thus the awakening and vigilance of historical consciousness is not something self-evident or pregiven in life. It is much more a task to be developed.

In a historical *[historische]* worldview, historical *[geschichtliche]* knowing becomes the principle for viewing all human things. History becomes universal history. Here the main question is: What is the sense of history, and what existential goals can be derived from it for the future? The derivation of life-goals from history has developed since the eighteenth century in Kant, Herder, Humboldt, and Hegel. The fundamental view here was ultimately that of a historical development whereby humanity overcomes its dependency and arrives at freedom (for Hegel, the humanity of European culture is embodied in the state). In this way the path was cleared for actual historical research, i.e., for the sciences that open up history theoretically and scientifically on the basis of sources secured in critical work (as in Wolff, Niebuhr, Savigny, Bopp, Bauer, Schleiermacher, Ranke, Jacob Grimm).

During the period 1780–1840, creative forces were unleashed that today we can no longer imagine. Then, with the collapse of Hegelian philosophy, reflection on historical reality subsided. What remained was positive, systematic work on history, and yet the question of the sense of historical being died out. Now it was the natural sciences that again took the actual lead in the formation of a worldview. When philosophy once again took stock of itself in the 1860s, this had the form of a historical return to Kant as the author of the three critiques and especially as the author of *The Critique of Pure Reason,* which offered a theory of the mathematical natural sciences. Philosophy was now understood as epistemology, a move carried out by the Marburg school of neo-Kantians. Philosophy no longer attempted to master the individual sciences, or to go beyond their results, but limited itself to a single domain of its own: theory of science. In his first critique, Kant had provided only a theory of the mathematical natural sciences. In the meantime, the historical sciences had developed. Thus the task at hand was to extend Kant's critique, i.e., to place a theory of the historical sciences alongside it. With the retreat from this way of formulating the question at the end of the nineteenth century and with the growth of concrete historical research, the need to raise the question of the sense of historical being became even more pressing. The question of formal foundations was superseded by that of material foundations (Troeltsch following upon Windelband and Rickert, who received their impulses from Dilthey; Spengler also derives from this position).

Modern philosophy of history owes its impulses and initiatives to Dilthey. Yet modern theory has not really understood the authentic tendencies of Dilthey's thought; in fact, it has seen to it that these tendencies have remained buried to this day.

We now will attempt to grasp the sense of the historical worldview in a more precise manner, i.e., we need to characterize this knowledge of the historical being of the world. The development of such knowledge is the task of philosophy and the historical sciences themselves. The possibility of a historical worldview is based on the attainment of clarity and transparency concerning the human condition. We need to make this presupposition very clear to ourselves. The struggle for a historical worldview is not played out in debates about the historical conception of the world but rather in those about the sense of historical being itself. And here we are speaking of the labors of Dilthey's research. We need to examine how philosophical questioning gains the transparency necessary for developing a historical worldview. We are raising the question: Which reality is historical in the authentic sense? And what does historical mean?

We will at first follow Dilthey on his paths of inquiry. It was Dilthey who, from the 1860s (along with Count Yorck), had a truly radical awareness of this problem. To gain an intimate understanding of Dilthey's work means that we ourselves question, that we ourselves formulate the questions that moved Dilthey. We need to ask whether he solved the problem and whether he at all possessed the philosophical resources necessary to do so. Thus we will be questioning beyond him, and indeed we will do this on the basis of phenomenology (Dilthey characterized the *Logical Investigations* as an epochal work).[2] We will see that the authentic historical reality is human Dasein itself, and we also will see what kinds of structures human Dasein possesses. The fundamental character of Dasein is nothing other than time. On the basis of this character of time, we will make clear that human being is historical. As we pursue this question of time, we will encounter another problem of time in the theory of relativity and will attempt to make clear its philosophical meaning. From the historicity of Dasein, we will return to Dilthey in order to inquire, in a critical way, into the whole of his work.

What we should achieve in all of this is a certain relation to the things themselves, in which we see that these things are things that concern human beings. Our aim is to awaken the consciousness that truly productive work exists in the modern sciences, and that there is no cause for resignation. Such work is done without window dressing or any racket, and because of this science is exemplary for the existence of our entire nation.

II

Outwardly, Dilthey's life was uneventful. What was present was his inner life and that which was alive in each of this philosopher's questions. That was able to express itself in his works and writings which, according to their aim, promoted the thematic treatment of specific problems. We will first present an external sketch of his life, then his "intellectual world," then the determining forces in his intellectual life, and lastly his works.

Born in 1833 as the son of a pastor, Dilthey first studied theology and later philosophy and the historical sciences (1850s and early 1860s). He was appointed to Basel in 1867, to Breslau in 1871, and to Berlin in 1882. Member of the Academy [of the Sciences] in 1887. Died on October 1, 1911 in the Tyrol. Sketches of his life in his student years in the diaries, *Ethica* (1854–1864), deal mostly with scholarly issues.[3] In his years as a university lecturer, involvement in the "Suicide Club" (Scherer, Grimm, Erdmannsdörffer, Usener). Correspondence with Yorck during the period 1877–1897, marked by a rare philosophical friendship.[4] Dilthey often wished for a quieter existence than the Berliners had. He was not one who easily finished his work. Rather, through the pressure of the Academy, he was forced to publish things he otherwise never would have.

Intellectual life was the only real existence for Dilthey. We will consider first his inner growth and impulses, then the determining forces stemming from history and the present. Dilthey was a theologian in the beginning and was thus provided with specific horizons and an openness for Dasein that remained effective later on. For him, theology had a relation to philosophy and to history, namely, the history of Christianity and its fundamental fact, the life of Jesus. Dilthey planned a history of Western Christianity, but this plan and his whole program of theological studies fell apart during his study of the Middle Ages. In the struggle between faith and knowledge, Dilthey sided with knowledge and this-worldliness. He renounced all closure and finality and was everywhere satisfied only with being able to explore, only with researching and "dying on the journey."[5] However, he took with him from theology essential impulses for understanding human life and its history. His passion remained open for the scientific investigation of human life.

This helps us understand his reaction to the contemporary forces of his time: positivism, the Historical School, the philosophy of Kant (as seen essentially through the eyes of Schleiermacher).

French *positivism* offered a critique of metaphysics; it sought a purely scientific form of knowledge and coincided with what we today call "sociology." What Dilthey took up in a positive way from this movement was its critique of metaphysics and its stress on things here below. But positivism misunderstood the life of the mind and its history. It sought to define mind as nature, and so it seemed to Dilthey that his task was to preserve the unique character of the world of the mind. He adopted a certain tendency from positivism, namely, that "one would not want to be hoodwinked by anything,"[6] but he rejected its desire to conceive of the mind as a product of nature. He took up positivism only as a principle of knowledge for defining things from out of themselves.

The *Historical School:* here Dilthey learned to think historically and experienced the living, effective force of the history of the mind, an impression that remained fresh for him during his whole life (see his "Seventieth Birthday Speech").[7] The world of history and his vital experience of historical research were the foundation for Dilthey's formulation of the question of history.

Dilthey approached *Kant's philosophy* basically in terms of the view that it formulated the question of the essence of knowledge. But, because of the influence of Schleiermacher, Dilthey saw knowledge within the context of the *whole* of life. The period of the 1860s was decisive, not in the sense of a neo-Kantianism but rather precisely because of Dilthey's tendency to understand the human condition on the basis of a full comprehension of human being. Thus Dilthey never shared the extreme attitude against Hegel that was prevalent among his contemporaries. He knew how to esteem Hegel's positive contribution long before neo-Hegelianism.

Dilthey remained open for everything of substance and closed his mind to all empty and groundless thinking that turns on its own axis and never engages the things themselves. This enabled him to formulate and foster in a new way a fundamental problem in philosophy. The effect of his work on others was at first slight. Only a few gifted people availed themselves of Dilthey's initiatives. One of them was Windelband, whose "Rectorial Address" of 1894[8] rendered Dilthey's inner aims superficial and turned them on their head. Following in Windelband's footsteps, Rickert attempted to delimit the natural sciences and the historical sciences over against each other in a wholly empty and formal way. This reception was tied just as much to the way his works were published. Only two major works were published in his lifetime, and they both stopped at volume one: *The Life of Schleiermacher*[9] and *Introduction to the Human Sciences.*[10] Besides this, he wrote essays, "Contributions To . . . ," "Ideas Concerning . . . ," "Attempts At. . . ." Everything preliminary, incomplete, and on the way. As a result, his work was ignored for a long time, and yet positive discoveries such as his cannot be repressed for long. Today we have the possibility of grasping the positive effects of his work—not merely repeating what he said but questioning beyond his work in a new way.

III

What sort of basic question did Dilthey formulate? What resources did he possess for answering it? We will attempt to understand Dilthey's formulation of his question by looking at the context of his own works and by contrasting it with the approaches of his contemporaries. We saw that all of his works are incomplete. So we must understand that any characterization of the contents of those works is impossible without recognizing the basic question raised by Dilthey. Thus at first it is only with an eye to this question that we will provide the historical sequence of his works.

Dissertation: "On Schleiermacher's Ethics."[11] We can already see that Dilthey's theme is not a theoretical one but rather a problem concerning the practical situation of human being. In the same period, he wrote the essay for a prize competition: "On Schleiermacher's Hermeneutics," i.e., on the scientific theory of historical understanding and interpretation of texts. It was Schleiermacher who first worked out this theory as a universal theory of understanding. Hermeneutics is a discipline that will acquire fundamental significance at the present time and in the future.[12] Dilthey never published this work, although he later used a portion of it in a *Festschrift* for Sigwart: "The Rise of Hermeneutics."[13] The connection here with history is clear, for history as a science is an interpretation of sources that have been secured for it in advance by the critical-historical work of philology. In 1864, he wrote the habilitation thesis: "Attempt at an Analysis of Moral Consciousness."[14] Here again Dilthey chose a theme that forced him to grapple with the problem of the being of human beings. He also wrote essays on Novalis, Hölderlin, and Goethe *(Poetry and Experience)*.[15] These writings, which appear to depart from Dilthey's other works, have their own special place in his corpus. In them an attempt is made to understand concrete historical individuals from their intellectual core ("from their center," as one says in the George circle). During this period, Dilthey also wrote about empirical psychology, and in 1870 he published his biography of Schleiermacher. In 1875, he wrote essays that contain the central thoughts of his *Introduction to the Human Sciences:* "Concerning the Study of the History of the Sciences of Man, Society, and the State."[16] The *Introduction to the Human Sciences* has the subtitle *Attempt at Laying a Foundation for the Sciences of Society and History.* Book One gives an overview of the individual human sciences and poses the problem of the foundation for this group of sciences. Book Two deals with the topic of metaphysics as the foundation of these sciences, its dominance as well as its decline. Human beings cannot be understood as historical beings if they are classified within the structures of the world as a part of nature. Volume Two of this book was never written, hence the book ends with a discussion of the medieval era.[17] In a series of essays, Dilthey made further ventures in this direction toward an anthropology: "Conception and Analysis of Human Being . . . ,"[18] "The Natural System of the Human Sciences."[19] Anthropology is for Dilthey a kind of historical research whose goal is to understand how the human being was viewed in the past. "Contributions to the Solution of the Question of Our Belief in the External World," written in 1890,[20] raised the question: How is one to characterize the fundamental relation of the human being to the world? "Ideas Concerning a Descriptive and Analytic Psychology" written in 1894 (will concern us more closely later).[21] Following this, Dilthey wrote "Contributions to the Definition of Human Individuality."[22] At the same time, he continued work on the biography of Schleiermacher, on the "History of German Idealism," and on "The History of the Young Hegel."[23] "Studies on the Foundations of the Human Sciences" in 1905 revealed a new current in Dilthey's thinking.[24] Perhaps this can be traced back to the effect of Husserl's *Logical Investigations,* which Dilthey read at that time and called an epochal work, holding seminars on it for years with his students. In his foundational work of 1907, "The Essence of Philosophy," Dilthey reflected on his own activity as a philosopher.[25] "The Structure of the Historical World in the Human Sciences" was written in 1910.[26]

What was the inner connection in this diversified productivity? Not a conceptual system but rather a vital questioning after the sense of history and human being. *Questioning* is a kind of searching in the realm of knowledge that has as its goal the discovery and defining of reality. In every question something is *interro-gated* [be*fragt*], and it is interrogated from a determinate point of view, i.e., what is interrogated is questioned *about* [ab*gefragt*] something. Thus to formulate a question requires that one have an originary intuition of the object that one is interrogating. Now where does one find the object "history," so that one might read off it the sense of its being, i.e., read off its historical being? It is the above sense of questions that also constitutes the sense of a scientific crisis. Every crisis is defined by the fact that previous concepts begin to totter, that phenomena are revealed that lead to a revision of these concepts.

On which paths of inquiry did Dilthey open up for himself access to history so that he could read off the sense of its being? On the following three:

1. a path of inquiry focusing on the history of the sciences;

2. an epistemological path of inquiry;

3. a psychological path of inquiry.

The first two paths are grounded in the third and presuppose it. We will see later how they point to it. But for Dilthey psychology means something very specific, and the first requirement for understanding it is to ask just what Dilthey himself meant by it.

Dilthey's formulation of the question of history *in terms of the history of the sciences* began with his essays on Schleiermacher's hermeneutics and those dealing with the study of the history of the sciences, etc. These essays are not simply historical research on the history of the sciences but rather attempts to understand how in earlier times human life was interpreted. Their ultimate theme is a question about the concept of life. The history of the historical sciences has a different sense than that of the natural sciences. When the history of the historical sciences is investigated, life itself is investigated with respect to its knowledge. As knowing, life investigates itself in its history. The knower is the known. That is the sense that belongs to the history of the sciences of human being and to its structure.

Dilthey's *epistemological* formulation of the question of history had the same motive. Here too we need to emphasize his question about the concept of life. This tendency of his thought has been misunderstood to this day. Dilthey's question appeared in the form of the traditional demarcation of the natural and human sciences that already had been attempted by J. S. Mill, who sought to understand history with the help of concept-formation in the natural sciences. Dilthey sought to assert a unique status for the human sciences. But his interest was not a doctrine of method and system; he was not concerned with the question of how to classify particular sciences within different domains. Such matters later became the interest of Rickert. Dilthey's central problem was how to see historical reality in its own reality. He sought to salvage the unique character not of a science but of reality. He sought to make comprehensible the process of human self-knowledge. To the sense of human being belongs not only consciousness of the world but also, as included in this consciousness, a knowing of oneself. Historical knowledge is a distinct form of self-knowledge. Dilthey's real interest lay here; he was not seeking an isolated theory of the sciences. On this point, his intentions have been so widely misunderstood that his own followers have not understood the real sense of his theory of science. Rather, they have emphasized that Dilthey, in contrast to Windelband and Rickert, drew his theory from a real knowledge of historical knowing. That is indeed correct, but it is self-evident and inessential. What mattered to Dilthey was to discover a concept of life, even on this epistemological path of inquiry. Characteristically, Dilthey was open to all stimuli. Hence, even Windelband's and Rickert's philosophy of history, which was influenced by Dilthey, was able to exert a reverse effect on him, so that in the end he misinterpreted the tendencies of his own work. Thus his real intentions remained unrealized.

The goal of both the above-mentioned directions of Dilthey's research shows itself clearly to be the apprehension and illumination of the phenomenon of life. This also is what Dilthey attempted to tackle in his psychology and indeed in sharp contrast to traditional psychology, where the unique being of life is relinquished.

IV

Dilthey's basic question concerns the concept of life. This question about the concept of life is one about the conceptualizing of life. Thus it is necessary to first

gain an originary access to life in order then to grasp it conceptually. Dilthey
understood this task under the traditional heading of psychology. Psychology
is the science of the soul or, in its modern conception, the science of experience. Insofar as these two conceptions appear in a certain continuity, one
speaks of the stream of experience (James). Experiences are a reality that does
not exist in the world but rather is accessible only in the inner observation of
reflection, in the consciousness of oneself. Thus this entire region of experiences also is described as consciousness. (Descartes—*res cogitans*). As a science,
psychology is the science of the contexts of experience, the science of consciousness. Dilthey had still another description of this science, which shows
more clearly what was at issue for him: anthropology. He was not seeking to
observe psychological processes side by side with physiological ones; rather,
his theme was the human being as a spiritual being, and it was the *structures*
of this being that he wanted to research. This also is the meaning of the definition: empirical psychology. Dilthey thereby disassociated himself from the
specific conception of psychology as a natural science. With these intentions,
he drew on earlier attempts in psychology, and yet this does not detract from
an interpretation of his approach as constituting something fundamentally
new. In 1874 there appeared Brentano's *Psychology from an Empirical Standpoint,* a book written in the spirit of positivism, which stressed the necessity
of taking stock of the psychical states of affairs before proceeding to inquire
into the laws governing the course of psychical events. In order to read off the
constitution of such laws, one must first know the primary structures. Originally, Brentano was a Catholic theologian, a student of Trendelenburg, leaving theology in 1870 and moving to the study of philosophy. However, the
historical tradition, with which he came into contact in his theological studies, remained vital for him (the Middle Ages and Aristotle). Greek psychology
was something wholly different from experimental psychology. Psychology
was here a doctrine of life and of human being itself. (Brentano's psychology,
which did not seek to explain psychical sequences of events but sought to
describe fundamental constitutive states of mind, decisively influenced not
only Dilthey but also Husserl.) Dilthey sought to research the structures of the
psychical, and what is essential here is that he saw in them not mere empty
forms of psychical being *[Dasein]* in terms of which they are classified; rather,
he saw them as belonging to the reality of psychical life itself. This signifies
the most extreme position to which Dilthey advanced in his concept of life:
structures as the primary vital unity of life itself and not as the mere classificatory schemata for understanding life.

In his "Ideas Concerning a Descriptive and Analytic Psychology" (1894),
Dilthey undertook the demarcation of his own psychology from the positivist
conception of psychology as a natural science. His psychology is *descriptive* and
not *explanatory, analytic* and not *constructive.* The conception of psychology as a
natural science transfers the methods of physics to psychology and seeks to grasp

laws in its measurement of regularities. Because it does this without first interrogating the psychical with respect to its being, this kind of psychology has to transplant certain hypotheses and prejudgments that are not and cannot be demonstrated. A hypothesis is justified on the basis of its results. Now, insofar as the hypothesis is not, however, grounded by a prior intuition of the thing inquired into, everything constructed upon it is only of hypothetical certainty. This psychology can never be the fundamental science of the human sciences. This is the kind of psychology that Wundt attempted in his *Physiological Psychology*,[27] where the psychical is treated in connection with the physical, and both are supposed to be made accessible through the same method.

Dilthey called his psychology "analytic" in contrast to construction, which is the basic approach of psychology as a natural science. The latter attempts, much like physics, a reduction to ultimate elements. As physics constructs nature on the basis of elements, so one tries to do the same thing with the psyche. One sees the ultimate element in the sensible impression. From complexes of impressions, one seeks to assemble phenomena such as "will," "hate," etc. It is no accident that this psychology saw sense data as the primal elements, for here the methods of comprehension through measurement in the natural sciences are most likely possible. Psychology as a natural science is therefore essentially a psychology of the senses. (Today even this kind of psychology—influenced in part by phenomenology—has arrived at new ways of formulating questions and has a wholly different look than it had in Dilthey's era). So for it, too, construction was the way to explain psychical contexts of experience.

Against these tendencies, what was important for Dilthey was that one begin by looking at the psychical context. Context was for him what is primary; it was the whole of life itself. It is always already there and is not first constructed out of elements. It is to be grasped first, and its component parts are to be loosened free from it. This breaking loose is no breaking loose of elements but a loosening up of primary structures. Psychical life is originally always given in its wholeness and, indeed, according to three fundamental characteristics:

1. It develops itself.

2. It is free, and

3. it is defined by an acquired context, i.e., it is historical.

For the sake of contrast, we can describe the way one usually attempts to understand "seeing." One believes that one is able to understand it in terms of amassing sense impressions. One does not see that it is seeing itself that is primary and first determines the assimilation and interpretation of sensory data. The same can be said for memory and recollection, which one usually tries to explain through association. On the contrary, the related comprehension of two states of affairs at different times is already recollection, and association is only a particular occurrence of recollection.

The fundamental character of psychical context is the self, the self-sameness of the person, of the ego, which is conditioned by the external world. It influences the self, and the self in turn influences it. There exists a certain effective correlation between the self and the external world ("On the Origin of Our Belief in the Reality of the External World and Its Justification"). This whole context of self and world is there *[ist da]* at every moment. Yet this being-there *[Dasein]* does not necessarily mean that life knows this fundamental structure. The context is a continuous one; something is always present for consciousness. For states of consciousness, taken at a cross-section, so to speak, there emerges at every moment a comportment that is equally noetic, emotive, and volitional. The intimate relationship between these moments constitutes the real structure of consciousness. This structure is something that is experienced by life itself. It is experience, i.e., the self-experience of psychical life itself, i.e., nothing other than the self-experience of the human being, insofar as the latter is determined by a world. This determination is not, however, causal; the context is much more tied to motive and motivation. Psychical life is defined by a context of purposes, a characteristic that is at first in motion (?) in individual life. Insofar as life is life with others, the structures of this life with one another need to be established. How is the life of the other originally given? In epistemological terms, the question presents itself as one concerned with the knowledge of an alien consciousness. But this way of formulating the question is mistaken, because it overlooks the fact that life is primarily always already life with others, a knowledge of one's fellow human beings. Yet Dilthey never pressed this question any further. The essential thing for him was that the structural context of life is acquired, i.e., it is defined by its history.

We now ask, how was Dilthey's fundamental research received? The Marburg school of neo-Kantians, whose main interests focused on epistemology, did not concern itself with Dilthey at all. But the Southwest German school of neo-Kantians, which was influenced by Kant as well as by Fichte, took up Dilthey's impulses. Windelband, "Rectorial Address." Rickert, *The Limits of Concept-Formation in Natural Science.*[28] Here Dilthey's basic problem was misunderstood beyond the point of recognition. Dilthey's ultimate interest was historical being, but Rickert never really concerned himself with knowledge of history, only with its manner of presentation. The upshot of Rickert's inquiry was to show that the historian presented unique individuality, whereas the natural scientist presented the universal; the one sought individuation, the other generalization. This is merely a formal taxonomy which, though so obviously true that it cannot be challenged, is so empty that nothing can be gleaned from it either. For both Windelband and Rickert, psychology is a generalizing science and hence a natural science. It cannot, therefore, serve as the basis of the human sciences, for a science of the universal cannot provide the basis for a science of the particular. This analogical inference—taken from the relationship of mathematics and physics—wholly overlooks the fact that even in this relationship universality is a purely formal, empty designation. The universality of mathematics is wholly different from that of physics; in mathematics, universality is merely a formalization, while in physics it is to be understood as a generalization. What is really essential here, however, is that the neo-Kantians of the Southwest German school did away with the positive tendency of Dilthey's thought with one stroke. They didn't concern themselves with the fact that Dilthey wanted to develop a psychology that neither wanted to be nor could be a natural science. They simply said: for us psychology is a natural science. The inner consequence was that Rickert launched superficial attacks against philosophy of life that did not carry research any farther, but that—and this was typical!—were true in principle. He maintained that the important factor for philosophy was to form a concept of the thing it researches. And here Rickert was right. Yet obviously philosophy of life also seeks to develop a concept of life and to work out its conceptuality. The demand for concept-formation is, however, an empty one; the real substance of science is its relation to the *thing* it researches. A change in this relation is also the primary factor in every transformation of a science.

If we now view Dilthey's life work as one of research, then we need to formulate a critical question and ask, how far did Dilthey get in his research, and where and in what way did he fail? We need to repeat his questioning and to do this on the basis of a type of research—namely, *phenomenology*—that provides us with the suitable resources for advancing further than Dilthey's own position.

V

The formation of a historical worldview is grounded in historical research. (Yorck: "Our common interest is to understand historicity").[29] What is important is to work out the being of the historical, i.e., historicity rather than the historical, being rather than beings, reality rather than the real. What is of concern is thus not the question of empirical research on history; even in universal history, one still would not have historicity. Dilthey penetrated into that reality, namely, human Dasein which, in the authentic sense, is in the sense of historical being. He succeeded in bringing this reality to givenness, defining it as living, free, and historical. But he did not pose the question of historicity itself, the question of the sense of being, i.e., concerning the being of beings. It is only since the development of phenomenology that we are in a position to pose this question clearly. Thus we need to look at this type of research that prepares the ground for our question.

The expression "phenomenology" is at first complicated and strange, but its meaning is simple. We will clarify the sense of this thing called "phenomenology" in terms of the following five themes, to be able then to understand the name:

1. The fundamental attitude of phenomenology as a new direction of philosophical research and its relation to traditional philosophy today.

2. The first breakthrough to it in Husserl's *Logical Investigations.*

3. The characterization of its decisive discoveries: intentionality and categorial intuition.

4. The name "phenomenology."

5. The limits of previous phenomenological research.

The fundamental attitude of phenomenological research is defined by a principle that appears self-evident: *to the things themselves.* Accordingly, in the question of historicity, it is a matter of bringing historical reality to givenness so that the sense of its being can be read off it. To derive concepts from things, and to philosophize from out of the things themselves, seems to be something self-evident. But this really only seems to be the case. Research and life have the strange tendency to leap over what is simple, originary, and genuine and to get hung up on what is complicated, derivative, and non-genuine. That is true not only today but for the whole history of philosophy. Contemporary philosophy is traditional; its newness lies in its renewal of previous philosophy, not in any new way of formulating questions about things. Traditional philosophy begins with opinions about things, i.e., with concepts that are not examined regarding their original appropriateness in the past. In contrast, phenomenology postulates an advance into the things themselves.

This obviously is not done with a postulate. At first, phenomenology was not a program but an undertaking. It treated apparently quite primitive and elemental things. But returning to self-evident things concealed from the consciousness of everyday life is always the genuine path to great discoveries. Every great discoverer poses an elementary question. With its new principle, which was concealed since the classical era and discovered again from it, phenomenology aimed not so much to place itself outside of history as to remain unaffected by it. But that is not possible, since every discovery stands in a historical continuity and is codetermined by history. Historical motives are alive in phenomenology and, in part, have determined its traditional way of formulating questions and starting points, concealing from it a genuine access to things. Phenomenology needs, first of all, to enter more and more into the possibility of extricating itself from the tradition in order to free up past philosophy for a genuine appropriation. The result of this kind of phenomenological research is necessarily a variety of directions, i.e., directions of inquiry. But there is no phenomenological school. There are different directions of work that subject themselves to reciprocal critique. Every proposition is valid only insofar as it can be demonstrated. One is of course never able to suspend personal opinions entirely, but they have no weight.

The first breakthrough in this kind of research was in 1900–1901 with the publication of Husserl's *Logical Investigations.* The *Logical Investigations* in fact constitute the fundamental book of phenomenology, but here we cannot really discuss the content of this work. That would even contradict the phenomenological principle since, according to it, one cannot demonstrate what is merely reported in a lecture; and it is precisely this pursuit of the things themselves that is essential. That requires a certain schooling which is neither sorcery nor a clever trick but a scientific method for which, as for every method, a certain aptitude is of course required. This aptitude can, however, only be developed by working with the things themselves over many years.

We will attempt in a roundabout way to make clear the two decisive discoveries that will allow us to formulate Dilthey's question in a new phenomenological way: intentionality and categorial intuition. *Intentio* is an aiming at something. In the Middle Ages, this expression was used to designate a characteristic of psychical comportment. All thinking is a thinking *about* something, all willing is a willing *of* something, all experience is an experience *of* something. This self-evident proposition is of fundamental significance. When we bring to mind this directedness toward something, the toward-which of this directedness is simultaneously given just as it is intended in the act in question. We experience what is intended in the determinations of its being-intended. That is, we have the possibility of interrogating the experienced world with respect to its being-there *[Dasein]*. Here we can learn to see beings in their being. Thus a scientific basis is acquired for the question of the being of beings. Phenomenological research does not simply observe one region of being; what matters to it, rather, is to investigate all regions with regard to the structure of their being. In this way, philosophy once again has the possibility of being in advance of the sciences. It no longer needs to say in an inadequate and a more general way what the individual sciences have already said with more precision and in a better way. As Plato once opened the way for geometry, so now philosophy again has the possibility of opening up the respective regions of the sciences and providing the main themes of their research through fundamental definitions. Thus phenomenology has its place in research at the universities. It seeks to make of students not philosophers but rather scholars with a consciousness of their own science. And this is precisely the effect that Plato and Aristotle had in the Academy and Lyceum.

The second discovery, categorial intuition, can be touched upon only briefly. Earlier we differentiated being from beings by observing that being, unlike beings, is not accessible through sensory intuition. Nonetheless, the sense of being that is meant when I say the word "is" must somehow be capable of demonstration. I must be able to show what the meaning of being is when I use the expression "is." The act that opens up access to this demonstration is categorial intuition.

According to the demands of phenomenology, philosophy should be concerned not with polishing concepts, making use of them in a superficial manner, but rather with making accessible that which is intended in them so that it can show itself from itself: φαινόμενον [phenomenon]—λόγος [discourse]. Phenomenology is therefore an addressing and defining of that which shows itself from itself. Thus in its Greek name one can already see an allusion to its basic

principle: to the things themselves. In its earliest breakthrough, phenomenological research confined itself essentially to theoretical experiences, i.e., to thinking.
It then later brought in emotional experiences as well. Yet one can see without
much effort that there is nothing really new here except a more radical formulation of traditional psychology. Phenomenology was still working to a great extent
within the framework of the older psychological tradition when the discovery of
intentionality was made, a discovery that shifted its research to another plane,
however. Husserl himself misunderstood his own work when he wrote the foreword to *Logical Investigations*.[30] Here he put forward the completely mistaken
interpretation of phenomenology as a better kind of psychology.

VI

For Dilthey, authentic historical being is human Dasein. Dilthey managed to
draw attention to certain structures in life, but he never formulated the question
of the reality of life itself, namely, what is the sense of the being of our own
Dasein? Because he doesn't pose this question, he never offers an answer to the
question of historical being, a question also neglected by previous phenomenological research. Phenomenology presupposed life. When it asked the question,
what is man?, it offered the traditional answer: *animal rationale*. Sensibility,
understanding, and reason as more exact definitions (in Kant). What holds these
realms together? What is the character of being that belongs to the whole being?
Phenomenology defined the human being as a context of experiences held
together through the unity of the ego as a center of acts. But it did not inquire
into the character of being that belongs to this center.

    What we would like to attempt now is a preliminary definition of the
being of human being that will serve as a basis for the more authentic definition
in which the sense of the being of human being will be shown to be time. We
will attempt, phenomenologically, to set forth characteristics of the being of
human being and to see human Dasein just as it shows itself in its everyday existence *[Dasein]*. This is a fundamental task that appears to move in the realm of
what is most self-evident and closest to us, but this realm of what is closest to us
is in fact what is least uncovered for us. This reality has been forgotten due to the
sediment of traditional modes of questioning. That is why we will begin with certain faulty interpretations in order to arrive at a genuine interpretation.

    One fundamental interpretation has the human being as an ego. It derives
from Descartes who, in his *Meditations,* sought a secure foundation of certitude
and found it in his understanding of the ego as *res cogitans*. Starting from this
Cartesian foundation and proceeding via Kant's mode of questioning, modern
epistemology has tried to understand how the subject comes out of itself to the
object, i.e., how it can know the object. By moving along this path of inquiry,
modern epistemology believes itself to be eminently critical. What was at issue in
Descartes' orientation to geometry was the acquisition of certain principles from

which inferences could be made; what mattered was not a presentation of the total being of human beings but an axiom for deduction. This interpretation, namely, that at first only the ego is given, is uncritical. It is based on the presupposition that consciousness is similar to a box, where the ego is inside and reality is outside. But natural consciousness knows nothing of all this; rather, the primal givenness of Dasein is that it is in a world. Life is that kind of reality which is in a world and indeed in such a way that it has a world. Every living creature has its environing world not as something extant next to it but as something that is there [da ist] for it as disclosed, uncovered. For a primitive animal, the world can be very simple. But life and its world are never two things side by side; rather, life "has" its world. Even in biology this kind of knowledge is slowly beginning to make headway. People are now reflecting on the fundamental structure of the animal. But we miss the essential thing here if we don't see that the animal has a world. In the same way, we too are always in a world in such a way that it is disclosed for us. An object such as a chair, for example, is merely extant; all life, on the other hand, is there [ist da] in such a way that a world also is there for it.

Now it is important to see the fundamental structures in which this being in the world is played out. How is the world originally given? Not as an object of theoretical knowledge but as an environing world in which I look around and act, set up something, care for it. These objects are not in the first place objects of theoretical knowledge but are things with which I am involved and which carry within themselves references to what they are used for and directives for their use, their usability. What is given at first is not material things in the sense of physics. The extraction of nature from the world as it is given immediately to us is originally a complicated process. The world that is closest to us is one of practical concern. The environing world [Umwelt] and its objects are in space, but the space of this world is not the space of geometry. It is essentially defined by moments of nearness and distance as we go about our everyday dealings [Umgang], i.e., by possibilities of turning to something and the like. It doesn't have the homogeneous structure of geometric space; rather, it has definite and distinct places. The distances between pieces of furniture, for example, are not given as measurements but rather in dimensions that are disclosed in going about dealings with them (they can be reached by a touch of the hand, one can walk between them, etc.). It is to the task of uncovering the space in the environing world that the painter is dedicated. It is on the basis of this space that geometric space is first worked out through a specific process.

The being-there [Dasein] of life is further defined by the being-there-with-us of other realities that have the same character of being that I myself have: other human beings. We enjoy a peculiar kind of being-with-one-another. We all share the same environing world; we are in the same space. Space is there for us as we are with one another, and we are there for one another. But the chairs in this space are, on the contrary, merely present, they are not there for one another, and though they are of course all in the same space, this space is not there for them.

Being-in-the-world is thus being-with-one-another. The former is characterized by this being-with-one-another even when there is in fact no other person there. In my natural way of living, I myself am not given to myself in such a way that I observe my experiences. I am initially given to myself in that with which I am involved, in that with which I tarry from day to day. There is a certain character of familiarity to the world (room, house, city, etc.). It is in this world, having faded into it as it were, that I see myself as something real. I encounter myself in my environing world. The environing world [Umwelt] is initially given in practical circumspection [Umsicht]. The possibility of theoretical research arises here only through a certain reorientation. I can reorient myself by detaching my circumspection from my own concerns and allowing it to become merely a kind of looking around, i.e., θεωρία [theory]. This move toward the autonomy of sight is the real source of any science. Science is the development of this way of merely looking at a thing.

But who is this Dasein? Initially and for the most part, we are not ourselves. We live in terms of what *everyone* says, what *everyone* judges to be the case, how *everyone* sees things, what *everyone* wants. It is this indeterminate "everyone" that rules over Dasein. Initially and for the most part, this everyone enjoys a thorough dominance over Dasein. Even science lives in terms of it. In tradition, we are shown how *everyone* asks questions and how everyone takes up research. This *publicness* of Dasein that rules over our being-with-one-another makes it clear that we are, for the most part, not ourselves but the Others: our lives are lived in terms of the Others and are lived as it were by them. Who is this everyone? It is imperceptible, indefinable, no one—however, it is not nothing but rather the most real reality of our everyday Dasein. This everyone-Dasein has the tendency to lose itself in its concerns with the world and to fall away from its own self. The human being is inauthentic in its everyday world, and it is precisely this fact that defines the primary reality of human Dasein. This becomes most evident in a structure of human being that the Greeks saw and used in their definition of human being. The human being is a ζῷον λόγον ἔχον [a living creature that has discourse]. For the Greeks, who liked to talk a lot, the human being is defined as speaking. Discourse is not understood here as the fundamental structure of our being. (Here one should, however, not understand discourse to be mere sound after the fashion of psychology as a natural science.) Discourse is always discourse about something and expressing oneself about something, and it is always with and to someone. Through discussion, what is discussed is uncovered and made accessible to others. Λόγος [discourse] is δηλοῦν [making visible]. The possibility of mere talk means for human beings precisely a tendency toward fallenness. This is *the* possibility that the everyone seizes upon. Typically, discourse does not, for the most part, arise from any original knowledge of things, for it is in fact impossible to have seen and documented everything for oneself. A considerable amount of discourse originates from hearsay. What characterizes this rote saying is that in being circulated the validity of what has been said becomes calcified and simultaneously gets disengaged from the very thing about which it was said. The more rote saying dominates, the more the world is covered over. It is in this way that Dasein has the tendency to cover over the world and, along with this, itself. This tendency to cover over is nothing other than Dasein's flight from itself into publicness, a flight that has important consequences for understanding the phenomenon of time.

Here we are not discussing acts or experiences of consciousness but certain ways of being-in-the-world. We are defining this Dasein in the first place in terms of its dealings and concern with the world. This concern also is always a concern with myself. *Care* is the authentic kind of being which characterizes Dasein. The concept and experience of care are ancient, but this phenomenon has long since been covered over, and it has never been taken up primordially as a point of departure.

Here we need to formulate a critical question: Can one, by following this path of description, arrive at any concepts that will help define human Dasein as a whole, as a unified reality? I can only define human Dasein as a living being that always has before it a not-yet being. When I am no longer alive, however, I will no longer be in a position to experience this whole *[Ganzheit]*. When life is finished, completed *[ganz]*, then it is no longer. One cannot evade this difficulty. How can human Dasein be given as a whole? For only in this way can one form a concept of life. The particulars of another life lived to its end provide only poor information. For, first, this life is of course no longer there and, second, one can never substitute another life for one's own. Dasein is in each case one's own Dasein, my Dasein, which is given at a particular time; this characteristic is inseparable from Dasein. We must hold fast to this point if we are to discover the ultimate meaning of Dasein, i.e., its authentic existence. How can we grasp human Dasein, which is always one's own, as a whole?

VII

Dasein's circumspection is guided by a type of interpretation that reigns within publicness. Defined by this interpretation, the world is accessible to everyone in an average way. The public character of the ways in which Dasein has been interpreted also defines life in the public arena. Moreover, individual life has the tendency to sink away into this publicness and to become lost in it. When Dasein speaks about itself, it sees itself as a thing in the world, like other things. Thus life is in the first place reflected upon in terms of concepts of the world and not in terms of concepts that originally belong to it. One finds oneself at first in one's concerns, in what one does, in one's career, and so on. The world of concerns yields the initial concept of what Dasein is. Thus the human being is first defined as an animal, while its peculiar kind of being is described only as rationality—a definition that is wholly characterized by the world. Kant understands this definition of the human being as a unity of the sensory world with understanding and reason. Thus these characteristics are no doubt viewed together as being unified in a single reality, but the question of the sense of the being of this unity is never raised. It remains merely a sum in which the parts precede the whole; the whole is merely supplementary. In contrast, a whole is something through which the parts are first determined. For example, a machine cannot be understood as the sum of gears and the like, which are somehow combined; rather, the meaning of the whole determines the type and arrangement of the individual parts. The main point here is to see life as a whole. We must ask about the structural moment that defines life as a whole and about the sense of this whole, i.e., whether perhaps it is this whole that marks our being at every moment. We saw earlier that life is essentially still incomplete; there is always part of it that still lies ahead. A whole requires, however, a sense of being finished. Yet when life comes to be finished in *death*, then it is no longer. We usually are accustomed to thinking that something really "is" only when it is finished. Yet life doesn't fit this case; when all of its possibilities have been exhausted, it "is" no longer. The dead person has departed from the world. The question of immortality or non-immortality does not play a role here. Earlier we saw that we could not find a way out of this predicament by living the life of another, whose death we experience, since their death is not my death—and there is no such thing as "death itself." Death is always in each case my death at the particular time. When one overlooks this, one has lost the very theme under discussion.

Just as every Dasein discovers the world for itself, so too every life is given to itself as its own. Earlier we spoke of death as a limit. In so doing, we tacitly understood life as a process that ceased somewhere or other. Here life is understood as a context of experiences coming to an end somewhere. In so doing, however, we once again have relinquished our earlier theme. Dasein is not a process, nor is death something that comes afterward at the end some time. Death is something that stands imminently before human beings; it is something that life itself knows. Having said this, however, we still have not provided a definition of death. Many things are imminent for me, but here there is a difference! When an event is imminent for me, it is something that concerns me and that I encounter in the world. But death is not something that comes to me from somewhere; it is rather what I myself am. I myself am the possibility of my own death. Death is the utmost end of what is possible in my Dasein; it is the most extreme possibility of my Dasein. There lies in Dasein a possibility which is imminent for it and in which human Dasein itself stands imminently before itself in its most extreme possibility. Here we are not concerned with moods or dispositions but rather with seeing the movements which Dasein makes in the consciousness that death is the most extreme possibility of itself that stands imminently before it. I myself am my death precisely when I live. Here it is less important to describe types of death than to understand death as a possibility of life. Our aim here is not to offer a metaphysics of death but to understand the ontological structures of death within life. For the difficult thing is not to die but to deal with death in

the present. We will need to keep this idea of death in mind for the following discussion. If death is such a thing, namely, the most extreme possibility that Dasein
itself is, then Dasein must have different possible ways of standing before its
death. First we need to see how the everyday life of the individual caught up in
the everyone stands before its death, as well as how death shows itself in this
standing-before-death, i.e., how it is encountered in everyday life. We saw that
what defines everydayness is the fact that here Dasein loses itself in its world.
Death is encountered daily in everyday life. We see it and know, in a rather indifferent way, that dying is a departure from this world that can perhaps someday
affect even us. In this indifference lies the moment of our thrusting death aside.
Here Dasein evades death and pushes it aside as a possibility. This fleeing from
death goes so far that in everyday life one tries to persuade the dying person that
he or she will not die and thus to talk the person out of his own death. One
believes that by doing this one has rendered a service to the dying person. Dasein
not only tranquilizes itself before the prospect of death but also seeks to thrust it
aside through a certain interpretation of it. Thinking about death is considered a
kind of cowardice or a form of escapism. Life tranquilizes itself regarding death
and by interpreting it in a certain way as something alien pushes it away from the
horizon of life. In its concerns, Dasein cares for itself; to the structure of care
belongs the fact that Dasein also is simultaneously concerned with itself and with
others. Dasein cares for itself by making sure that the possibility of its death stays
away. It is continually taking care that it *omits* the possibility of taking hold of
death in a more radical fashion. It is precisely in this flight from death that the
being-there *[Da-sein]* of death shows itself. Death shows itself in the *from-which*
of our fleeing. How is death there for us in our constant flight from it? What are
the characteristics of its peculiar form of being present? Its indefiniteness: this
possibility of Dasein is indefinite. *When* death will come is wholly indefinite for
Dasein. But at the same time this possibility stands imminently before us as a certainty that surpasses all other certainties we might think of. It is for Dasein a certainty that it will die its death. This certainty neither does away with the indefiniteness nor diminishes it. On the contrary, it increases it. Everydayness attempts
to thrust aside this indefinite certainty. It reckons with all that still remains for
Dasein. It pushes away the indefiniteness of death into the realm of postpone-
ment and suppresses its certainty in an attitude of "not thinking about it."

Thus death shows itself as the most extreme, indefinite, and yet certain
possibility of Dasein in which Dasein stands before itself.

This definition of the structure of death is not an arbitrary one but rather
must be grasped in a priori fashion as a definition that is fundamental to any interpretation of death, even those in which faith must be taken into account. This
holds for Christianity as well. It was through Christian theology that the problem
of death first appeared in connection with the question of the sense of life.

We have defined Dasein in its publicness as inauthenticity. This inauthentic way of standing-before-death is a kind of evasion. But what constitutes the

kind of standing-before-death that belongs to authenticity, and what meaning does this have for gaining a fundamental understanding [of the constitution?][31] of human Dasein?

VIII

Should the task of defining the being of Dasein be successful, then this task becomes a matter of grasping Dasein as a whole. A whole is defined by limits. Death is just such a limit that is there for Dasein itself. Standing before this limit as an indefinite and yet certain possibility is what characterizes the kind of being that is characteristic of human life. In its everydayness, Dasein evades this possibility, a phenomenon that we have characterized as an inauthentic stance toward death. Is there an authentic way of approaching death that is not defined by publicness but rather is a way in which Dasein always stands before itself as in each case something individual, ownmost, and "my own"? What is implied here is grasping the actuality of this possibility and holding fast to it. To stand before a possibility means to grasp it *as* a possibility. To *endure* the possibility of death means to have it there for oneself in such a way that it stands before one purely as what it is—indefinite regarding its "when" and certain regarding its "that." To let this possibility exist as a possibility and to not turn it into an actuality, as is done in suicide, for example, means to *run forward toward it* in an anticipatory manner. Here the world withdraws, collapsing into nothingness. The possibility of death means that I will, at some time, depart from this world, that the world will have nothing more to say to me, that everything to which I cling, with which I busy myself, and about which I am concerned will have no more to say to me and will no longer be of help to me. The world, as something on the basis of which I am able to live, will then no longer be there. I have to deal with this possibility purely on my own. Here we see that the possibility of *choice* is given in advance for Dasein. At every moment Dasein can comport itself in such a way that it chooses between itself and the world; it can make each decision on the basis of what it encounters in the world, or it can rely on itself. Dasein's possibility of choosing offers the possibility of fetching itself back from its having become lost in the world, that is, from its publicness. When Dasein has chosen itself, it has thereby chosen both itself and choice. To have chosen to choose means, however, to be *resolved.* Thus running forward anticipatorily means choosing; to have chosen means to be resolved—not to die but to live. This choosing and this being resolved is the *choice* of *responsibility* for itself that Dasein takes on and that consists in the fact that in each instance of my acting I make myself responsible through my action. Choosing responsibility for oneself means to choose one's *conscience* as a possibility that the human being authentically is. It is an error on the part of phenomenology (Scheler) that it has misunderstood the genuinely anthropological structure of Kantian ethics. Kant saw that the fundamental sense of Dasein is possibility, i.e., to be possibility itself and to be able to grasp it. To choose one's conscience means at the same time, however, *to become guilty*. As Goethe once said, "He who acts is always without conscience, irresponsible." Every action is at the same time something marked by guilt. For the possibilities of action are limited in comparison with the demands of conscience, so that every action that is successfully carried out produces conflicts. To choose self-responsibility, then, is to become guilty in an absolute sense. Insofar as I am at all, I become guilty whenever I act in any sense.

What do these connections mean? This anticipatory running forward into the most extreme possibility of myself, which I am not yet, but will be, means *to be futural*. I myself am my future by virtue of this anticipatory running forward. I am not in the future but rather am myself futural. Being guilty is nothing other than carrying *the past* around with oneself, for being guilty is a kind of being past. In this state of being guilty, we can see how one holds onto the past and how along with this human Dasein, through its actions, comes authentically into *the present*. In being resolved, Dasein is its future, in being guilty it is its past, and in acting it comes into the present. The *being-there* of Dasein *is* nothing other than *being-time*. Time is not something that I encounter out there in the world, but is what I myself am. In running forward anticipatorily, being guilty, and acting, time itself is there for us. Time characterizes the whole of Dasein. At any particular time, Dasein is not only in the moment but rather is itself within the entire span of its possibilities and its past. It is remarkable how, in acting in the direction of the future, the past comes alive and the present vanishes. Those who act authentically live from out of the future and also can live from out of the past; the present takes care of itself. Time constitutes the whole of my Dasein and also defines my own being at every moment. Human life does not happen in time but rather is time itself. This will become clearer if we can show that even in its everyday manner of being, Dasein is characterized by time.

How is time there for us in everyday life? It is obviously there for me when I decide or determine something about it, when I look at the *clock* and say *"now."* What is going on in this *now?* What is that time which is ascertained when Dasein is arranged in terms of timetables, days, weeks, and years? In these means of orienting oneself, one can already see that all life is defined in a peculiar manner by time. These ways of arranging time are characterized by concern. Concern means to bring that which has been placed under one's care into the *present;* by a certain way of managing it, one makes available that which is not yet available. In care there lies a certain anticipation or awaiting, that is, a certain relation to the *future*. I await something from the future that affects me; it is not something that I am but rather something I have to deal with. To concern oneself in this way with the future is at the same time to *forget*. What is of concern loses its character of having-become what it is; it is simply there for us. Its history is covered over. It becomes an everyday matter. The counter-phenomenon to this awaiting is thus not memory but forgetting. Everyday life always lives in the present, which provides the measure with which the future is calculated and the past is forgotten. This tendency to stay within the present is what has brought about the use of clocks. Why are there clocks? Because everyday life wants to have the course of the world available in the "now." Now and then, and then, and then. . . . Nothing but more nows that one wants to make available in the realm of the everyone. To make these nows universally accessible requires a clock.

What is the genesis of the clock? What are the genuine motives of calculating time? Plato, *Timaeus:* time is the heavens. This definition grows out of a primordial experience, but Plato could not grasp its meaning conceptually. Everyday life orients its concern to the now. The circumspection of concern is characterized in its possibilities by its being-day-to-day. For primitive humanity, night is the time of rest. The day and the course of the day determine daily tasks. Morning, afternoon, and evening are not astronomical facts but rather points of orientation for going about one's dealings, now-points for certain kinds of concern. Insofar as humanity defines this now with reference to the heavens, its assertions about time appeal to the heavens. Time is the heavens. For the Greeks, further determinations of time established themselves as the time of the market and the time of political assembly, which again were oriented around concern. As this sense of shared concern grew, it became more urgent to have agreed-upon determinations of time and the now. The Greeks invented the tree clock (?) for this. Shadows measured in terms of footsteps served as the measure of time. The more that everyday Dasein becomes absorbed in shared concerns, the less time it has and the more precise the clock becomes. In determining time, it also is important that no time be lost (pocket watch). Authentic temporal being does not amount to acting in time and calculating with time, for using a clock means to turn all time into the present. This is clearly shown by the fact that we use the clock to objectively define processes of nature. Dasein attempts to define the world with the help of the clock. Why does Dasein define the world in terms of clock-time? And what kind of time is it that is measured in the natural sciences? What does the use of the clock, i.e., this kind of periodical system of calculation, signify? It means that one makes a possibility available within the framework of the now. But life thereby loses its sense for the time that it itself authentically is. To look at the clock means: to say "now." This now is not, however, my now, but the "now" of the clock that we can speak about together, the public now of being-with-one-another. This time is the time of the everyone that belongs to publicness. This time of the everyone, because of which we are agitated and rushed by existence *[Dasein]*, shows in an extreme sense the dominance of publicness in our Dasein. This kind of time is nothing other than our being-with-one-another itself, i.e., the time that we are with one another.

IX

The being of Dasein as being-there in the world is characterized by circumspective concern. Here Dasein has the possibility of looking away from its concern and making its circumspection autonomous. This is how philosophy and science can emerge at all. Philosophy is observation of the world, disclosing it in terms of its being. Here the real being of the world is nature as that which *always* is; a science of the world is in the first place therefore an unlocking of nature. Nature has to be made present and accessible in its perpetual being and regularity in such a way that all of those moments are excluded which, though conditioning our access to the observation of nature, interfere with it. This tendency first developed in such a way that rather than erecting a nexus of particular laws, it secured fundamental concepts. This happened in Greek philosophy.

Modern physics led to the discovery of laws of motion, defining them in a way that was free of any reference to the contingencies of its access, measurement, and defining of them. The *theory of relativity* took seriously this idea of an *absolute* knowledge of nature. It is not a theory about the relative validity of physical laws; rather, it inquires into those conditions of definition and measurement that make it possible for nature to be grasped purely in terms of itself and for its laws of motion to be understood. What is the philosophical significance of this theory spawned by one of the individual sciences? This question is legitimate since every genuine science is only a kind of concrete philosophy and is genuine only to the extent that it is philosophically grounded. To date, the theory of relativity has been little proven by the facts. Nonetheless, it has provided confirmation of two important insights: (1) the curving of light rays by gravity; (2) the deviation of the orbit of Mercury. Mathematically, the theory of relativity depends upon achieving a radical conception of geometry. Not every spatial property of a figure is geometrical. For Euclidean geometry, above, below, right, and left are unimportant. Its results are independent of displacement, rotation, and reflection. In contrast to these transformations, its theorems are *invariant*. On the basis of these facts, the mathematician Klein worked out a geometry that was a theory of invariants for a certain class of transformations. This way of formulating the question was occasioned by the controversy over the axiom of parallel lines, which could not be proved. As a result, the methodical hypothesis was asserted that this axiom could not be valid, and two new geometries were established that were in themselves free of contradiction within their own spheres: (1) *elliptical* geometry, which was based on the hypothesis that a parallel line cannot be drawn through a point at any degree (here the sum of the angles in a triangle < 180°); (2) *hyperbolic* geometry, which was based on the hypothesis that one can draw several parallel lines through a point at any degree (here the sum of the angles in a triangle > 180°). In the problem of defining the laws of motion, one proceeds from a system of coordinates with time as the fourth coordinate and formulates the question of whether a static system is preferable or whether the equations of a dynamic system should be preserved. The Newtonian laws were transformed by an accelerated motion in the system of measurement. The tendency to preserve the laws of motion led to modifying space and time (as conditions of measurement) in such a way that the laws of motion are preserved with respect to all motions in the system of measurement. How must the system of coordinates be defined for this? The necessary condition here is that the time that I measure alters with the movement, as do the very standards for measuring it. Space and time vary; they are dependent on matter. Hence, it becomes necessary to redefine the concepts of matter and field of force.

What is to be found in these definitions regarding time? Here the Kantian concept of time is no longer adequate. The new discovery in the theory of relativity is that time is always local time; it always depends upon the site where it is measured. Measuring means to consult a standard of measurement in such a way that the quantity of the thing measured becomes visible; the latter is made accessible through number and brought into the present. Measuring is a way of making something present. The idea that time is really local time becomes more comprehensible if we see that the self is authentic time. Time is not something that happens outside of us, a kind of receptacle of being; we ourselves are time. The processes of the world are encountered in time. They are encountered within a kind of understanding that is capable of saying "now."

Thus time, even thought of as the time of nature, does not have to be conceived of in an absolute metaphysical fashion. This is one of the basic discoveries of the theory of relativity. Physical time is a one-dimensional, irreversible multiplicity of earlier and later moments. Each "now" is unrepeatable and has its own distinct position. The ultimate character of these nows is their openness, which is without beginning and end. Minkowski attempted to reform geometry on the basis of these aspects of time. With the help of time as the fourth coordinate, he developed geometry into a theory of relativity.

It is this world-time that everyone can agree upon. Though this measured time is not authentic time, Bergson is wrong in thinking that here time is spatialized. Time is rather transferred from the future into the now. It is not an accident that the first scientific definition of time deals with the time of nature. Aristotle fully understood what he was really measuring in the measurement of time. The sundial displays a moving shadow that constantly changes place—it is now here, now here, now here. Time, says Aristotle, is what is counted in motion with respect to before and after. This definition has remained essentially unchanged up to modern times. Kant, too, defines time by starting from an understanding of nature. But it is essential that we understand time as the reality of our own selves. The inauthentic being of time is the customary one—each of us is this inauthentic time. Yet a difficulty arises here: if in each case Dasein itself is time, how is it that there can be such a thing as measured time? This is a question about how the specific character of individual Dasein is to be understood in terms of the phenomenon of being-with-one-another in time. In any case, what we have ascertained so far should suffice for our question about the sense of historicity.

X

Dilthey's real question concerns the sense of history. It is bound up with his tendency to understand life in terms of itself and not in terms of a reality alien to it.

This implies that the way in which life itself is constituted must be made visible. Dilthey emphasized that the fundamental character of life is historical being. But he merely left it at that and neglected to ask what historical being is. Nor did he show in what way life is historical. We have attempted to formulate this question on the basis of phenomenology, and we have prepared ourselves for it by providing an analysis of Dasein and its authentic reality, namely, time. In this way, we have provided a sufficient basis for raising the question of historicity, which we will discuss in three stages:

1. history and historicity;

2. historicity and historical science;

3. an example of historical [historischer] knowledge as a possibility of historical [geschichtliche] being: namely, research on the history of philosophy.

In preparation, let us first define the meaning of two terms: history [Geschichte] and historical science [Historie]. Each word has a very different origin, and yet both are used interchangeably. However, this is not merely by chance. History signifies a happening [Geschehen] which we ourselves are and in which we are involved. There is a difference between history and motion (e.g., the motion of the heavenly bodies). Only when the term is taken in a very broad sense can it be said that there also is a "history" of the world. History is, formally speaking, a particular kind of motion. It is a happening which, as something past, is still there and which we know about in a particular manner, carry with us, and endure. In the word "past," the moment of time manifests itself.

Historical science (ἱστορεῖν: ascertaining, making known that which has happened) means knowledge of certain happenings. This mode and method of knowledge that enables something past to be made known is called historical [historisch]. It is accomplished in the discovery, critical testing, and interpretation of sources as well as in the presentation of what is found in these sources. But why is the expression "knowledge of a happening" used of this happening itself? Because it is a happening with us ourselves. This happening is preserved in our knowledge of it.

In order to define history in a scientific manner, we first would need to distinguish it from movement. But here we must be satisfied with a few short comments. Earlier we distinguished merely being-extant from being-in-the-world. Motion is the broader concept; it means the phenomenon of change and of alteration from one thing to another. Motions transpire in the world. History happens to me; I am this happening. Anticipatory running forward is a motion that Dasein carries out in its own future. This going-forth-in-advance-of-oneself is the fundamental motion from which history arises, for it is through this going-forth that the past is uncovered. This happening is not mere change or a sequence of events; rather, insofar as we go forth in advance of ourselves, we are this very happening. That we know about ourselves in it belongs to the structure of the happening. The happening is originally discovered there. We need to understand this structure of historicity along the same lines as we did time. We are history, i.e., our own past. Our future is lived from out of the past. We carry the past with us. That clearly can be seen in being-with-one-another within a generation. Dilthey discovered that this concept of generation was important for the phenomenon of historicity. Each of us is not only his own self but also belongs to a generation. The generation precedes the individual, is there before the individual, and defines the Dasein of the individual. The individual lives in terms of that which has been in the past, drags himself or herself through the present, and finally is overtaken by a new generation.

The past can be seized upon and understood in an explicit manner. That is, this context of being, in terms of which life is lived, can be opened up as a theme for research. The past is immediately there for one as a present that has passed away. Understanding the past is always caught up in certain limits. This possibility is determined by how we ourselves understand and define our own Dasein. For example, Spengler's notion of the universal observation of history is determined by an interpretation of cultures that basically characterizes them as symbols, i.e., as expressions of the souls of the respective cultures. This way of interpreting the phenomena in question no longer allows for a genuine characterization of them. Here the soul of a culture is understood in purely biological terms. Spengler's notion of historical observation is an aesthetic kind of observation that does not investigate dynamic contexts of history but rather amounts to a type of botany masquerading as history. One's own present is only one among others. These theses in Spengler's interpretation of history are certainly contestable; here we only want to show that from the outset whatever is researched stands within a certain interpretation. If the past is to be disclosed authentically in terms of what it is, we will have to avoid bringing in questions that ignore the present historical situation. This implies that fundamental reflection on historical research also includes reflection on the possibility of developing a concept of Dasein for the possibility of interpreting its history. Developing a basis for this possibility is a fundamental part of historical method. For the most part, objective historical research proceeds from the naive assumption that the concepts it adopts and uses are self-evident. This is precisely what the Marburg school did in its history of philosophy when it tried to understand this history in terms of Kantian concepts. In Catholic philosophy, Aristotle has been interpreted from a Thomistic standpoint. And in the rivalry between these schools, the one played up Plato as an idealist, and the other played up Aristotle as a realist. Within the historical present of one's research there lies the danger of obstructing history, of not uncovering it but rather rendering it inaccessible. We are faced with the critical task of freeing ourselves from preconceptions and reflecting instead on those conditions that enable us to understand the past. What is required of philosophical research is that it be a critique of the present. In disclosing the past in a primordial manner, the past is no longer seen to be merely a present that preceded our own present. Rather, it is possible to emancipate the past so that we can find in it the authentic roots of our existence and bring it into our own present as a vital force. Historical consciousness liberates the past for the future, and it is then that the past gains force and becomes productive. And only because Dasein is in itself historical [geschichtlich] and can have its own past are unhistorical [unhistorische] epochs at all possible. Here one does not see the past as such; rather, the past is absorbed in the present, something that is only a particular kind of temporal being and historical being.

To bring home the meaning of historical research and its possibilities we choose as our example the history of philosophy. We do not choose this example arbitrarily but rather because phenomenology, one of the most genuine and radical tendencies in philosophy, is characterized by a lack of history, even an animosity toward history, for it believes itself to be capable of discarding what has been as irrelevant and coming to the things themselves on its own. But here phenomenology remains entangled in traditional ways of formulating questions. And yet it belongs to the very sense of phenomenological research that it must constantly reflect upon itself and throw off all spurious tradition in order to activate the genuine sense of the past.

We focus our treatment of the history of philosophy on a fundamental problem, one that we already constantly have had in view but have not expressly formulated, namely, the question of the *being of beings*. A question concerning the being of a particular realm of beings is, however, not yet radical, since I still do not know what I really want to know with the term "being." Plato was the first to formulate this central question in *The Sophist*. With the decline of philosophical research, this question also falls into decline. Today one simply says: Being is the most universal concept and hence is indefinable. But what is decisive for a concept is not definition but its demonstration in terms of how things stand with the subject matter. This critical, foundational question is the central question of philosophy. It is at the same time a question about the way in which the sense of being can be experienced. By formulating the question in this way, the otherwise chaotic appearance of the history of philosophy becomes very simple. What is striking here is how the Greeks interpreted being in terms of time: οὐσία [being] means presence, the present. If this is what being signifies, then authentic being is that which is never not there, i.e., what is always there (ἀεὶ ὄν [perpetual being]). Within the tradition, this concept of being was employed to understand historical reality, a reality that, however, is not always there. It is clear that if the Greek doctrine of being is uncritically accepted as absolute, then it becomes impossible for research to understand a reality such as historical Dasein. Descartes offers proof of how the Greek doctrine of being can be kept alive in the present. He made use of the Thomistic doctrine of being, whose fundamental concepts are entirely Greek. Descartes neglected to ask about the sense of the being of the "I am" that he discovered. Here he simply employed the concept of being that meant being-extant in the world. This omission and confusion was transmitted through subsequent philosophy to phenomenology. Husserl, too, fails to formulate the question of the being of consciousness. So it can be shown that a certain interpretation of being pervades the history of philosophy and determines its whole conceptuality.

Thus the question of historical inquiry in philosophy is referred back to the fundamental question of being itself. We need to formulate this question in such a way that we can preserve its continuity with the first scientific formulation of the question of being in the Greeks, investigating the legitimacy of this formulation and its fundamental limits. If we succeed in returning scientific philosophy to its real themes, then this kind of research certainly will be fruitful for the sciences once again. Logic will then no longer be a supplementary formulation of methods in the sciences but something that runs ahead of the sciences, guides them, and discloses their fundamental concepts. For this, we need the history of philosophy, i.e., we need to understand the ancients anew. We must push on until we are once again a match for the questioning of the Greeks. Yorck von Wartenburg had perhaps an even better idea than Dilthey of this urgent need for historical reflection. He writes on August 21, 1889: "It appears to me that the oscillations brought about by the principle of eccentricity, which led to a new era more than four hundred years ago, have become extremely broad and flat. Knowledge has progressed to the point where it annuls itself, and human beings are so removed from themselves that they can no longer see themselves. 'Modern man,' i.e., man since the Renaissance, is ready for burial."[32] And on February 11, 1884: "Since to philosophize is to live, there is in my opinion—do not be alarmed!—a philosophy of history: but who would be able to write it? . . . That is also why there can be no real philosophizing which is not historical. The distinction between systematic philosophy and historical presentation is essentially false. . . . I am alarmed at the monastic cell of modern man in these times where life's waves surge so high and where, if at all, knowledge would be power. But if science has a ground, it is to be found in the world of the past, in *antiquity*."[33]

NOTES

EDITOR'S INTRODUCTION

1. This term was subsequently expanded into a central philosophical theme in my interpretation of Heidegger's early writings in YH 14ff.

2. On Heidegger's early philosophy of translation, which has provided the main principles of translation in the present volume, see my "Translator's Epilogue" in OHF 91–99.

3. For elaboration on this sense of "supplements," see YH 14ff.

4. GA1 55; translated as "A Recollection,'" in Sheehan 1981, p. 21.

5. *Zur Sache des Denkens* (Tübingen: Max Niemeyer, 1976), pp. 81ff.; translated as *On Time and Being,* tr. Joan Stambaugh (New York: Harper & Row, 1972), pp. 74ff.

6. For elaboration on the following overview of Heidegger's Student Period, see YH chs. 3–6; Steven Galt Crowell, "Making Logic Philosophical Again," in RHFS ch. 3; and Sheehan 1988, pp. 77–137.

7. GA2 553 n. 4/BTMR 471 n. v/BTS 384 n. 5.

8. For the influence of Braig, Hegel, Nietzsche, and Dilthey, see Heidegger's 1957 chronology of his early development in GA1 55–57; translated as "A Recollection," in Sheehan 1981, pp. 21–22.

9. For elaboration on the following overview of Heidegger's Early Freiburg and Marburg periods, see YH chs. 7–15 and RHFS chs. 4ff.

10. See YH ch. 2 for elaboration on this terminological schema of "content," "relation," "actualizing," and "temporalizing" which, though used in his student writings, Heidegger first introduces as precise technical terms around 1920 (see chapter 7 of this volume, p. 87), adding "temporalizing" around 1922 (see chapter 9 of this volume, p. 112), and continuing to use all of them in *Being and Time* and in later texts such as *Contributions to Philosophy,* even if in a less technical sense.

11. For an overview of Heidegger's turn to Kant in 1925–1926, see YH 363–67, as well as Daniel O. Dahlstrom, "Heidegger's Kant-Courses at Marburg, in RHFS ch. 16 and Frank Schalow, "The Kantian Schema of Heidegger's Late Marburg Period, in RHFS ch. 17.

12. Hans-Georg Gadamer, "Martin Heidegger's One Path," tr. P. Christopher Smith, in RHFS 26.

13. GA56/57 11–12; GA61 35. For an overview of Heidegger's first postwar courses of 1919, see George Kovacs, "Philosophy As Primordial Science in Heidegger's Courses of 1919," in RHFS ch. 5.

14. For an overview of Heidegger's destruction of traditonal ontology in the twenties, see YH ch. 7; Jeffrey Andrew Barash, "Heidegger's Ontological 'Destruction' of Western Intellectual Traditions," in RHFS ch. 6; Robert Bernasconi, "Repetition and Tradition: Heidegger's Destructuring of the Distinction between Essence and Existence in *Basic Problems of Phenomenology*," in RHFS ch. 7; and Otto Pöggeler, "Destruction and Moment," tr. Daniel Magurshak, in RHFS ch. 8.

15. Heidegger had known his friend and colleague, Father Engelbert Krebs, since the early teens, co-teaching a seminar with him in SS1916. A year later, Krebs married Heidegger and his fiancée Elfride Petri on March 21, 1917 in a quiet, wartime wedding in the university chapel. Before the wedding, Heidegger's fiancée had expressed to Krebs her wish to convert from Lutheran Protestantism to Catholicism, but she was told that she should wait to make such a difficult decision. Then, during the Christmas of 1918, she again visited Krebs, this time with the news that "my husband no longer has his faith in the Church, and I did not find it," and that "both of us now think in a Protestant manner (i.e., without a fixed, dogmatic tie), believe in the personal God, pray to him in the spirit of Christ, but without Protestant or Catholic orthodoxy." Reminding Krebs of this recent stormy visit from his wife, and referring to the last two troubled years in which he performed military service and did not teach but engaged in soul-searching reflection, Heidegger's letter of January 9, 1919—preceded two days earlier by Husserl's request to the Ministry of Education that Heidegger be appointed his salaried assistant—explains his profound confessional and philosophical turn from Catholicism to free Protestantism and from the phenomenological neo-Scholasticism of his postdoctoral dissertation to a fundamentally historical phenomenological philosophy and phenomenology of religion. See Ott 1988/1993, pp. 99–108/99–109.

16. Heidegger had originally intended to publish this essay in the journal *Göttingischen Gelehrten Anzeigen,* but it never appeared there and was published only decades later in 1973 in an anthology on Jaspers' philosophy (see the entry on this essay in chapter 1). The bibliographic note to its reprinting in GA9 reads: "A critical review from the years 1919–21 the author sent to Karl Jaspers in June of 1921." Indeed, the published correspondence shows that it was a lively topic of conversation between them in the early twenties. See Martin Heidegger and Karl Jaspers, *Briefwechsel 1920–1963,* ed. Walter Biemel and Hans Saner (Frankfurt: Klostermann, 1990), pp. 15ff. The bibliographic note in GA9 also highlights that "the foreword to the third edition (1925) of Jaspers' *Psychology of Worldviews* . . . provides, without naming names, a response to Heidegger's review."

This new edition is an unaltered reprint of the second edition. Allow me to make a few purely personal comments about why a revised edition would be difficult.

The result would be a new book. In representing worldviews as moments or dimensions of the one true worldview, which comprehends the whole only vaguely and never explicitly, I attempted at that time to formulate all of this on the basis of intuition and to communicate it to my readers without any second thoughts. The particulars of what was presented in this manner still seem to me today to be true. I would be unable to do it better today. I could only do it differently. Following this first endeavor, which used an immediate, intuitive approach, I have for quite some time been concerned with the methodological issue of venturing the second step of providing a logically precise elucidation of our modern consciousness of existence. Therefore, allowing my youthful undertaking to remain in its original form would seem to be the more natural thing to do. Without my being aware of it or wishing it at the time, my whole approach in the book and my method of analysis expressed a hidden ideal. I fully acknowledge this, now that I have become aware of it. However, the limits found in the nature of this kind of presentation demand that the same content should appear in different form. I am presently endeavoring to come up with a new form, and the wrong way to do this would be to revise what has already been published. In my subsequent work, I have become a different person not in my cast of mind but rather in the realm of knowledge and logical form. And I would rather leave my earlier work untouched in the hope that, after this first attempt to provide a psychological explanation and foundation for philosophical existence, I also will be able to present a logically systematic clarification and foundation.

Another possible result of a revised edition would be damage to the book. Since the book has certain flaws (in its arrangement, methodological comments, and historical digressions, i.e., in matters that should be considered unessential with respect to the purpose of the book), I would want to correct these in a revised edition, taking advantage of my present insights into the book. Pages and sentences that are weak could be deleted, a lot of the terminology could be altered, and above all lacunae could be filled and the systematics of the whole book could be rearranged without effecting the particulars, but the result would be a hybrid form, and the book would suffer because of this. In return, it would gain only a certain correctness in its outward appearance and in peripheral matters.

Years later, Jaspers again responded to the review in his autobiography with the recollection that he found much of it incomprehensible. See Karl Jaspers, *Philosophische Autobiographie*, 2d ed. (Munich: R. Piper & Co., 1977), p. 95, translated by Dale Ponikvar as "On Heidegger" in *Graduate Faculty Philosophy Journal* 7 (1978): 110.

17. For an overview of the development of Heidegger's phenomenology of religion, see YH chs. 7–8, as well as Theodore Kisiel, "Heidegger (1920–21) on Becoming a Christian: A Conceptual Picture Show," in RHFS ch. 10 and John D. Caputo, "Sorge and Kardia: The Hermeneutics of Factical Life and the Categories of the Heart," in RHFS ch. 18.

18. For an overview of Heidegger's transformation of Husserl's phenomenology in the early twenties, see YH ch. 9; István M. Fehér, "Phenomenology, Hermeneutics, *Lebensphilosophie:* Heidegger's Confrontation with Husserl, Dilthey, and Jaspers" in RHFS ch. 4; Daniel O. Dahlstrom, "Heidegger's Critique of Husserl" in RHFS ch. 13; Rudolf Bernet, "Phenomenological Reduction and the Double Life of the Subject," tr. François Renaud, in RHFS ch. 14; and Jacques Taminiaux, "The Husserlian Heritage in Heidegger's Notion of the Self," tr. François Renaud, in RHFS ch. 15.

19. For an overview of Heidegger's reading of philosophy of life in the early twenties, see David Farrell Krell, "The 'Factical Life' of Dasein: From the Early Freiburg Courses to *Being and Time*," in RHFS ch. 20.

20. For an overview of Heidegger's early concept of formal indication, see YH ch. 14, as well as Th.C.W. Oudemans, "Heidegger: Reading against the Grain," in RHFS ch. 2

and Jean Grondin, "The Ethical and Young Hegelian Motives in Heidegger's Hermeneutics of Facticity" in RHFS ch. 19.

21. For background material on Heidegger's preoccupation with Luther in the early twenties, see my "Martin Heidegger, Martin Luther" in RHFS 159–74.

22. This text, which Heidegger himself cited as his "Aristotle-introduction" and was known to Heidegger scholars as the famous lost "Natorp-Report," has a curious history. See the epilogue of the German editor, Hans-Ulrich Lessing, in *Dilthey Jahrbuch* 6: 270–74. In 1922, Paul Natorp at the University of Marburg and Georg Misch at the University of Göttingen wrote to Husserl asking for information about the teaching activities and publication plans of his assistant Martin Heidegger, who was being considered as a candidate for positions at the two universities, even though he had not published anything since the printing of his revised postdoctoral dissertation on Duns Scotus in 1916. The result was that over the course of three weeks, between September and October of that year, Heidegger hurriedly wrote an introductory outline of the large book titled "Phenomenological Interpretations in Connection with Aristotle," which he was planning to publish the following year in vol. 7 of Husserl's *Jahrbuch für Philosophie und phänomenologische Forschung* and was to have been composed by drawing on the manuscripts of his lecture courses on Aristotle in WS1921–22 (GA61) and SS1922 (GA62) and his seminars at the time. The original typescript, which Heidegger relayed to Natorp at the University of Marburg through Husserl and so was largely responsible for his receiving his position as associate professor there in WS1923–24, was passed on to Natorp's student, the young Hans-Georg Gadamer, but then later lost during World War II in a bombing raid on Leipzig. The other copy sent to Misch in Göttingen was passed on to Misch's student Josef König in 1964, and having been filed away among his papers and forgotten, it finally was discovered there in the late eighties. As for the planned book on Aristotle, for which Heidegger wrote this introduction, it never appeared, though he worked on it until as late as 1925. But it, too, has become available to us in certain versions, namely, the lecture courses of WS1921–22 (GA61), SS1922 (GA62), and SS1924 (GA18), as well as the first part of the lecture course of WS1924–25 on Plato's *Sophist* (GA19 21–188; translated by Richard Rojcewicz and André Schuwer as *Plato's Sophist* [Bloomington: Indiana University Press, 1997]. It also is cited and elaborated on in the course of SS1923 (see my explanation in OHF 1 n. 1, 37 n. 41).

23. For an overview of Heidegger's reading of Aristotle in the early twenties, see YH ch. 10; Franco Volpi, "*Being and Time:* A 'Translation' of the *Nicomachean Ethics?,*" tr. John Protevi, in RHFS ch. 11; and Walter Brogan, "The Place of Aristotle in the Development of Heidegger's Phenomenology," in RHFS ch. 12.

24. See also the translations of the WS1924–25 course *Plato's Sophist* and the SS1925 course *History of the Concept of Time: Prolegomena,* tr. Theodore Kisiel (Bloomington: Indiana University Press, 1985), as well as the 1924 talk *The Concept of Time,* tr. Will McNeill (New York: Basil Blackwell, 1992) and the following courses currently being translated: *Toward a Definition of Philosophy,* tr. E. H. Sadler (Athlone Press), containing lecture courses from KNS1919 and SS1919; *Phenomenology of Religious Life,* tr. Jennifer Gossetti (Indiana University Press), containing lecture courses from WS1919–20, WS1920–21, and SS1921; and *Phenomenology of Intuition and Expression,* tr. E. H. Sadler (Athlone Press), containing the lecture course from SS1920.

25. GA2 97 n. 1/BTMR 102 n. i/BTS 67 n. i.

26. GA2 399 n. 7/BTMR 301 n. xv/BTS 277 n. 17.

27. GA2 331 n. 2/BTMR 293 n. vi/BTS 231 n. 6.

28. GA2 313 n. 6, 447 n. 2/BTMR 278 n. vi, 388 n. iii/BTS 217 n. 6, 311 n. 3.

29. GA2 252 n. 3/BTMR 235 n. iv/BTS 178 n. 4.

30. GA2 264 n. 3/BTMR 243 n. vii/BTS 185 n. 7.

31. GA2 185 n. 3/BTMR 178 n. v/BTS 131 n. 6.

32. GA2 252 n. 3, 59 n. 1/BTMR 235 n. iv, 69 n. i/BTS 178 n. 4, 41 n. 1.

33. GA2 331 n. 2/BTMR 293 n. vi/BTS 231 n. 6.

34. GA2 252 n. 3, 406 n. 1/BTMR 235 n. iv, 354 n. ii/BTS 178 n. 4, 283 n. 2.

35. GA2 264 n. 3/BTMR 243 vii/BTS 185 n. 7.

36. GA2 227 n. 1/BTMR 215 n. xi/BTS 160 n. 12.

37. GA2 553 n. 4/BTMR 471 n. v/BTS 384 n. 5.

38. GA2 52 n. 2, 63 n. 1, 67 n. 9, 103 n. 1, 220 n. 1, 289 n. 15, 324 n. 1, 480 n. 10/BTMR 63 n. v, 73 n. ii, 75 n. x, 108 n. ii, 209 n. x, 261 n. xxxiv, 288 n. iii, 414 n. xxiii/BTS 34 n. 5, 44 n. 2, 47 n. 10, 72, n. 3, 155 n. 11, 201 n. 34, 227 n. 3, 332 n. 22.

39. See Richardson 1963, pp. viii–xxiii.

40. For Heidegger's suggestions that "Heidegger II" was a return to a Heidegger before "Heidegger I," see also GA1 55–57, translated in part as "A Recollection," in Sheehan 1981, pp. 21–22; GA12 81–146, translated as *On the Way to Language,* tr. Peter D. Hertz (New York: Harper & Row, 1971), pp. 1–54; GA13 87–90, translated by Thomas F. O'Meara and Thomas J. Sheehan as "The Pathway," *Listening* 8 (1973): 32–39; *Zur Sache des Denkens,* pp. 81–90, translated as *On Time and Being,* pp. 74–82.

41. For elaboration, see YH chs. 2 and 16, and "Translator's Epilogue" in OHF.

42. Cf. GA65 §§62–69, 105, 153–54, 179, 212.

43. GA26 219; translated as *The Metaphysical Foundations of Logic,* tr. Michael Heim (Bloomington: Indiana University Press, 1984), p. 171.

44. GA12 81–146; translated as *On the Way to Language,* pp. 1–54.

45. On hermeneutics in Heidegger's early and later thought, see Will McNeill, "The First Principle of Hermeneutics," in RHFS ch. 22.

46. *Zur Sache des Denkens,* pp. 81–90, translated as *On Time and Being,* pp. 74–82. The untranslated work *Seminare* returns to the appropriation of Husserl in the early twenties (GA15 334–39, 372–400). For Heidegger's early notion of truth, see John Sallis, "The Truth that is not of Knowledge," in RHFS ch. 21.

47. GA9; translated as *Pathmarks,* ed. Will McNeill (New York: Cambridge University Press, 1998). See also the untranslated anthologies *Aus der Erfahrung des Denkens* (GA13), which opens with texts from 1910, and *Reden und andere Zeugnisse eines Lebenswege 1910–1976* (GA16), which also opens with texts from the Student Period.

48. See, for example, GA65 §§32, 42, 134–35, 218, 242; translated by Parvis Emad and Kenneth Maly as *Contributions to Philosophy (From Enowning)* (Bloomington: Indiana University Press, 1999).

49. *The Question Concerning Technology,* tr. William Lovitt (New York: Harper & Row, 1977).

50. *Poetry Language Thought*, tr. Albert Hofstadter (New York: Harper & Row, 1971).

51. GA1 55–57, translated as "A Recollection,'" in Sheehan 1981, pp. 21–22; Sheehan 1988, pp. 86–88.

52. Quoted in Sheehan 1988, p. 88.

53. See chapter 1 in this volume, pp. 18–19, 21–26.

54. GA56/57 46, 70–76, 132–34, 207; GA58 32, 58, 65, 69, 76, 85, 111, 205; GA60 301–37.

55. GA20 375–76, translated by Theodore Kisiel as *History of the Concept of Time: Prolegomena* (Bloomington: Indiana University Press, 1985), p. 272; GA2 22, 216/BTMR 37, 205/BTS 14, 152.

56. See my elaborations in OHF 5 n. 9, 90–93.

57. GA1 57, translated as "A Recollection," in Sheehan 1981, p. 22.

58. See note 24 above.

59. See chapter 1, which also functions as a primary bibliography.

60. For elaboration on the rediscovery of Heidegger's early texts and the issue of evaluating their philosophical importance, see YH ch. 1 and the editor's following articles: "Is It an Objective or Subjective Genitive?," *International Philosophical Quarterly* XXXV (1995): 483–89; "What Does It All Come To? Response to Reviews of *The Young Heidegger*," *Philosophy Today* 41 (1997): 325–33.

61. In addition to the editor's works (YH, RHFS), see Sheehan, 1981, 1988; Sheehan and Palmer 1997; Caputo 1982, 1992; Krell 1986, 1992; Taminiaux 1991; Schalow 1992; Kisiel 1993; Dahlstrom 1994; Bambach 1995; McNeill 1999; and Crowell 2001.

62. For this concept taken from Jacques Derrida, see YH 14–16.

CHAPTER ONE

1. All four sections are revised versions of Appendices I–IV in John van Buren, "The Young Heidegger," Ph.D. dissertation, McMaster University, 1989, p. 564ff. The first section is based on Bernhard Casper, "Martin Heidegger und die Theologische Fakultät Freiburg, 1909–1923," *Freiburger Diözesan-Archiv* 100 (1980): 534–41; Sheehan 1988, 77–137; Hugo Ott, "Der junge Martin Heidegger: Gymnasial-Konviktszeit und Studium" and "Der Habilitand Martin Heidegger und das von Schaezler'sche Stipendium" in *Freiburger Diözesanarchiv* 104 (1984): 315–25, and 108 (1986): 141–60; Ott 1988/1993. Sections 2–4 are based on Heidegger's "List of Lecture Courses" in Richardson 1963, pp. 663–65; the publisher's prospectus of March 2000 for Heidegger's *Gesamtausgabe;* corrections to these documents in Kisiel 1993, 461–69; and "Appendix I: Heidegger's Writings, Lectures, Courses, and Seminars" in Denker 2000, pp. 247–53.

2. For biographical sketches on Heidegger's teachers at the University of Freiburg, see Sheehan 1988, p. 90ff.

3. The curriculum vitae Heidegger submitted with his postdoctoral dissertation of 1915 refers to his health problem in 1911 as "severe exhaustion" and "my heart-trouble," which "broke out so severely that any later employment in the service of the Church was taken to be extremely questionable" (see Sheehan 1988, p. 79). Physically and mentally

exhausted after three semesters of intense studies and a prolific publication output for a freshman and sophomore (see section 2 of this chapter), the twenty-one-year-old Heidegger saw at the end of WS1910–11 a renewed outbreak of the "heart-trouble" that had earlier led to his being dismissed from the Jesuit Novitiate at Tisis in the fall of 1909. The director and doctor at the Theological Seminary where Heidegger lived described the problem as a psychosomatic "nervous heart condition" of an "asthmatic nature," a condition that would continue to plague him later in the wake of the denazification hearings after the collapse of Nazi Germany, when Heidegger went into therapy. After following the doctor's recommendation to spend time at home in Messkirch "to have complete rest," he returned in April to resume his studies in SS1911, but his condition worsened, and he apparently spent most of the summer semester at home convalescing, though still finding time to read Husserl's writings. The poems "Dying Splendor," "Hours on the Mount of Olives," and "We Shall Wait" that were published by Heidegger between October 29, 1910 and April 8, 1911, as well as the great interest his published book review of March 1910 shows in Johannes Jörgensen's autobiographical depiction of his intellectual turmoil and despair (see chapter 2 of this volume), give an important indication of Heidegger's own *Angst*-ridden state of mind and intellectual crisis. For example, "My life's hours on the Mount of Olives: often you have looked at me with the dark apparition of dejected apprehension" (GA13 6). Faced also with severe financial worries, and to the great disappointment of his parents, who had even dreamt that their gifted son might one day become a bishop, the twenty-one-year-old Heidegger took the advice of his superiors to abandon the idea of becoming a priest and withdrew from the seminary and the Department of Theology. For the details of this first intellectual "turn" in Heidegger's development, see Ott 1988/1993, pp. 67ff./64ff. and Sheehan 1988, pp. 95–96.

4. In his curriculum vitae of 1915, Heidegger states that beginning in WS1911–12 he attended "a great quantity of lecture courses in philosophy" (see Sheehan 1988, p. 79f.).

5. Heidegger later recalled that "I did attend one lecture course in theology even in the years after 1911, the course on dogmatic theology by Carl Braig." See *Zur Sache des Denkens* (Tübingen: Max Niemeyer, 1976), p. 82; translated by Joan Stambaugh as *On Time and Being* (New York: Harper & Row, 1972), p. 75.

6. For this and the following course, see the curriculum vitae Heidegger sent to Georg Misch in 1922 (GA16 41–42).

7. In a later recollection of his student years, Heidegger mentioned attending at least one lecture course given by Vöge, who asserted a "decisive . . . influence" on him. See GA1 57; translated as "A Recollection,'" in Sheehan 1981, p. 21.

8. The curriculum vitae Heidegger submitted with his doctoral dissertation of 1913 mentioned attending "lecture courses in mathematics, physics, chemistry, and botany." See Sheehan 1988, p. 106.

9. This curriculum vitae can be found in German and English translation in Sheehan 1988, pp. 106, 115 and in *Martin Heidegger/Heinrich Rickert: Briefwechsel 1912 bis 1933*, ed. Alfred Denker (Frankfurt: Klostermann, 2002), p. 92.

10. The German text of Schneider's evaluation of the doctoral dissertation can be found in Sheehan 1988, p. 115, as well as in *Martin Heidegger/Heinrich Rickert: Briefwechsel 1912 bis 1933*.

11. For Heidegger's letters of application for Von Schaezler grants, see Ott, "Der Habilitand Martin Heidegger und das von Schaezler'sche Stipendium," pp. 315–25.

12. See Sheehan 1988, p. 111.

13. Heidegger's seminar paper can be found in *Martin Heidegger/Heinrich Rickert: Briefwechsel 1912 bis 1933*, pp. 77–79.

14. See Sheehan 1988, p. 113.

15. Published in *Martin Heidegger/Heinrich Rickert: Briefwechsel 1912 bis 1933*, pp. 81–90; also in GA80 (forthcoming).

16. This curriculum vitae can be found in German and English translation in Sheehan 1988, pp. 78–80, 116f., as well as in GA16 37–39.

17. The German text of Rickert's evaluation of the postdoctoral dissertation can be found in Sheehan 1988, p. 117f., as well as in *Martin Heidegger/Heinrich Rickert: Briefwechsel 1912 bis 1933*.

18. For the history of the composition of *Being and Time*, see Kisiel 1993, p. 489.

CHAPTER TWO

1. *Lebenslüge und Lebenswahrheit* (Kirchheim, 2d ed., 1903).

2. *Parabeln* (Kirchheim, 2d ed., 1905, p. 78f.).

3. *Reisebuch* (Kirchheim, 1898).

CHAPTER THREE

1. *Sur les chemins de la croyance: I^(re) étape (l'utilisation du positivisme)* (Paris, 8th ed., 1910), p. 25 note. [Tr.'s n.: When Heidegger in this and the following chapters provides only the place and the date of publication, separating them with a comma, this format has been retained.]

2. *Prolegomena* (Leipzig), p. 34 [*Prolegomena to Any Future Metaphysics*, trans. Lewis White Beck (Indianapolis: Bobbs-Merrill, 1950)].

3. Tr.'s n.: Defending Oswald Külpe's "critical realism" in the present essay, Heidegger in 1916 argues for the need to critically supplement it with the viewpoint of "transcendental idealism" (see chapter 5 in this volume, p. 64, n. 5), but then in 1922 he dismisses it completely as a "misbegotten epistemology" (see chapter 9, p. 131, n. 14). For a sketch of this little-known thinker, see *The Encyclopedia of Philosophy*, vol. 4 (New York: Macmillan, 1967), pp. 367–68.

4. Cf. Fr. Klimke, *Der Monismus und seine philosophischen Grundlage* (Freiburg, 1911), p. 382ff. This work, the title of which is not even remotely indicative of the wealth of thought through which it works, deals in Book IV (pp. 371–533) with the movements of conscientialism *[Konszientialismus]* and phenomenalism that will be examined in what follows, although Klimke's treatment is admittedly carried out from the standpoint of epistemological monism.

5. ". . . the chief question is always simply this: what and how much can understanding and reason know apart from all experience?" *Kritik der reinen Vernunft* (Leipzig, 2d ed.), "Preface to the First Edition," p. xvii [*Critique of Pure Reason*, trans. Norman Kemp Smith (London: Macmillan, 1978), p. 12]. For the three parts of the main transcendental problem, see Kant's *Prolegomena*, p. 57ff. [*Prolegomena to Any Future Meta-*

physics, p. 28ff.]. Külpe correctly observes that Kant, who so vehemently warned against overstepping limits, was untrue to himself and allowed a theory of formal science to become a theory of science *in general.*

6. Cf. E. Walz, "David Hume und der Positivismus und Nominalismus," *Philosophisches Jahrbuch* XXIII (1910): 161–82.

7. Tr.'s n.: Though *Wirklichkeit* is customarily translated as "reality," it is here rendered as "actuality," since Heidegger, following Oswald Külpe's terminology in his *Einleitung in die Philosophie* (Leipzig: Hirzel, 1907), pp. 147–65 [*Introduction to Philosophy: A Handbook for Students of Psychology, Logic, Ethics, Aesthetics, and General Philosophy*, tr. W. B. Pillsbury and E. B. Titchener (London: Swan Sonnenschein, 1897), p. 172], uses it in this essay to refer specifically to the "actuality" of consciousness and its contents, contrasting it to *Realität*, that is, "reality" in the sense of that which exists independently of consciousness. Accordingly, "reality" has been reserved for *Realität.*

8. *Die Philosophie der Gegenwart in Deutschland* (Leipzig, 5th ed., 1911), p. 136. [*The Philosophy of the Present in Germany*, tr. M. L. Patrick and G. T. W. Patrick (London: George Allen, 1913), p. 251.]

9. A. Ruge, "Unter den beiden Türmen." On the philosophical congress in Bologna, see *Der Tag*, no. 99 (1911).

10. Hereafter we shall use the following abbreviations of Külpe's works in references: K = *I. Kant* (Leipzig, 2d ed., 1908); E = *Einleitung in die Philosophie* (Leipzig, 5th ed., 1910); EN = *Erkenntnistheorie und Naturwissenschaft* (Leipzig, 1910); Ph = *Die Philosophie der Gegenwart in Deutschland* (Leipzig, 5th ed., 1911).

11. *Erkenntnistheoretische Logik* (Bonn, 1878).

12. *Philosophie als Denken der Welt gemäss dem Prinzip des kleinsten Kraftmasses* (Berlin, 2d ed., 1903); *Kritik der reinen Erfahrung* (Leipzig, 2d ed., 1907); *Der menschliche Weltbegriff* (Leipzig, 2d ed., 1905).

13. A thorough critique of Mach can be found in Ph 23ff. [*The Philosophy of the Present in Germany*, p. 35ff.] and in Klimke, ibid., p. 416ff.

14. *Beiträge zur Analyse der Empfindung* (1906), p. 17f.

15. See E 149ff. [*Introduction to Philosophy*, p. 194ff.] A summary account can be found in Klimke, ibid., pp. 431–51.

16. Külpe distinguishes between logical, empirical, formal, teleological, and genetic arguments.

17. *Grundlagen der Logik und Erkenntnislehre* (Münster, 1909), p. 62.

18. Geyser, *Grundlagen der Logik und Erkenntnislehre*, p. 275. For the general problem touched upon here, cf. E. Husserl, *Logische Untersuchungen*, vol. 1 (1900), sect. 17ff. [*Logical Investigations*, vol. 1, tr. J. N. Findlay (London: Routledge & Kegan Paul, 1970)], and A. Messer, *Empfindung und Denken* (Leipzig, 1908), p. 163ff.

19. Cf. W. Wundt, *Grundriß der Psychologie* (Leipzig, 10th ed., 1911), p. 34f.

20. Ph 27. [*The Philosophy of the Present in Germany*, p. 49 (modified).]

21. *Kritik der reinen Vernunft*, p. 17ff. (A edition), 31ff. (B edition) [*Critique of Pure Reason*, p. 65ff.].

22. Ibid., pp. 66 (A edition), 91 (B edition) [*Critique of Pure Reason*, p. 103].

23. A. Messer's *Einführung in die Erkenntnistheorie,* in *Philosophische Bibliothek,* vol. 118, chap. 2, sect. 4, p. 14ff., provides a good orientation regarding the "objective nature of thought." In the same book, the author treats naive and critical realism (pp. 41–61). The reservations expressed about naive realism are especially lucid; however, the first objection "from the viewpoint of religious doubt" does not seem especially convincing.

24. *Grundlegung der empirischen Psychologie* (Bonn, 1902), p. 89.

25. In the area of psychology, the work of the Würzburg school of psychology concerning higher intelligent life has led to a vigorous attempt to escape from the sensationalistic psychology that considers sensations and their reproductions the only elements of consciousness. Cf. Geyser, *Einführung in die Psychologie der Denkvorgänge* (Paderborn, 1909), as well as N. Kostyleff, "Les traveaux de l'école de Wurzbourg. L'étude objective de la Pensée," *Rév. philos. XXXV* 12 (1910): 553–80.

26. The influence of Ed. von Hartmann and his "transcendental realism" has done the most in philosophy to pave the way for a realist type of thought.

CHAPTER FOUR

1. Medieval thinking really was never quite as removed from empirical method as is oftentimes believed. It certainly knew how to appreciate the processing of experience, or at least the registering of facts. There was, even if it was not explained on a theoretical level, a consciousness of the value of mathematics for research into nature, and there was a familiarity with experiments. However, in all of this the proper way to formulate problems in the natural sciences was still missing.

2. *Acht Vorlesungen über theoretische Physik* (Leipzig: Hirzel, 1910), p. 8. [*Eight Lectures on Theoretical Physics,* trans. A. P. Willis (New York: Columbia University Press, 1915), p. 8 (modified).]

3. Ibid., p. 9. [*Eight Lectures on Theoretical Physics,* p. 9 (modified).]

4. *Unterredungen und mathematische Demonstrationen über zwei neue Wissenszweige, die Mechanik und die Fallgesetze betreffend. 3. und 4. Tag* (1638), translated and edited by A. von Öttingen, in *Ostwalds Klassiker der exakten Wissenschaften,* no. 24 (Leipzig: Engelmann, 1891), p. 7. [Galileo, *Two New Sciences,* tr. S. Drake (Madison: University of Wisconsin Press, 1974), p. 154.]

5. A. Einstein, "Zur Elektrodynamik bewegter Körper," *Annalen der Physik* 17 (1905); rep. in *Fortschritte der mathematischen Wissenschaften in Monographien,* edited by O. Blumenthal, vol. 2: *Das Relativitätsprinzip* (Berlin and Leipzig: Teubner, 1913), p. 28. [H. A. Lorentz, A. Einstein, and H. Minkowski, *The Principle of Relativity,* tr. W. Perrett and G. B. Jeffery (New York: Dover, 1952), pp. 38–39.]

6. Planck, *Acht Vorlesungen über theoretische Physik,* p. 117. [*Eight Lectures on Theoretical Physics,* p. 120 (modified).]

7. *Wissenschaft und Wirklichkeit* (Berlin and Leipzig: Teubner, 1912), p. 168.

8. *Kleine Schriften* (Halle: Niemeyer, 1910), p. 42.

9. *Methodus ad facilem historiarum cognitionem* (1607), chap. 7, "De temporis universi ratione," p. 431. [*Method for the Easy Comprehension of History,* tr. B. Reynolds (New York: Columbia University Press, 1945), p. 303 (modified).]

10. *Grundriß der Historik*, 2d ed. (Leipzig: Viet, 1875), p. 79f. [*Outline of the Principles of History*, tr. E. B. Andrews (New York: Fertig, 1967), p. 111 (modified).]

11. O. Redlich, *Urkundenlehre* (Berlin and Munich: Oldenbourg, 1907), part I, p. 21f.

12. E. Bernheim, *Lehrbuch der historischen Methode*, 5th and 6th eds. (Leipzig: Duncker & Humblot, 1908), p. 393.

13. *Augustin. Die christliche Antike und das Mittelalter in Anschluß an die Schrift "de civitate Dei"* (Berlin and Munich: Oldenbourg, 1915).

14. Ibid., p. 6f.

15. Ibid., p. 172.

16. Tr.'s n.: The German term is *bedeutsam*, which derives from *bedeuten* ("to mean," "to signify"). When Heidegger has in mind the meaning of terms and concepts, *bedeuten* is translated as "to mean" and the noun *Bedeutung* as "meaning," but when he is discussing the more practically oriented meaningfulness of the world and experience, *bedeuten* is rather translated as "to signify," the adjective *bedeutsam* as "significant" or "of significance," and the noun *Bedeutsamkeit* as "significance." These renderings are used consistently throughout this volume.

17. Rühl, *Chronologie des Mittelalters und der Neuzeit* (Berlin: Reuther and Reichard, 1897), p. 24.

18. Regarding this fundamental concept of concept-formation in history, cf. H. Rickert, *Die Grenzen der naturwissenschaftlichen Begriffsbildung: Eine logische Einleitung in die historischen Wissenschaften*, 2d ed. (Tübingen: Mohr, 1913), p. 333ff. [*The Limits of Concept-Formation in Natural Science: A Logical Introduction to the Historical Sciences (abridged edition)*, tr. Guy Oakes (London: Cambridge University Press, 1986), p. 99ff.]

CHAPTER FIVE

1. Tr.'s n.: See chapter 4, p. 59, n. 16 on the term *Bedeutung*.

2. Novalis, *Fragmente*, Vol. II (Minor), p. 111. [*Novalis: Philosophical Writings*, tr. Margaret Mahony Stoljar (Albany: State University of New York, 1997), p. 23 (modified).]

3. Even O. Külpe emphasizes "difference in the domain of the validity of the categories." See "Zur Kategorienlehre" in *Sitzungsberichte der Kgl. Bayr. Akad. d. Wissensch. philos.-hist. Klasse* (1915), p. 46ff. This very valuable work, which was Külpe's last, appeared only *after* the present investigation was completed. The significance of Külpe's essay and of the general philosophical position that this scholar who died too young won for himself calls for comment, but this will be done only to the extent that the following train of thought requires it. We may emphatically note, just in case this is needed, that respect for the author will thereby not in the least be infringed upon.

4. I hope to be able to show on another occasion how *Eckhartian mysticism* is given its proper philosophical interpretation and assessment only from this point of view and in connection with the metaphysics of the problem of truth we shall touch on below.

5. The lack of attention paid to the fundamental importance of the problem of judgment for the *grounding of objectivity* [Objektivität] also is the reason Külpe succeeded as lit-

tle in his book *Realisierung* (1912), as in his previously mentioned essay, "Zur Kategorien-lehre," in refuting transcendental idealism and could not succeed. Right at the crucial point where Külpe rejects the term "picture theory" as an unsuitable description of critical real-ism and emphasizes that "the objects of the real world to be represented and defined [!] in knowledge are not components of perception already discoverable in it, i.e., are not simply given in consciousness, *but rather can be grasped only through a process of knowing and espe-cially through scientific research*" [emphasis added] ("Zur Kategorienlehre," p. 42), he here bases his position on an argument that transcendental idealism has consciously made the focal point of the problem. If critical realism could be brought to the point where it takes judgment into account in a fundamental manner in its treatment of the problem of knowl-edge and if, on the other hand, transcendental idealism could manage to incorporate organ-ically into its basic position the principle of the material determination of form, then we would succeed in lifting up into a higher unity these two "directions" of epistemology that are the most significant and fruitful ones in our present times.

6. See Külpe, "Zur Kategorienlehre," p. 52. In the present times, it is especially H. Rickert in his *Gegenstand der Erkenntnis* who has made us aware of the necessity of includ-ing the logical judging subject. We shall have to refrain from making any definitive com-ment on the problem of "judging consciousness in general" and of "unquestionable affir-mation" (ibid., pp. 318ff. and 334ff.) until the general foundations necessary for all of this have been made available in the theory of value Rickert is presently working out. Roughly the same holds for Husserl's valuable theses about "pure consciousness" (*Ideen*, p. 141ff.), which offer a penetrating, decisive look into the riches of "consciousness" and destroy the often expressed view that consciousness in general is something empty of content.

7. Tr.'s n.: In the present essay, *Geist* has been rendered as "spirit," *Geistesgeschichte* as "intellectual history of spirit," and *geistig* and the associated term *seelish* as "spiritual" to reflect Heidegger's attempted grounding of epistemology in the metaphysical relation of "the soul" to God and the influence of Hegel, who is explicitly cited later on. Though in preceding and following texts in this volume, *Geist* usually has been rendered simply as "mind," *geistig* as "mental" or "psychical," *Geistesgeschichte* as intellectual history, and *seel-ish* as "psychical," the reader should keep in mind the above connotations of these terms.

8. The author hopes shortly to be able to contribute some fundamental theses on this problem in a more detailed investigation about being, value, and negation.

9. Unfortunately, even Külpe—as is clear from his constant preference for "objec-tive logic"—was not able to deal with precisely *this* problem, just as he never paid any attention to Lask's *Lehre Vom Urteil* (1912), an investigation to which I would have to attribute a *more* far-reaching importance for the theory of categories than that of his *Logik der Philosophie*. This book on judgment is unusually rich in fruitful perspectives, for which reason it is all the more regrettable that Külpe, with his distinguished and exemplary style of critical analysis, was no longer allowed the chance to present to the experts his position on Lask regarding what is, in my opinion, the all-decisive problem of judgment. Indeed, what Külpe in his last work wrote of Lask holds true today for himself: "Surely the highly talented researcher would not have been able to avoid this consequence of his deeply pen-etrating train of thought [about the problem of the differentiation of forms] in the course of his later development if he had not been torn from us all too early by a harsh fate" ("Zur Kategorienlehre," p. 26, n. 2).

10. See *Gesamtausgabe*, vol. 1: *Frühe Schriften*, p. 255ff.

11. It is from this point of view that we can also, for the very first time, analyze and define the concept of "philosophia perennis" in theory of science, something that to this day has *not* even been done in a roughly adequate fashion. Just as little to this day has the problem of *providing a study of Catholic theology within theory of science*—something closely connected with what was discussed above—been seen as a problem, to say nothing, then, of a solution having been ventured. The reason for this is in part the all too traditional manner in which *logic* has until now treated its subject matter and its blindness to problems. The first fundamental reorientation in the area of logic has been undertaken by Geyser, whose *Grundlagen der Logik und Erkenntnislehre* (1909) already has been singled out in an earlier writing. See my review "Neuere Forschungen über Logik," *Literarische Rundschau für das katholische Deutschland,* ed. J. Sauer, vol. XXXVIII, no. 11 (1912): 522ff.; repr. in *Gesamtausgabe,* vol. 1: *Frühe Schriften,* p. 35ff.

CHAPTER SEVEN

All notes are by the translator.

1. See chapter 5, p. 65, n. 7 on the terms "psychical," "mental," "mind," and "spirit" used in the present chapter.

2. See Heidegger's helpful explanation of this early terminus technicus *Bekümmerung* (later replaced by *Angst* [anxiety] in *Being and Time*) in chapter 9 of this volume, p. 118, n. 5. See also my elaboration in OHF 13 n. 17.

3. Heidegger uses two German words interchangeably for history in this 1920 essay and in the 1922 essay in chapter 9, namely, *Historie* and *Geschichte.* He does not clearly distinguish between them, as he does later in his 1925 lectures on Dilthey's philosophy of history in chapter 10 (see p. 148, n. 1). There, *Historie* usually is reserved for the "science of history" and *Geschichte* for the actual "happening" of history. In the present chapter and in chapter 9, I have translated both terms and their variants in the same way without indicating which German term is being employed at the time, since Heidegger allows the context of their usage to define which sense of history is meant.

4. Anticipating the terminology in *Being and Time,* this essay and the one from 1922 in chapter 9 already use *Dasein* as a central term, playing on its literal meaning as "being-there" and that of the verb *dasein* as "to be there," though these German terms normally mean simply "existence" and "to exist," respectively. Thus following existing translation practice, in both essays I have either used the German term *Dasein* without italics or rendered it as "being-there." The verb *dasein* usually has been translated as "to be there (for us, one)." The English term *existence* has been reserved for *Existenz.* See my elaboration in OHF 2 n. 7.

5. The German neologism that Heidegger employs is *Da sein.* When he places special emphasis on the dynamic, verbal sense of *Sein,* it is rendered with "be-ing." See my elaboration in OHF 2 notes 5 and 7.

6. See chapter 4, p. 59, n. 16 on the term *bedeutsam.*

CHAPTER EIGHT

1. M. Luther, "Quaestio de viribus et voluntate hominis sine gratia disputata" (1516) in *D. Martin Luthers Werke,* vol. 1 (Weimar: Hermann Böhlau, 1883), pp.

142–51. [Tr.'s n. : The above-cited volume of the Weimar edition of Luther's works will be abbreviated "WA1."]

2. The Latin words cannot be found as quotations in Luther's text in WA1, p. 145ff.

3. M. Luther, "Disputatio contra scholasticam theolgiam" (1517) in WA1, pp. 221–28. ["Disputation against Scholastic Theology," trans. Harold J. Grimm in *Luther's Works*, ed. Jaroslav Pelikan and Helmut T. Lehmann, vol. 31: *Career of the Reformer* (Philadelphia: Concordia, 1957), pp. 9–16.]

4. WA1, p. 225, l. 1f. ["Disputation against Scholastic Theology," p. 10: "17. Man is by nature unable to want God to be God. Indeed, he himself wants to be God and does not want God to be God."]

5. WA1, p. 225, l. 15f. ["Disputation against Scholastic Theology," p. 10: "25. Hope does not grow out of merits, but out of suffering which destroys merits *(merita destruentibus)*."]

6. WA1, p. 225, l. 29f. ["Disputation against Scholastic Theology," p. 11.]

7. Tr.'s n.: WA1, p. 226, l. 3f. ["Disputation against Scholastic Theology," p. 11: "37. Nature, moreover, inwardly and necessarily glories and takes pride in every work which is apparently and outwardly good."]

8. WA1, p. 226, l. 26. ["Disputation against Scholastic Theology," p. 50.]

9. M. Luther, "Disputatio Heidelbergae habita" (1518) in WA1, pp. 350–74. ["Heidelberg Disputation," tr. Harold J. Grimm, in *Career of the Reformer*, pp. 39–70.]

10. WA1, p. 362, l. 35.

11. WA1, p. 362, l. 21.

12. WA1, p. 362, l. 22. ["Heidelberg Disputation," p. 53 (modified): "21. A theologian of glory calls evil good and good evil. A theologian of the cross says what the matter actually is . . . 22. That wisdom which sees the invisible things of God in works as perceived by man is completely puffed up, blinded, and hardened."]

13. Ibid. ["Heidelberg Disputation," p. 53.]

14. Faith, hope, and charity (see 1 Cor. 13:13).

15. M. Luther, *In primum librum Mose enarrationes = Enarrationes in Genesin*, cap. I–IV, 7 in M. Luther, *Exegetica opera latina*, curavit Christoph Steph. Theoph. Elsperger, tom. I (Erlangen, 1829) (= EA1); cf. WA42–44. [*Lectures on Genesis*, tr. George V. Schick, in *Luther's Works*, ed. Jaroslav Pelikan and Helmut T. Lehmann, vols. 1–8 (Saint Louis: Concordia, 1958).]

16. EA1, p. 209. [*Lectures on Genesis*, vol. 1, pp. 164–65.]

17. Tr.'s n.: see EA1, p. 210 and *Lectures on Genesis*, p. 166: "But see what follows if you maintain that original righteousness was not a part of nature but a sort of superfluous or superadded gift *(donum superadditum)*. When you declare that righteousness was not a part of the essence of man, does it not also follow that sin, which took its place, is not part of the essence of man either? Then there was no purpose in sending Christ, the Redeemer, if the original righteousness, like something foreign to our nature, has been taken away and the natural endowments remain perfect. What can be said that is more unworthy of a theologian?"

18. EA1, p. 210. [*Lectures on Genesis*, vol. 1, p. 166 (modified): "Therefore let us shun those ravings like real pests and a perversion of the Holy Scriptures, and let us rather fol-

low experience, which shows that we are born from unclean seed and that from the very nature of the seed we acquire ignorance of God, smug carefreeness, unbelief, hatred against God, disobedience, impatience, and similar grave faults. These are so deeply implanted in our flesh, and this poison has been so widely spread through flesh, body, mind, muscles, and blood, through the bones and the very marrow, in the will, in the intellect, and in reason, that they not only cannot be fully removed but are not even recognized as sins."]

19. EA1, p. 178. [*Lectures on Genesis,* pp. 141–42 (modified): "But these words show how horrifying the ruinous fall *(horribilis ruina)* of Adam and Eve was; for through it we have lost a most beautifully enlightened reason and a will in agreement with the Word and will of God. . . . The most serious loss consists in this, that not only were those benefits lost, but man's will turned away from *(aversio)* God. As a result, man wants and does none of the things God wants and commands. Likewise, we have no knowledge about what God is, what grace is, what righteousness is, and finally what sin itself is. These are most horrible losses *(defectus),* and those who not realize and see them are blinder than moles. Experience, of course, teaches us about this calamity. . . . Therefore it is a cause for great errors when some men minimize this evil and speak of our depraved nature in the manner of the philosophers, as if it were not depraved. Thus they state that the natural endowments have remained unimpaired not only in the nature of man, but also in the devil."]

20. EA1, p. 184. [*Lectures on Genesis,* p. 147 (modified).]

21. EA1, p. 217. [*Lectures on Genesis,* p. 171 (modified).]

22. Tr.'s n.: see *Lectures on Genesis,* pp. 169–71 (modified): "*And when they had heard the voice of the Lord, who was walking in Paradise at the breeze of the day, Adam and his wife hid among the trees of Paradise from the face of the Lord.* . . . After their conscience had been convicted by the Law, Adam and Eve were terrified by the rustling of a leaf (Lev. 26:36). We see it to be just so in the case of frightened human beings. When they hear the creaking of a beam, they are afraid that the entire house may collapse; when they hear a mouse, they are afraid that Satan is there and wants to kill them. By nature we have become so thoroughly frightened that we fear even the things that are safe. . . . When the conscience is truly and thoroughly frightened, man is so overcome that he not only cannot act but is unable even to do any thinking. They say that such a thing happens in battle when soldiers who are overcome by fear cannot move a hand but permit themselves to be slain by the enemy. . . . Oh, what a grievous downfall, to plunge from the utmost carefreeness . . . into such horrifying fear *(horribilem pavorem)* that man flees from the sight of God more than from the sight and presence of the devil!"

23. EA1, p. 217f. [*Lectures on Genesis,* p. 172 (modified): "Nor can we have any doubt that their intellect was depraved when we look at the stratagem by which Adam and Eve think they are safe. Or is it not the height of folly, in the first place, to attempt the impossible, to try to flee from God, from whom they are unable to flee?"]

24. EA1, p. 218. [*Lectures on Genesis,* pp. 172–73 (modified): "9. *And the Lord God called Adam and said to him: Where are you?* . . . After Adam had become terrified through the awareness of his sin, he flees from the sight of God and realizes that not only Paradise but the entire world is too narrow to be a safe hiding place. And now, in that anxiety *[anxietate]* of soul, he reveals his folly by seeking relief from sin through flight from God. But he had already fled too far from God. Sin itself is the actual withdrawal from God, and it would not have been necessary to add any further flight."]

25. Ibid. [*Lectures on Genesis*, p. 172 (modified).]

26. Ibid. [*Lectures on Genesis*, p. 173.]

27. EA1, p. 221. [*Lectures on Genesis*, p. 175 (modified).]

28. EA1, p. 223. [*Lectures on Genesis*, p. 177.]

29. EA1, p. 221. [*Lectures on Genesis*, p. 175.]

30. EA1, p. 225. [*Lectures on Genesis*, p. 178.]

31. EA1, p. 226. [*Lectures on Genesis*, p. 179.]

32. EA1, p. 227. [*Lectures on Genesis*, p. 179.]

33. EA1, p. 229. [*Lectures on Genesis*, p. 181 (modified): "He does not drive Adam away from Himself because of his sin, but He calls him and calls him back from his sin. . . . It is the highest grace that after Adam's sin God does not remain silent but speaks *(locquitur)*, and in many words *(verbis)* indeed. . . ."]

34. Tr.'s n.: See *Søren Kierkegaard's Journals and Papers*, vol. 3, ed. and tr. Howard V. Hong and Edna H. Hong (Bloomington: Indiana University Press, 1975), pp. 669–72.

CHAPTER NINE

1. Tr.'s n.: Itself confirming what Heidegger says below about the inevitable "plurivocity" of words, his neologism *das woraufhin* has both the directional or intentional meaning of "the toward-which" of interpreting and the horizonal meaning of "that on the basis of which" or "that with respect to which" something is interpreted. The single occurrence of this term here and the frequent occurrences below of its abbreviated form *das Worauf* have been rendered as "the toward-which," though the reader also should keep in mind its above horizonal meaning. When the preposition *auf,* from which these neologisms are formed, is used in conjunction with them, it has been translated as "with respect to," which has the advantage of expressing its double meaning of "toward" and "on the basis of." See my elaboration in OHF 1 n. 3, 21 n. 29. Regarding my neologistic translations here and below of Heidegger's own neologisms, which are themselves sometimes translations of Aristotle's own neologisms, see Heidegger's comments on p. 127 about the hermeneutical value of employing such apparently unnatural modes of expression when they are demanded by the content of the text being translated.

2. Tr.'s n.: The verb *zeitigen,* rendered here as "to temporalize and unfold," is related to the nouns *Zeit* (time) and *Zeitlichkeit* (temporality) and more closely to the adjective *zeitig,* which means timely, seasonable, ripe, or mature. Heidegger accordingly intends it both in its meaning of "to temporalize" and in its more common vegetative sense, namely, to unfold, ripen, mature, or bear (fruit) in season, at the right time (e.g., the ripening of grapes or blooming of flowers in season). It is bound up with Heidegger's terms *jeweilig* and *jeweils,* which have respectively been rendered in most occurrences as "at the particular time" and "at any particular time"; with his use of the phrase *es kommt auf . . . an,* which is connected with the sense of temporalizing as a "not yet" or a *Zukunft* (a "future," but literally "a coming toward us"), and which accordingly has been rendered simultaneously as "what is at issue" and "what it comes to"; and even more intimately with a number of vegetative terms that he employs in connection with temporality, namely, *erwachsen (aus),* which has been rendered as "to grow (out of)"; *anwachsen* ("to bourgeon"); *entspringen* ("to spring from"); *Verwurzelung* ("being rooted in"); and *Boden* ("soil" or

"basis"). This concomitant vegetative sense of *zeitigen* again comes to the fore when Heidegger puts it to work to interpret and translate the basic concepts of Aristotle's treatment of βίος [life] and more specifically of human life in his "natural philosophy" (*Physics, De anima,* and *De motu animalium*), as well as the basic concepts of his "metaphysics," "logic," and "ethics" (as Heidegger states, his view is that the latter disciplines "grew out of" Aristotle's natural philosophy). The most notable of these concepts in Aristotle's natural philosophy are φύσις (nature, but more literally, that which grows or springs forth), γινόμενον (becoming), ἀρχή (origin, first principle, though Heidegger himself translates it with the neologism *Vonwoaus* [the "from-out-of-which"]), κίνησις (motion, namely, that of life from δύναμις [potentiality] to ἐνέργεια [actuality], the latter term being translated by Heidegger as *Vollzug* ["actualization" or "actualizing"]), and καιρός (the right season, the moment, timeliness). Thus it is in order to express something of its rich double meaning of "to temporalize" and "to unfold (in season, at the right time)" that *zeitigen* has for the most part been rendered into English with the hendiadys "to temporalize and unfold."

3. Tr.'s n.: The somewhat clumsy technicus terminus *(sich) bekümmern* (to worry oneself, to be worried), which Heidegger had been using at least since his 1920 essay on Jaspers (see this volume, p. 74ff.), is defined in note 5 as the anxious and resolute "care of [human] existence" for itself. In subsequent writings, including *Being and Time,* it was replaced with the perhaps more natural term *Angst* ("anxiety" or "anxiousness" about existence). Though *sich bekümmern* has been rendered as "to worry," other possible translations include "to trouble oneself" as well as "to be troubled," "to concern oneself," and "to be in distress about" or "anxious about." However, "anxious" has been reserved for translating the term *Besorgnis,* which is an intensive form of *Besorgen* and accordingly sometimes has been rendered not simply as "concern" (about the world) but more strongly as "anxious concern" or "concern and apprehension" (about the world). Note that the etymological connection between these two German terms, on the one hand, and *Sorgen* and *Sorge,* on the other hand, is lost in my respective translations of the latter terms as "caring" and "care" (about the world or about human existence).

4. Tr.'s n.: On the term *begegnen* (to encounter), see my comments in OHF 65 n. 53.

5. "Worry" refers not to a mood in which one wears a woebegone expression but rather to a factical being-resolved, that is, seizing upon one's *existence* (cf. pp. 119–20) as something that one is and will be concerned about. If we take "care" to be *vox media* [in the middle voice] (which in itself, as a category of meaning, has its origin in the speech of facticity), then worry is the care of existence (*gen. ob.* [objective genitive]).

6. Tr.'s n.: The German term is *Öffentlichkeit,* which has the literal spatial meaning of "openness," on which Heidegger oftens plays in connection with the similarly spatial term *Dasein* ("being-there"). See my elaboration in OHF 25 n. 34, 78 n. 75.

7. Tr.'s n.: For an explanation of the term *das Man* ("the everyone"), see my comments in OHF 26 n. 36.

8. Tr.'s n.: The German term is *existenziell.* See my explanation of this term in OHF 13 n. 21.

9. "Atheistic" not in the sense of a theory such as materialism or the like. Any philosophy that understands itself in terms of what it is, that is, as the factical how of the interpretation of life, must know—and know it precisely if it also has an "intimation" of

God—that this throwing of life back upon itself which gets actualized in philosophy is something that in religious terms amounts to raising one's hand against God. But philosophy is thereby only being honest with itself and standing firm on this, that is, it is comporting itself in a manner that is fitting to the only possibility of standing before God that is available to it as such. And here, "atheistic" means: keeping itself free from the temptations of that kind of concern and apprehension that only talks glibly about religiosity. Could it be that the very idea of a philosophy of religion, and especially if it does not take into account the facticity of human being, is pure nonsense?

10. Tr.'s n.: Though the term that Heidegger is employing here, namely, *Verwahrung*, means simply "safekeeping" or "preservation" in everyday German, he also plays on its literal meaning of "true-ing" or, in archaic terms, "betrothing." This is especially the case when he uses it frequently below in his discussion of "truth" in Book VI of Aristotle's *Nicomachean Ethics*. Thus from this point onward it has been rendered as "true safekeeping" in the expectation that this somewhat clumsy translation will nonetheless put across what Heidegger is struggling to express in this early essay. See my elaboration in OHF 56 n. 48.

11. The hymnology and music of the Middle Ages, as well as its architecture and plastic arts, can be properly approached in intellectual history only on the basis of a primordial phenomenological interpretation of the philosophical and theological anthropology of this era, which was communicated within the environing world and the social with-world through sermons and schooling. "Gothic man" will remain a mere cliche as long as this anthropology has not been appropriated.

12. Tr.'s n.: The neologism Heidegger employs here, *Vonwoaus*, has a double meaning expressing the well-known double meaning of the Aristotelian term it translates, namely, Aristotle's term ἀρχή (origin and logical first principle). Like the neologism *das woraufhin* (see n. 1 above), it has, as Heidegger makes clear below (see especially pp. 133–34, 141), a directional meaning and a horizonal meaning, that is: (1) the directional meaning of "the from-out-of-which" or "point of departure" *(Ausgang)* both for the being of things and for our discourse about it (and in the latter sense it seems to be the Aristotelian equivalent of Heidegger's notion of one's "initial position of looking" that motivates one's "direction of looking" [see p. 112 above]); and (2) the horizonal meaning of "the from-the-point-of-view-of-which" on the basis of which beings are interpreted and understood in their being. It is therefore often translated below with the hendiadys "the from-out-of-which and point-of-view-of-which," though "point of view" also is used for *Hinsicht.*

13. Tr.'s n.: Cf. *The Basic Works of Aristotle*, p. 1024 (modified): "Let it be assumed that the states by virtue of which the soul is true by way of affirmation and denial are five in number, i.e., art, scientific understanding, prudence, wisdom, and intelligence; we do not include supposition and opinion because these can be false."

14. Tr.'s n.: See chapter 3 in this volume, p. 40, n. 3, regarding Heidegger's now explicit renunciation of his earlier adoption of Oswald Külpe's "critical realism."

15. Tr.'s n.: In the German text, this reference to Aristotle's *De anima* is followed by "see chap. 3," which apparently is an error on either the editor's or Heidegger's own part, since the reference already cites "chap. 3."

16. Tr.'s n.: Heidegger has in mind the fact that *orthotes* means not only "correct" but also "in a straight line toward . . . " and "hitting the mark." See the opening passage of

Book VI of the *Nicomachean Ethics*: "In all the states of having we have mentioned, as well as in all other matters, there is a mark the one who possesses discourse aims at, heightening or relaxing his activity accordingly, and there is a measure determining the mean states we say are intermediate between excess and deficiency, one which is in accord with correct discourse which hits its mark" (*The Basic Works of Aristotle*, p. 1022 [modified]).

17. Tr.'s n.: The published German text reads "chap. 3," but the context indicates that "chap. 7" is really meant.

18. Tr.'s n.: See *Simplicii in Aristotelis Physicorum Libros Quattuor Priores Commentaria* (Berlin, 1882), p. 395, l. 20.

19. Tr.'s n.: The passage Heidegger seems to be referring to, namely, *Met.* E 2, 1026b8–9, actually speaks of "the house [οἰκία] which has come into being" and "has been produced." In apparently substituting "being" (οὐσία) for "house," Heidegger also may have in mind his above interpretation of Aristotle's term οὐσία as a neologism whose original meaning is "the household."

CHAPTER TEN

1. Tr.'s n.: In this essay, Heidegger almost always distinguishes between the two German words for history, namely, *Geschichte* and *Historie,* and the two corresponding adjectives *geschichtlich* and *historisch.* For Heidegger, *Geschichte* means historical existence itself, i.e., the fact that human Dasein is marked by temporality, historicity, and the factical categories of life rather than by the lifeless, rigid categories of Aristotelian or neo-Kantian logic. To be historical *(geschichtlich)* is to be constituted by the various structures of sense *(Sinn)* that make up our temporal existence. In GA59 43–49, we find the young Heidegger speaking of six senses of history, and in GA60 34–45, and GA9 32–34 (see chapter 7 of this volume) we find him offering his own views on history. In these earlier texts, he has not yet begun to clearly distinguish between the terms *geschichtlich* and *historisch* (see chapter 7, p. 74, n. 3), nor has he done so in his very early essay "The Concept of Time in the Science of History" in chapter 4 of this volume. By the time of the Kassel lectures in 1925, *Historie* means the historiographical inquiry into the past, whereas *Geschichte* signifies something that, as he already put it in his 1920 essay on Jaspers, "we ourselves are" (GA9 34; see this volume, p. 95). See also the 1924 lecture "The Concept of Time": "Dasein, however, is in itself historical *[geschichtlich]* insofar as it is its possibility." *Der Begriff der Zeit* (Tübingen: Max Niemeyer, 1989), p. 25; translated by Will McNeill as *The Concept of Time* (New York: Basil Blackwell, 1992), p. 19. In order to avoid the sometimes infelicitous lexicon of Heideggeriana, I have in this translation abandoned the neologism "historiology" (used by Macquarrie and Robinson in their translation of *Being and Time*) to render *Historie.* Instead, I have translated *Historie* as "historical science" and *Geschichte* as "history." Likewise, I have departed from their use of the neologism "historiological" as an English equivalent of the German adjective *historisch,* and I have simply translated both it and the adjective *geschichtlich* as "historical." When the context does not make clear which of these two German adjectives is being used, or what Heidegger's meaning is, I have inserted the German term in brackets. The noun *Geschehen* has been translated as "happening" or "happenings."

2. Edmund Husserl, *Logische Untersuchungen,* 2 vols. (Halle: Niemeyer, 1900, 1901), now available in *Gesammelte Werke,* vols. XVIII, XIX/1, and XIX/2 (Hague: Mar-

tinus Nijhoff, 1975, 1984); translated by J. N. Findlay as *Logical Investigations*, 2 vols. (London: Routledge & Kegan Paul, 1970).

3. *Ethica: Aus den Tagebüchern Wilhelm Diltheys* (Berlin: Literaturarchiv-Gesellschaft, 1915), now available in *Der junge Dilthey: Ein Lebensbild in Briefen und Tagebüchern, 1852–1870*, ed. Clara Misch neé Dilthey (Leipzig and Berlin: Teubner, 1933).

4. *Briefwechsel zwischen Wilhelm Dilthey und dem Grafen Paul Yorck von Wartenburg, 1877–1897*, ed. Sigrid von Schulenburg (Halle: Niemeyer, 1923).

5. *Der junge Dilthey*, p. 87.

6. "Vorrede" (1911) in *Gesammelte Schriften*, vol. V (Stuttgart: Teubner, 1957), p. 3. [Tr.'s note: All volumes of Dilthey's *Gesammelte Schriften* will hereafter be referred to as "GS" with the appropriate volume number immediately following.]

7. "Rede zum 70. Geburtstag" (1903) in GS V, pp. 7–9.

8. Wilhelm Windelband, "Geschichte und Naturwissenschaft" (Strasbourg Rectorial Address of 1894) in *Präludien: Aufsätze und Reden zur Philosophie und ihrer Geschichte*, vol. 2 (Tübingen: J.C.B. Mohr, 1924), pp. 136–60; translated by Guy Oakes as "History and Natural Science" in *History and Theory* XIX (1980): 165–85.

9. *Leben Schleiermachers*, vol. 1 (Berlin: Reimer, 1870), now available in GS XIII.

10. *Einleitung in die Geisteswissenschaften: Versuch einer Grundlegung für das Studium der Gesellschaft und der Geschichte*, vol. 1 (Leipzig: Dunker & Humblot, 1883), now available in GS I; translated by R. Betanzos as *Introduction to the Human Sciences* (Detroit: Wayne State University Press, 1988).

11. "De principiis ethices Schleiermacheri," Ph.D. dissertation (Berlin, 1864). The first part of the German translation is unpublished. The second part has been published under the title "Kritik der ethischen Prinzipien Schleiermachers" in GS XIV, pp. 339–57.

12. "Das hermeneutische System Schleiermachers in der Auseinandersetzung mit der älteren protestantischen Hermeneutik" (1860), now available in GS XIV, pp. 597–787; translated as "Schleiermachers Hermeneutical System in Relation to Earlier Protestant Hermeneutics" in *Selected Works*, ed. R. Makkreel and F. Rodi, vol. 4, *Hermeneutics and the Study of History* (Princeton, N.J.: Princeton University Press, 1996), pp. 33–227. *Selected Works* will hereafter be abbreviated as "SW" with the volume number immediately following.

13. "Die Entstehung der Hermeneutik" in *Philosophische Abhandlungen: Christoph Sigwart zu seinem 70. Geburtstag 28, März 1900 Gewidmet* (Tübingen: J.C.B. Mohr, 1900), now available in GS V, pp. 317–31; translated as "The Rise of Hermeneutics" in SW IV, pp. 235–58.

14. "Versuch einer Analyse des moralischen Bewußtseins" (1864), now available in GS VI, pp. 1–55.

15. *Das Erlebnis und die Dichtung: Lessing, Goethe, Novalis, Hölderlin* (Leipzig: Teubner, 1906).

16. "Über das Studium der Geschichte der Wissenschaften vom Menschen, der Gesellschaft und dem Staat" (1875), now available in GS V, pp. 31–73. See also "Vorarbeiten zur Abhandlung von 1875" and "Fortsetzungen der Abhandlungen von 1875" in GS XVIII, pp. 17–37, 57–111.

17. Tr.'s n.: GS XIX and XX contain the drafts of the uncompleted sections of vols. 1 and 2 of the *Introduction to the Human Sciences*. For a discussion, see SW I, pp. 3–7.

18. "Auffassung und Analyse des Menschen im 15. und 16. Jahrhundert" (1890–91), now available in GS II, pp. 1–89.

19. "Das natürliche System der Geisteswissenschaften im 17. Jahrhundert" (1892–93), now available in GS II, pp. 90–245.

20. "Beiträge zur Lösung der Frage vom Ursprung unseres Glaubens an die Realität der Aussenwelt und seinem Recht" (1890), now available in GS V, pp. 90–138.

21. "Ideen über eine beschreibende und zergliedernde Psychologie" (1894), now available in GS V, pp. 139–240; translated by R. Zaner as "Ideas Concerning a Descriptive and Analytic Psychology" in *Descriptive Psychology and Historical Understanding* (The Hague: Martinus Nijhoff, 1977).

22. "Beiträge zum Studium der Individualität (Über vergleichende Psychologie)" (1895–96), now available in GS V, pp. 241–316.

23. See *Leben Schleiermachers*, vol. 2 in GS XIV, and *Die Jugendgeschichte Hegels und andere Abhandlungen zur Geschichte des deutschen Idealismus* in GS IV.

24. "Studien zur Grundlegung der Geisteswissenschaften" (1905), now available in GS VII, pp. 3–75.

25. "Das Wesen der Philosophie" (1907), now available in GS V, pp. 339–416; translated by S. Emery and W.T. Emery as *The Essence of Philosophy* (Chapel Hill, N.C.: University of North Carolina Press, 1961).

26. "Der Aufbau der geschichtlichen Welt in den Geisteswissenschaften" (1910), now available in GS VII, pp. 79–188.

27. Wilhelm Wundt, *Grundzüge der physiologischen Psychologie* (Leipzig: Engelmann, 1874).

28. Heinrich Rickert, *Die Grenzen der naturwissenschaftlichen Begriffsbildung* (Tübingen and Leipzig: J.C.B. Mohr, 1902); translated by G. Oakes as *The Limits of Concept Formation in Natural Science: A Logical Introduction to the Historical Sciences* (Cambridge: Cambridge University Press, 1986).

29. *Briefwechsel Dilthey-Yorck*, p. 185.

30. Introduction to vol. 2 of *Logical Investigations*.

31. Tr.'s n.: The German edition reads: ". . . die Grund[v?]erfassung des menschlichen Daseins. . . ."

32. *Briefwechsel Dilthey-Yorck*, p. 83.

33. Ibid., p. 251. This and the above quotation from Yorck were put into modern German by Walter Bröcker, who made the transcript of Heidegger's lectures.

GLOSSARY

This glossary lists only central or problematic German terms and only the most frequent English renderings.

Abbau	deconstruction
Anzeige	indication
Aussein auf	being out for something (and moving toward it)
bedeuten	to mean, to signify
bedeutsam	significant, of significance
Bedeutsamkeit	significance
Bedeutung	meaning
begegnen	to encounter, is being encountered
Bekümmerung	worry
Besorgnis	concern, anxious concern, concern and apprehension(s)
bestimmen	define, characterize, determine
Bezug	relation
Blickrichtung	direction of looking
Blickstand	the initial position of looking
Blickweite	scope
Dasein	Dasein, being-there
Existenz	existence
existenziell	existential
Gehalt	content
Geist	spirit, mind, intellect
geistlich	spiritual, mental, intellectual
Geltung	validity
Gerede	mere talk
Geschehen	happening, happenings
Geschichte	history

Geschichtlichkeit	historicity
Historie	historical science
historisch	historical
jeweilig	at the particular time, particular
(das) Man	the everyone
Mensch	human being(s), man
Mitwelt	with-world
Öffentlichkeit	publicness
Seiendes	beings
Sein	being, be-ing
Selbstwelt	self-world
Sinn	sense, meaning
Umgang	(going about) dealings
Umsicht	circumspection
Umwelt	environing world
Verwahrung	(true) safekeeping
Vollzug	actualizing, actualization
(das) Vonwoaus	the from-out-of-which, the from-the-point-of-view-of-which
Vorgriff	foreconception
Vorhabe	forehaving
Vorlaufen	running forward
(das) Worauf(hin)	(the) toward-which
zeitigen	temporalize (and unfold)
Zusammenhang	context, relation, nexus

Secondary Bibliography

This bibliography lists comprehensive studies of either Heidegger's early thought as a whole, his student years, his Early Freiburg Period, or his Marburg Period. Citations of these studies are made in short form in the body of the volume, which also contains references to more specialized secondary literature. Internet sites providing philological resources such as a chronology of Heidegger's life, a listing in German and English of the volumes of his *Gesamtausgabe*, bibliographies on selected topics, and a link to the Heidegger Archives at the Deutsches Literatur Archiv in Marbach, Germany, have been given at the end.

Bambach, Charles. 1995. *Heidegger, Dilthey, and the Crisis of Historicism: History and Metaphysics in Heidegger, Dilthey, and the Neo-Kantians*. Ithaca, N.Y.: Cornell University Press.

Caputo, John D. 1992. *Demythologizing Heidegger*. Bloomington: Indiana University Press.

———. 1982. *Heidegger and Aquinas: An Essay on Overcoming Metaphysics*. New York: Fordham University Press.

———. 1978. *The Mystical Element in Heidegger's Thought*. New York: Fordham University Press.

———. 1974. "Phenomenology, Mysticism and the *Grammatica Speculativa*," *Journal of the British Society for Phenomenology* 5: 101–17.

Crowell, Steven. 2001. *Husserl, Heidegger, and the Space of Meaning: Paths Toward Transcendental Phenomenology*. Evanston: Northwestern University Press.

Dahlstrom, Daniel O. 1994. *Das logische Vorurteil: Untersuchungen zur Wahrheitstheorie des frühren Heidegger*. Vienna: Passagen-Verlag.

Denker, Alfred. 2000. *Historical Dictionary of Heidegger's Philosophy*. Lanham, Md.: Scarecrow Press.

Dreyfus, Hubert L. 1990. *Being-in-the-World: A Commentary on Heidegger's Being and Time, Part I*. MIT Press.

Farías, Victor. 1989. *Heidegger and Nazism*. Edited by Joseph Margolis and Tom Rockmore and translated by Paul Burrell and Bariel R. Ricci. Philadelphia: Temple University Press.

Gadamer, Hans-Georg. 1994. *Heideggers Wege*. Tübingen: Mohr, 1983. Translated by John W. Stanley as *Heidegger's Ways*. Albany: State University of New York Press.

Gadamer, Hans-Georg et al. 1986–1987. "Vorträge, gehalten auf den Symposien 'Faktizität und Geschichtlichkeit'." *Dilthey-Jahrbuch* 4: 1–180.

Gudopp, Wolf-Dieter. 1983. *Der junge Heidegger: Realität und Wahrheit in der Vorgeschichte von Sein und Zeit*. Berlin: Akademie.

King, Magda, and John Llewelyn. 2001. *A Guide to Heidegger's Being and Time*. Albany: State University of New York Press.

Kisiel, Theodore. 1993. *The Genesis of Heidegger's Being and Time*. Berkeley: University of California Press.

Krell, David Farrell. 1992. *Daimon Life: Heidegger and Life-Philosophy*. Bloomington: Indiana University Press.

———. 1986. *Intimations of Mortality*. University Park: Pennsylvania State University Press.

Löwith, Karl. 1960. *Heidegger: Denker in dürftiger Zeit*. Göttingen: Vandenhoeck & Ruprecht.

McNeill, William. 1999. *The Glance of the Eye: Heidegger, Aristotle, and the Ends of Theory*. Albany: State University of New York Press.

Ott, Hugo. 1993. *Martin Heidegger: Unterwegs zu seiner Biographie*. Frankfurt: Campus, 1988. Translated by Allan Blunden as *Martin Heidegger: A Political Life*. New York: Basic Books.

Petkovšek, Robert. 1998. *Heidegger-Index (1919–1927)*. Slovenia: Theology Department of the University of Ljubljani.

Pöggeler, Otto. 1997. *Neue Wege mit Heidegger*. Freiburg/Munich: Karl Alber, 1992. Translated by John Baliff as *The Paths of Heidegger's Life and Thought*. New York: Prometheus Books.

———. 1987. *Der Denkweg Martin Heideggers*. Pfullingen: Neske, 1963; 3rd ed., 1990. Translated by Daniel Magurshak and Sigmund Barber as *Martin Heidegger's Path of Thinking*. Atlantic Highlands, N.J.: Humanities Press.

Richardson, William J. 1963. *Through Phenomenology to Thought*. The Hague: Martinus Nijhoff.

Schaeffler, Richard. 1970. *Frömmigkeit des Denkens? Martin Heidegger und die Katholische Theologie*. Darmstadt: Wissenschaftliche Buchgesellschaft.

Schalow, Frank. 1992. *The Renewal of the Heidegger–Kant Dialogue: Action, Thought, and Responsibility*. Albany: State University of New York Press.

Sheehan, Thomas (ed.). 1988. "Heidegger's Lehrjahre." Pp. 77–137 in J. C. Sallis et al., eds., *The Collegium Phaenomenologicum*. Dordrecht: Kluwer.

———. 1981. *Heidegger: The Man and the Thinker*. Chicago: Precedent.

Sheehan, Thomas, and Richard Palmer, eds. 1997. *Psychological and Transcendental Phenomenology and the Confrontation with Heidegger (1927–1931)*. Dordrecht: Kluwer.

Taminiaux, Jacques. 1991. *Heidegger and the Project of Fundamental Ontology*. Translated by Michael Gendre. Albany: State University of New York Press.

Van Buren, John. 1994. *The Young Heidegger: Rumor of the Hidden King*. Bloomington: Indiana University Press.

Van Buren, John, and Theodore Kisiel, eds. 1994. *Reading Heidegger from the Start: Essays in His Earliest Thought*. Albany: State University of New York Press.

Zimmerman, Michael E. 1981. *Eclipse of the Self: The Development of Heidegger's Concept of Authenticity*. Athens: Ohio State University Press.

INTERNET SITES

Ereignis: Heidegger Links. http://webcom.com/~paf/ereignis.html.

Heidegger, Burghard. *Heidegger-WWW-Server-Projekt*. http://www.heidegger.org.

ABOUT THE CONTRIBUTORS

CHARLES BAMBACH is associate professor at the University of Texas at Dallas. He is the author of essays on hermeneutics, Continental philosophy, and the history of philosophy. His book *Heidegger, Dilthey, and the Crisis of Historicism* was recently published by Cornell University Press.

PHILIP J. BOSSERT was formerly professor of philosophy at the University of Hawaii and is presently president of Strategic Information Solutions, Inc.

JOHN PROTEVI is assistant professor of French studies at Louisiana State University. He is the author of *Time and Exteriority: Aristotle, Heidegger, Derrida* (Bucknell University Press, 1994) and *Political Physics: Deleuze, Derrida, and the Body Politic* (Athlone Press, 2001), as well as the coeditor of *Between Deleuze and Derrida* (Athlone, forthcoming).

RODERICK M. STEWART is associate professor of philosophy at Austin College in Sherman, Texas. His research interests are in contemporary Continental philosophy (especially Heidegger, Nietzsche, and Gadamer) and more recently in the debates over multiculturalism and intellectual canons.

HARRY S. TAYLOR is professor of philosophy at Blue River Community College, Missouri.

HANS W. UFFELMANN is professor of philosophy and medicine at the University of Missouri.

JOHN VAN BUREN is associate professor of philosophy and director of environmental studies at Fordham University, the author of *The Young Heidegger: Rumor of the Hidden King*, editor of *Reading Heidegger From the Start: Essays in*

His Earliest Thought, translator of and commentator on Heidegger's 1923 lecture course *Ontology—The Hermeneutics of Facticity,* and editor (with Baird Callicott) of the State University of New York Press series *Environmental Philosophy and Ethics.*